I0868643

# The Making and Ending of Federalism

# Studies in Territorial and Cultural Diversity Governance

*Series Editors*

Francesco Palermo
Joseph Marko

*Editorial Board*

Mikhail Antonov (*HSE University St. Petersburg*)
Eva Maria Belser (*University of Fribourg*)
Ilze Brands Kehris (*United Nations, New York*)
Joshua Castellino (*Middlesex University and MRG International*)
Erin Delaney (*Northwestern University*)
Rosalind Dixon (*University of New South Wales, Sydney*)
Anna Gamper (*University of Innsbruck*)
James A. Gardner (*The State University of New York, Buffalo*)
Giuseppe Martinico (*Scuola Superiore Sant'Anna, Pisa*)
John McGarry (*Queen's University, Kingston, ON*)
Jaclyn L. Neo (*National University of Singapore*)
Petra Roter (*University of Ljubljana*)
Cheryl Saunders (*University of Melbourne*)
Nico Steytler (*University of Western Cape*)

VOLUME 20

The titles published in this series are listed at *brill.com/tcdg*

# The Making and Ending of Federalism

*Edited by*

Peter Bußjäger, Mathias Eller and Julia Oberdanner

BRILL | NIJHOFF

LEIDEN | BOSTON

Library of Congress Cataloging-in-Publication Data

Names: International Association of Centers for Federal Studies. Conference (2021 : Innsbruck, Austria), author. | Bussjäger, Peter, editor. | Eller, Mathias, editor. | Oberdanner, Julia, editor.
Title: The making and ending of federalism / edited by Peter Bußjäger, Mathias Eller and Julia Oberdanner.
Description: Leiden ; Boston : Brill/Nijhoff, 2024. | Series: Studies in territorial & cultural diversity governance, 2213-2570 ; volume 20 | Includes index. | Summary: "This compilation, The Making and Ending of Federalism, includes the main topics addressed by recognized experts on federalism at the Conference of the International Association of Federal Studies (IACFS) held in Innsbruck, Austria, on 28-30 October 2021. It analyzes how federal and quasi-federal systems are created and if there are common patterns or certain conditions that promote the emergence or the demise of federal systems, including case studies from Brazil, Spain, and Italy"– Provided by publisher.
Identifiers: LCCN 2024014509 (print) | LCCN 2024014510 (ebook) | ISBN 9789004528574 (hardback) | ISBN 9789004528581 (ebook)
Subjects: LCSH: Federal government–Congresses. | Exclusive and concurrent legislative powers–Congresses.
Classification: LCC K3185.A6 I585 2021 (print) | LCC K3185.A6 (ebook) | DDC 342/.042–dc23/eng/20240402
LC record available at https://lccn.loc.gov/2024014509
LC ebook record available at https://lccn.loc.gov/2024014510

Typeface for the Latin, Greek, and Cyrillic scripts: "Brill". See and download: brill.com/brill-typeface.

ISSN 2213-2570
ISBN 978-90-04-52857-4 (hardback)
ISBN 978-90-04-52858-1 (e-book)
DOI 10.1163/9789004528581

Copyright 2024 by Peter Bußjäger, Mathias Eller and Julia Oberdanner. Published by Koninklijke Brill BV, Leiden, The Netherlands.
Koninklijke Brill BV incorporates the imprints Brill, Brill Nijhoff, Brill Schöningh, Brill Fink, Brill mentis, Brill Wageningen Academic, Vandenhoeck & Ruprecht, Böhlau and V&R unipress.
Koninklijke Brill BV reserves the right to protect this publication against unauthorized use. Requests for re-use and/or translations must be addressed to Koninklijke Brill BV via brill.com or copyright.com.

This book is printed on acid-free paper and produced in a sustainable manner.

# Contents

## PART 3
## *The Making and Ending of Federalism – Theory and Case Studies*



## PART 4
## *Country Reports*

# Figures and Tables

## Figures



## Tables

## Notes on Contributors

*Eva Maria Belser*
Ph.D., is Professor of State- and Administrative Law at the University of Fribourg, Co-Director of the Institute for Federalism at the University of Fribourg and Holder of an UNESCO Chair for Democracy and Human Rights.

*Peter Bußjäger*
Ph.D., is Professor of Constitutional and Administrative Law at the University of Innsbruck, Director of the Institute for Federalism in Innsbruck and Judge at the State Court of the Principality of Liechtenstein.

*Paolo Colasante*
Ph.D., is Senior Researcher in Public Law at the National Research Council (ISSiRFA-CNR) in Rome, Italy.

*Vanessa Elias de Oliveira*
Ph.D., is Associate Professor at the Federal University of ABC (UFABC), Brazil, and was Coordinator of the Graduate Program in Public Policy.

*Mathias Eller*
Ph.D., is Assistant at the Institute for Federalism in Innsbruck.

*Gisela Färber*
Ph.D., was Professor of Economics, in particular General Economics and Public Finance, and Head of the Civil Service Research Center at the University of Administrative Sciences Speyer.

*Klaus Frey*
Ph.D., is Professor at the Federal University of ABC (UFABC), Center for Engineering, Modeling and Applied Social Sciences, Brazil.

*Anna Gamper*
Ph.D., is Professor of Public Law, State- and Administrative Law at the University of Innsbruck and Alternate Judge at the State Court of the Principality of Liechtenstein.

*Salome Hunkeler*
is Diploma Assistant and a PhD-Candidate at the Chair for State- and Administrative Law (Prof. Belser), University of Fribourg.

*Jordi Jaria-Manzano*
Ph.D., is Head of the Communication and Dissemination Area, Institute for Self-Government Studies (Government of Catalonia), Serra Húnter Associate Professor of Constitutional and Environmental Law, on leave (University of Rovira i Virgili) and Senior Researcher (Tarragona Centre for Environmental Law Studies, CEDAT).

*John Kincaid*
Ph.D., is the Robert B. & Helen S. Meyner Professor of Government and Public Service and Director of the Meyner Center for the Study of State and Local Government at Lafayette College in Easton, Pennsylvania.

*Karl Kössler*
Ph.D., is Senior Researcher and Group Leader at the Institute for Comparative Federalism of Eurac Research Bolzano/Bozen, Italy, and Alternate Member of the Council of Europe's Group of Independent Experts on the European Charter of Local Self-Government.

*Julia Oberdanner*
LL.M., is Assistant at the Institute for Federalism in Innsbruck and Assistant and Ph.D.-Candidate at the Institute for Public Law, State- and Administrative Science at the University of Innsbruck.

*J. Wesley Leckrone*
Ph.D., is Professor at Widener University in Chester, Pennsylvania.

*Patricia Popelier*
Ph.D., is Professor at the Law Faculty of the University of Antwerp and Director of the Research Group of Government and Law.

*Gilberto M.A. Rodrigues*
Ph.D., is Professor of International Relations at the Federal University of ABC (UFABC), Brazil, and Research Productivity Fellow at the National Council for Scientific and Technological Research, Brazil.

# PART 1

## *Introductory Remarks*

# The Making and Ending of Federalism

*Peter Bußjäger, Mathias Eller and Julia Oberdanner*

Since the founding of the United States of America, many federal states have been created, but by no means in the 'classic' way through a constitutional compact agreed upon by all the states.[1] This is also accompanied by a trend towards asymmetrical and quasi-federal states that follow different approaches of regionalism and federalism. Although the number of federal and quasi-federal systems significantly increased over the last decades,[2] one might ask whether the founding model of the United States is no longer relevant or even outdated today. In this context, it is also interesting to ask whether the 'classical' way of founding has an impact on federalism and makes a federation more stable, symmetrical, stronger, or not.

In this context, on the one hand, the historical processes of formation would have to be dealt with in more detail. While in some cases founding conventions with representatives of the states were envisaged, other federally organized states came into being through a constitutional treaty or even a mere reform of the Constitution. On the other hand, the factors driving the emergence of federal states are crucial. Examples include civil wars or an inefficiency of unitary states. Moreover, the following questions arise in the process of the emergence of federal structures:

- Are there current constitutional founding processes and how are they shaped?
- How do the founding modalities affect the constitutional design, the organization, the functions and the political system in federally or quasi-federally organized states?
- How can modern findings from research on constitution-making processes be used (eg involvement of civil society, experts, digital participation etc)?
- What role do referendums play in this context?
- How are federations, confederations and quasi-federations distinguished?

1 See David Benner, *Compact of the Republic: The League of States and the Constitution* (2nd edn, Life and Liberty Publishing Group 2014), although the US Supreme Court rejected the idea that the Constitution is a compact among the states, but has argued in favor of the 'contract theory', which holds that the United States was formed by the people of the United States.

2 Various recent studies (for example, the Regional Authority Index) indicate a slight tendency towards decentralization of state power.

© PETER BUßJÄGER ET AL., 2024 | DOI:10.1163/9789004528581_002

- What conditions of emergence are needed for federalism to become functional?
- Does the way a federal system comes into being also correspond to the way it ends?
- Have federal systems already 'perished' and why?

The Conference of the International Association of Federal Studies (IACFS) held in Innsbruck, Austria, from 28–30 October 2021 mainly dealt with these kinds of issues. Unfortunately, not all speakers of the conference were able to contribute to this volume. The editors were therefore even more eager to ensure that the main topics addressed during the conference are included in this conference volume. With the quality of the contributions received, this requirement was undoubtedly met.

The second part of this publication focuses mainly on the emergence of federal systems. The papers belonging to this part therefore analyze how federal and quasi-federal systems are created and if there are common patterns or certain conditions that promote the emergence of federal systems. Eva Maria Belser and Salome Hunkeler deal with the question why the world did not come together through a world constitution and analyze the failures of the 'Committee to Frame A World Constitution'. Gisela Färber then focuses mainly on economic and fiscal factors in the development of federal constitutions and what can be learnt from the history of the German *Reich* and the European Union, followed by Karl Kössler, who analyses the categorizations of federalism based on the formation process as well as the effects that the dynamics of formative processes have on the distribution of powers between the national and subnational levels of government. Patricia Popelier deals with federal dynamics and stability, presenting propositions as to which structures are most adequate, and on how a system best moves towards another type of formal structure. John Kincaid and J. Wesley Leckrone examine the Iroquois Confederation including the question of whether it really was a confederation or if the term 'confederation' was not rather the label applied to the Iroquois arrangement by Europeans.

The third part of this book includes not only a theoretical contribution by Anna Gamper about the constitutional eschatology of federalism, focusing on constitutional ways of abolishing federalism in formal constitutional terms, but also a case study concerning the federal system in Brazil. Klaus Frey, Vanessa Elias de Oliveira and Gilberto M.A. Rodrigues present the role of municipalities in Brazilian cooperative federalism, especially their performance in public policies as well as the problems and challenges faced.

In the fourth part, Jordi Jaria-Manzano demonstrates the influence of the centralized judiciary in Spain on the Spanish decentralization process and shows, how historical dynamics affect the development of systems of territorial distribution of powers. Paolo Colasante deals with the making of Italian Regionalism, analyzing the foundation, evolution and perspective through a compact among the constituent units.

The editors hope that this conference volume has given new stimulus to the discussion on the emergence and dynamics of federalism in its various forms. We would like to express our special thanks to the speakers at the conference and to the authors of this volume for their contributions. Additionally, we would like to thank Ms. Lauren Danahy and Ms. Akiko Hakuno at Brill for their excellent support during the publication process.

# PART 2

## *The Emergence of Federalism*

CHAPTER 1

# Why the World Did Not Come Together

## *The Failures of the 'Committee to Frame a World Constitution'*

*Eva Maria Belser and Salome Hunkeler*

> The people of the earth having agreed
> that the advancement of man
> in spiritual excellence and physical welfare
> is the common goal of mankind;
> that universal peace is the prerequisite
> for the pursuit of that goal;
> that justice in turn is the prerequisite of peace,
> and peace and justice stand or fall together
> that iniquity and war inseparably spring
> from the competitive anarchy of the national states;
> that therefore the age of nations must end,
> and the era of humanity begin;
> the governments of the nations have decided
> to order their separate sovereignties
> in one government of justice,
> to which they surrender their arms;
> and to establish, as they do establish,
> this Constitution
> as the covenant and fundamental law
> of the Federal Republic of the World.
>
> Preamble of the Preliminary Draft of a World Constitution (1948)

## 1 Introduction

Federal scholars are mostly interested in federal achievements and success stories and have, so far, taken little interest in failed plans and attempts to federalise countries or regions. Nevertheless, most experts share the view that it is

© EVA MARIA BELSER AND SALOME HUNKELER, 2024 | DOI:10.1163/9789004528581_003

of equal importance for federal scholarship and practice to understand better why states or other entities do not come together (or federalise otherwise).[1] The relatively unexplored field of failed-federalism studies indeed has a lot to offer: by identifying circumstances and processes that do not give rise to a federal system despite of manifest federalisation aspirations and obvious federal drivers we can better grasp what the federal momentum is all about.[2]

If a coming-together federation fails, units remain independent states (confederatively cooperating or not with each other) despite of considerable interests or even crucial imperatives to strengthen cooperation and jointly design rules for purposes of common interest. If a holding-together federation does not arise, a unitary government survives regardless of significant claims of some or all communities to enjoy (more) autonomy and relevant interests for strengthening regional influence at the centre.[3] It is very likely that federal scholars and other experts interested in constitutional power-sharing

1 Eg Thomas M. Franck (ed), *Why Federations Fail: An Inquiry into the Requisites for Successful Federations* (New York University Press 1968) xv, 213, where he and Professors Spiro, Flanz and Trager discuss the failed Federations of East Africa, Rhodesia and Nyasaland, the West Indies and the Federation of Malaya. See also Peter Bußjäger, *Föderale Systeme. Über Entstehung, Scheitern und Erfolg von Föderalismus* (Jan Sramek Verlag 2017).

2 See for studies in the field eg Wallace, who examined the reasons for the failure of the West Indies Federation, first and foremost the lack of a general sense of national unity and the obvious imbalance in the distribution of power (Elisabeth Wallace, 'The West Indies Federation: Decline and Fall' [1962] 17 International Journal 269); Palmer, who examined the reasons for the short-lived nature of the Arab Republic, which he found, among other things, in the clear imbalance of the partners. The Union – negotiated by a small cadre of the Syrian military and political elites, pressured by communism and the Syrian right, as well as by the allocation of political power, which had led to an impasse and made progress in the country extremely difficult – was a testament to the weaker position of the Syrians, who optimistically entered into a union treaty that quickly lost the initially strong popular support. This was followed by harsh environmental conditions, operational factors that hampered economic development (eg great loss of income from oil transport due to the Suez crisis, loss of value of the Syrian currency and mass exodus of capital), the administrative incapacity of an overly centralised system, ever-increasing political restrictions (eg the practical ban on most Syrians leaving the country) and the growing disintegration of the two nations, which eventually led to the collapse of the Arab Union. (Monte Palmer, 'Arab Republic: An Assessment of Its Failure' [1966] 20 Middle East Journal 50); Riker, who sees reasons for the failure of federalisation in non-existing or no longer existing military objectives (though only recognizing military objectives as valid reasons for a federalization and excluding others such as economic reasons altogether; William H. Riker, 'Federalism' in Robert E. Goodin, Philip Pettit and Thomas Pogge [eds], *A Companion to Contemporary Political Philosophy* [2nd edn, Blackwell Publishing Ltd 1993] 614f).

3 Francesco Palermo and Karl Kössler, *Comparative Federalism: Constitutional Arrangement and Case Law* (Bloomsbury Publishing 2017) 164ff.

arrangements could gain important insights about self-rule and shared rule, the federal essentials of compromise and subsidiarity, and even governance more generally, by detecting mistakes and shortcomings of failed federalising processes. It is probably as much from failures to federalise as from success stories that federal experts and practitioners can learn about the appeal of federalism, its rebuff, and its rationales, enabling them to better assess the likelihood of a successful federalisation process.

Coming-together-federations – and only those are the focus of this contribution – are formed when formerly independent units conclude that they are better off cooperating in a larger union but want to preserve parts of their sovereignty and secure a relevant say at the (new) centre. Their drafters usually entrench a compromise between actors aiming at a new unitary government and actors preferring regional independence. Hence, a federation is born when the proponents of stronger cooperation accept a shared future based on internal diversity and a joint making of unity, and when the supporters of independence consent to limit their sovereignty and accept the primacy of federal law. It goes without saying that such acceptance or consent not necessarily constitutes a free and deliberate act. The new union can be imposed on (some) of the uniting members who would have preferred a unity without diversity, and on members who were not convinced that an overwhelming need for cooperation exists and would have preferred a looser or no alliance. The new regime might also have been imposed on (some) communities (for instance majorities or intra-unit minorities) or on regional elites fearing a loss of power and resources, either by the regional or federal population aspiring better cooperation, or by other powerholders.

States aggregate into a federation when the proponents of either position – creating a new and larger unitary government versus preserving the independence of the units – both have considerable bargaining power due to their political or economic strength, military threat potential or international support. For the old federations, it was such conflict between unitarist and independentist which gave rise to a combination of self-rule and shared rule (and in new federations, the banning of secessionisms as a legitimate position is likely to be a reason for weak or fragile federalism).[4] The combination of self-determination and co-determination, as controversial it might be in practice, is attractive to most in theory. 'Because federalism', as Ronald Watts famously put it in-1998-, 'combines a shared government (for specified

4 See Nico Steytler and Jaap de Visser, "Fragile Federations' and the Dynamics of Devolution' in Francesco Palermo and Elisabeth Alber (eds), *Federalism as Decision-Making, Changes in Structures, Procedures and Policies* (Brill/Nijhoff 2015).

common purposes) with autonomous action by constituent units of government that maintain their identity and distinctiveness, more and more peoples have come to see some form of federalism as the closest institutional approximation to the multinational reality of the contemporary world'.[5] The famous statement is still valid today. More and more people, reluctantly or not, see federalism as the best or only way to effectively govern together, to face common threats or to deal with separatism or internal conflict without questioning the different identities composing them.[6] The toolbox of federalism is well-stocked and offers ideas and instruments to states and peoples willing to solve common problems without oppressing diversity.

The people of the world, however, confronted with global concerns and multinational *par excellence*, however, constitutes an exception. World federalism, ie the combination of a shared world government for certain common purposes with simultaneous autonomy of states in all other respects, is not seen by the states and peoples of the world as a solution to global governance problems such as the inefficiency of international cooperation. It is hard to deny the strong interest of the peoples of the world to share a government for purposes such as peace, security, human rights, environment, climate, health, migration, common heritage of humankind, and its joint interest in cherishing its diversity. It is nonetheless impossible to oversee that humankind has not come together in a federation and, more generally, struggles to effectively cooperate. Instead of sharing a government dealing with common issues, the governments of the world rather continue to insist on their unimpaired sovereignty thereby threatening common global goods.

This contribution is an attempt to better understand the failure of the peoples of the world to federalise despite of convincing motives to federate. Our contribution will focus on the trials and tribulations of the so-called *Committee to Frame A World Constitution* and their work as an example to show how the right ideas can go wrong. It was neither the first effort to draft a world constitution, nor the last.[7] The Chicago Committee and the draft constitution it

5 Ronald L. Watts, 'Federalism, Federal Political Systems, and Federations' (1998) 1 Annual Review of Political Science 117, 118.

6 See eg Soeren Keil and Sabine Kropp (eds), *Emerging Federal Structures in the Post-Cold War Era* (Palgrave Macmillan 2022); for further reading see also the complete series: Soeren Keil and Eva Maria Belser (eds), *Federalism and Internal Conflicts* (Palgrave Macmillan 2019–2023).

7 A prominent example is the first world federalist organization, the Campaign for a World Government, founded in 1937 by feminists and peace activists Rosika Schwimmer and Lola Maverick Lloyd; Megan Threlkeld, '"Chaos, War, or a New World Order?" A Radical Plan for Peace and World Government in the 1930s' (2018) 43 Peace & Change 473.

produced, however, constitute a particularly remarkable case to investigate why states do not come together but stay apart.

The story begins in November 1945, when politicians under the shock of World War II were ratifying the UN Charter and judges in Nurnberg investigating crimes against humanity. It was then that a committee of eleven illustrious men and an eminent secretary started to meet at the University of Chicago to draft a constitution for a world federation. The Committee's aim was to go beyond the UN Charter and to create a world state able not just to sanction but to prevent crimes against humanity, to advance human wellbeing, to guarantee universal peace and to provide justice for all. In 1948, just before the Universal Declaration of Human Rights was proclaimed, the Committee published its Preliminary Draft of a World Constitution. The attempt to unite the world provoked some comments and critics, anger, and ridicule, and not much else. The Committee to Frame a World Constitution and its attempt to federate the nations of the world was a complete failure.

To better understand what went wrong, we will first recall the constitution-drafting process (2.) and present the draft constitution (3.). We will then have a closer look at the draft's shortcomings, such as its difficulty to conceptualise the constitution maker (4.), the struggle to bridge the widening ideological divide between West and East (5.), the rejection of the states and the weak role of self-rule (6.), and finally the design of the federal institutions and the confusion about the shared rule (7.). Before claiming that the reasons world federalists asserted after World War II in support of a shared world government are more compelling today than ever before (9.), we will again refer to the historical context and illustrate how rapidly a window of opportunity to federalise closes (8.).

## 2 The Failure of the Interwar International Order and the Renaissance of Global Federalism

Just like World War I, resulting in the founding of the League of Nations and the International Labour organisations, World War II had cruelly demonstrated that the fate of humanity was deeply intertwined, and that the well-being of a people also depended on decisions made by other governments. The global conflict with its devastating effects led again in front of all eyes that one state – even a strong, good-willed, and democratically governed one – was not able to effectively guarantee security or liberty to its citizens. Due to the connectedness of states, economies and societies, the wrongdoings of one (despotic) government could have tremendous effects on the wellbeing of all others. This insight was not new, but the Second World War had clearly demonstrated the failure of the interwar international order.

The League of Nations, founded in 1920 by the Paris Peace Conference, had not been able to fulfil its mission of guaranteeing global peace. It obliged all members to respect the territorial integrity and political independence of other members and prohibited external aggression but proved tragically uncapable of constraining its member state Italy illegally invading the member state Abyssinia in 1936. When the Italian army began the bombing in Ethiopia, employed banned weapons such as mustard gas and dumdum bullets, and targeted red cross establishments, the emperor Haile Selassie unsuccessfully appealed to the League of Nations in Geneva. His solemn appeal that justice be done to the people of Ethiopia, and his warning of a doom awaiting states tolerating a brutal war of one member against another, earned him the title of Time Man of the Year,[8] not more. The authority of the League was lost when it formally condemned the Italian attack but secretly allowed Italy to take over Abyssinia. Its credibility was further weakened by the fact that many states, including the USA, opted not to join the organisation, and others, such as Japan, Germany, and Italy, chose to withdraw. When the League proved incapable of preventing the aggressions of the Axis powers, it diminished into insignificance.

Therefore, during World War II, the insight became widespread again that the states and peoples of the world were in dire need of more binding international cooperation. On 21 September 1943, the House of Representatives of the United States passed a resolution stating: 'Resolved by the House of Representatives (the Senate concurring), that the Congress hereby expresses itself as favouring the creation of appropriate international machinery with power adequate to establish and to maintain a just and lasting peace, among the nations of the world, and as favouring participation by the United States therein through its constitutional processes'.[9] The House of Representatives' and other governments calls for new and more adequate international cooperation was later picked up by politicians and diplomats designing the Bretton

8 Murielle Schlup, 'Emperor Haile Selassie, God of the Rastafarians' (*Nationalmuseum Schweiz*, 28 January 2022) <https://blog.nationalmuseum.ch/en/2022/01/emperor-haile-selassie-god-of-the-rastafarians/> accessed 20 September 2023.

9 'The Fulbright Resolution (House Concurrent Resolution 25, Seventy-Eighth Congress. September 21, 1943)' printed in: Army Information School, *Pamphlet No 4, Pillars of Peace. Documents Pertaining To American Interest In Establishing A Lasting World Peace. January 1941-February 1946* (Book Department, Army Information School, Carlisle Barracks, Pa 1946) 11.

Woods institution and the United Nations. However, the leaders of the world failed to establish a machinery with adequate power to guarantee lasting global peace and instead settled on loose confederal arrangements allowing states to cooperate or not.

While world leaders debated the new international order, the idea of federalising the world also gained momentum in intellectual circles, among physicians, mathematicians, biologists, philosophers, writers, and artists. The German born physicist and Nobel prize winner Albert Einstein's activism for world federalism was driven by the threat atomic power constituted for global peace. He was convinced that unshackled national sovereignty and world peace were two incompatible concepts and world federalism a necessity.[10] Similarly, Robert Oppenheimer pushed for an effective international control of nuclear power. When he was recruited to work on the Manhattan Project in 1942 and to direct the Los Alamos Laboratory in New Mexico, tasked with the development of a nuclear bomb, he insisted that such invention required global rules on its use. The Nobel prize winning novelist Thomas Mann, an exile from Nazi Germany, was also amongst the world federalists of the time. Mann considered nationalism, racism and authoritarianism as most hazardous threats to global peace and hoped for a world government to jointly fight ruthless and dangerous autocrats. He claimed that mankind had to learn how to combine the concept of the nation with the concept of liberty. It was precarious, he warned, to take democracy for granted and expedient to protect and promote it globally.[11] Mahatma Gandhi was also member of the illustrious circles of world federalism. In his famous 'Quit India Speech' of 1942, Gandhi – who was killed before he could receive a Nobel prize – stressed that Indians did not want to 'remain frogs in a well' but aimed at a world federation. He forcefully argued that future

10 On 23 May 1946, Albert Einstein sent a telegram to hundreds of prominent Americans urging them to support the Emergency Committee of Atomic Scientists and argued: 'The unleashed power of the atom has changed everything save our modes of thinking, and thus we drift toward unparalleled catastrophe'; 'Atomic Education Urged by Einstein; Scientist in Plea for $200,000 to Promote New Type of Essential Thinking' *The New York Times* (New York, 25 May 1946) 13.

11 Thomas Mann spoke out in favour of a world democracy in various texts. One example is his speech '*Deutsche Ansprache*' (German Address) from 1943, which he delivered as part of a radio series for foreign broadcasting. In this speech, he emphasized that a 'reasonable world politics' was only possible on the basis of a 'world political democracy' (Thomas Mann, *Deutsche Hörer!, Radiosendungen nach Deutschland aus den Jahren 1940 bis 1945* [Fischer Verlag 1987]); Thomas Mann gives his unqualified approval to the draft of the world constitution, a 'first-rate document, honour-saving for human reason under all circumstances', and concludes accordingly, '[t]herefore my yea and amen' (Thomas Mann, *Brief über den Entwurf einer Welt-Verfassung* [Fischer Verlag 2011]).

peace, security and orderly progress of the world demanded a world federation of free nations as on no other basis the problems of the modern world would be solved.[12] The prominent peace activists Rosika Schwimmer and Lola Maverick Lloyd founded the 'Campaign for a World Government' in 1937, leading an international campaign headquartered in New York as well as a national campaign in Chicago advocating for the establishment of a democratic federal world government. Disillusioned with the lack of effectiveness of the League of Nations, demonstrated by the way in which it had abandoned Ethiopia, they advocated a federal world government to directly represent the interests of the world's people rather than the interests of states.[13]

The World War II generation of world federalists all shared a sense of urgency and hoped for rapid and effective success. The drawbacks, however, came fast and were overwhelming. World federalism soon went out of fashion and the initial enthusiasm died.[14] Before we join the era of political realism and settle for global institutions that are unable to combine the concept of national sovereignty with universal rights and freedoms and of guaranteeing peace, it is worth looking at the failed attempt of the Committee to Draft a World Constitution in Chicago. The unsuccessful Committee was a private and particularly ambitious initiative, composed of world federalists aiming at a scholarly-driven federalisation of the world. The aims and objectives of the drafters were compelling, the process of constitution-making and its outcome, however, severely flawed. Scholars, it seems, are too far away from power to effectively plan for the dividing and sharing of it.

12 'Such a world federation would ensure the freedom of its constituent nations, the prevention of aggression and exploitation by one nation over another, the protection of national minorities, the advancement of all backward areas and peoples, and the pooling of the world's resources for the common good of all. On the establishment of such a world federation, disarmament would be practicable in all countries, national armies, navies and air forces would no longer be necessary, and a world federal defence force would keep the world peace and prevent aggression.'; Mahatma Gandhi, 'Quit India Speech' (8 August 1942) at the Gowalia Tank Maidan in Bombay (now Mumbai), India; see Mahatma Gandhi, 'Quit India' in Ramachandra Krishna Prabhu and U. R. Rao (eds), *Quit India* (Padma Publications Ltd 1942).

13 Eva Maria Belser, 'Rosika Schwimmer - Erinnerungen an eine Frau ohne Grenzen und ohne Heimat' in Eva Maria Belser, Pascal Pichonnaz and Hubert Stöckli (eds), *Le droit sans frontières – Recht ohne Grenzen – Law without Borders* (Stämpfli 2022) 55ff.

14 Jean-Francis Billion, 'The World Federalist Movements from 1945 to 1954 and European Integration' (1991) 33 The Federalist 28.

## 3 The Making of the Draft and Its Failure

On Sunday, 6 August 1945, the very day the atomic bomb Little Boy containing 64 kilos of uranium detonated over the city of Hiroshima, Robert Maynard Hutchins, the chancellor of the University of Chicago and author of the best-selling book 'The atomic bomb versus civilisation', gave a radio speech on the atomic energy and its relevance for mankind. Like Albert Einstein, Robert Oppenheimer and many other global federalists, Chancellor Hutchins was convinced that the new atomic threat to the survival of humankind required a new global governance regime. He argued that only a global coalition for the control of nuclear weapons could prevent a 'world suicide'.[15]

Only a few days after the radio speech, at a Round Table Discussion on 12 August 1945, Hutchins stressed the need for a world government.[16] The speech and the discussion encouraged two members of the University of Chicago, Giuseppe Antonio Borgese and Richard Peter McKeon, to issue a memorandum urging the university to financially and morally support an Institute for a World Government. They both claimed that a World State was the only alternative to the permanent threat of world destruction.[17] The Chicago university, as the memorandum claims, had played a crucial role in the making of the atomic age. The same intellectual courage which led to the division of the atom, it urged, should now be used to unite the world.[18] The request fell on receptive ears. In his support letter to the cause, Hutchins claims that university meant universality and declared that when there was no future, it was up to universities to create one.

The Committee to Frame a World Constitution consisted of six professors of the University of Chicago, four professors from other US American universities and one professor of the University of Toronto.[19] The work of the eleven

15 Robert Maynard Hutchins, 'Hutchins' Radio Discussion (with R. Gustavos and R. Ogburn) on "Atomic Force: Its Meaning for Mankind" (August 18, 1945)' CFWC, box 46, document 1.

16 Hutchins (n 15).

17 Committee to Frame a World Constitution, *Preliminary Draft of a World Constitution* (University of Chicago Press 1948) VII.

18 Giuseppe Antonio Borgese and Richard Peter McKeon, 'BorgeseMcKeon Memorandum to Hutchins (September 16, 1945)' CFWC, box 46, document 2.

19 The 'Brief History of the Committee', which was published in the Committee's own monthly periodical Common Cause, states that it was by no means intended that the great majority of the Committee should be from the United States, nor that its members should all belong to high educational institutions. Invitations to scholars and political leaders abroad could simply not be extended because of practical and technical reasons, and the challenge of immediately developing a common language and skill among people of diverse backgrounds limited the chances of finding a diverse collection of members

men was supported by a most capable secretary, Elisabeth Mann Borgese, the daughter of Thomas Mann. Mann was married to Guiseppe Antonio Borgese, presumably the strongest driving force behind the project, and, like the Manns, an antifascist intellectual. Borgese had been forced to leave Italy for the USA in 1931 after having refused to swear the fascist oath at the University of Milan. When he married Mann, a pianist fleeing from Nazi Germany, the two saw their relationship as a symbol of the spiritual alliance between the Italian and the German anti-fascists.

In 1945, the Committee to Frame a World Constitution began its work, seeing its central task in preparing a preliminary draft of a world constitution, which would then be submitted to governments and public opinion. The first version of the preliminary text was printed in a 350 copies confidential edition 'not for public circulation or use' and sent to selected experts for comment. In 1948, a slightly adapted preliminary draft was published in the committee's own monthly journal 'Common Cause' and subsequently in 'The Saturday Review of Literature'.[20] The draft was dedicated to the world federalist Mahatma Gandhi who, the same year, had been assassinated by a Hindu nationalist.

The publication of the draft was accompanied by an international debate and raised comments from persons such as Albert Einstein, Winston Churchill, Henry Usborne, Hans Morgenthau, three-time Prime Minister Léon Blum, and many others.[21] The Editor of 'The Saturday Review of Literature', Norman Cousins, who was himself a word federalist, praised the draft highly as a 'work of tremendous importance' that should be discussed in regional conventions across the world.[22] However, the proposal was nowhere near as sensational as the authors had hoped.[23]

According to one of the most outspoken critics of the draft, Ely Culbertson, the committee had worked in mental isolation and had made little effort to bring in the views and works of others thinking about world governance and

---

from the outset, the Journal claims ('Brief History of the Committee' [1947] 1 Common Cause 13f).

20 Committee to Frame a World Constitution (n 17) v.

21 Or Rosenboim, *The Emergence of Globalism: Visions of World Order in Britain and the United States, 1939–1950* (Princeton University Press 2017) 168.

22 Norman Cousins to Giuseppe Antonio Borgese (6 January 1948) CFWC, box 35. Cousins (1915–1990) was the president of the World Federalist Association, a great supporter of the constitution and published it in the popular Saturday Review. In 1945, he published a pamphlet that launched his public antinuclear campaign (Norman Cousins, *Modern Man Is Obsolete* [Viking 1945]).

23 Analysis by Ray Garrett, 'A World Constitution: Analysis of the Draft by the Hutchins Committee' (1948) 34 American Bar Association Journal 563, 564.

shaping its institutions in places such as Paris, New York, and Geneva.[24] It is not readily possible to assess the veracity of the accusation. According to the Guide to the collection of Records, the committee members studied and debated for three years, aided by research staff and, near the end, a large panel of critics.[25] In contrast, the effects of the work of the committee can easily be evaluated. Apart from a few, mostly sarcastic comments, the draft did not generate any consequences. This failure had its reasons in the tense political world situation, but the non-transparent procedure and its outcome also contributed to the fiasco.

## 4 The Trouble with the Constitution-Maker

According to the preamble of the draft, the 'people of the earth' have agreed that the advancement of mankind and its welfare is the common goal of all, that universal peace is the prerequisite for the pursuit of such goal and that justice is in turn the prerequisite of peace. The preamble thus resonates with the powerful link between universal peace and social justice that also guided the drafters of the 1918 Versailles Peace Treaty, Part XIII of which established an International Labour Organisation. Similarly, the preamble of the ILO states that there is a need to improve social justice globally, as conditions of labour involving injustice, hardship, and privation to large numbers of people produced unrest imperilling the peace and harmony in the world. It equally – and convincingly – emphasized that one nation's failure to implement humane working conditions was an obstacle to other nations seeking to improve the conditions in their own countries, and that progress therefore must be made jointly.[26] The world federation set out to overcome the weaknesses of the interwar international order and to establish a world government with the power to set and implement the rules on which world peace depended. When Culbertson claimed that the grandiloquent preamble was neither good poetry

24 Ely Culbertson, 'The Preliminary Draft of a World Constitution, by the Committee to Frame a World Constitution' (1949) 24 Indiana Law Journal 474. Culbertson, however, did not think that this was the main reason for the 'dismal failure' (ibid) of the project as so many other problems stood in the way of the establishment of a World Federal Republic.

25 William Tucker Dean, Jr., 'Preliminary Draft of a World Constitution by Robert M. Hutchins, G. A. Borgese, Mortimer J. Adler, Stringfellow Barr, Albert Guérard, Harold A. Innis, Erich Kahler, Wilber G. Katz, Charles H. McIlwain, Robert Redfield, Rexford G. Tugwell' (1949) 35 American Bar Association Journal 656.

26 Eva Maria Belser, 'The White Man's Burden: Arbeit und Menschenrechte in der globalisierten Welt' (Habilitation thesis, Universität Freiburg 2007) 29ff and 31ff.

nor good international law,[27] he probably did not refer to its references to global dependencies, but to the grim attitude that the authors displayed towards the nation state. According to the preamble, the 'age of nations must end, and the era of humanity begin' because war and injustice 'inseparably spring from the competitive anarchy of the national states'.[28]

For federal scholars, it is fascinating to see that the drafters had major difficulties defining the *pouvoir constituant* of the Federal Republic of the World. They also displayed great ambiguity when it came to referring to the federal units. This conundrum is already evident in the preamble, which refers to the peoples of the earth uniting for world peace, but at the same time provides that 'the governments of nations' resolve to arrange their separate sovereignties in a government of justice. The first Article of the draft makes it clear that the Federal World Republic is 'indivisible and one'[29] but based on a 'pluralistic unity'.[30] Nation states must not only 'surrender their arms'[31] and delegate a limited set of competences to the new global tier of government as it would normally be the case in a coming-together federation. They must disappear. This, the drafters insisted, is the main purpose of the undertaking, claiming that the nation-state is 'by definition and nature the enemy and antagonist of the World State'.[32] If the nation-states are to disappear, however, a unitary state, not a federation, emerges. This decidedly unitary attitude, which lacked any federal spirit,[33] surely contributed to the postwar failures of the world federalists. The refugees of fascism and Nazism had lost trust in the nation-state and shied away from granting the actor, which had repeatedly brought immeasurable misfortune upon the world, a constituting role in the world republic.

What are thus the building blocks or component units of the 'federal' world republic? The drafters, none of whom were federal scholars, were not able to answer the question, which, however, is – or would have been – an essential one for any federation. The constitution alternatively mentions 'regions'

27 See also Garrett (n 23) 564: 'The preamble gives the impression that perhaps preambles should be done away with altogether'.

28 Culbertson (n 24) 475.

29 Art 1 para 1 of the Preliminary Draft of a World Constitution.

30 Art B of the Preliminary Draft of a World Constitution.

31 Preamble of the Preliminary Draft of a World Constitution.

32 In addition, they claim that only few of the so-called nation-states were 'really national', most were products of chances and bargains, mere coincidences of histories, and some not more than corporations of vested interests ('First Comments' [1948] 1 Common Cause 347).

33 See on its importance Michael Burgess, *In Search of the Federal Spirit: New Theoretical and Empirical Perspectives in Comparative Federalism* (Oxford University Press 2012).

(Art B), 'national or regional' tenure (Art C), 'component communities and territories', 'component units' and – surprise – 'states and unions thereof' (Art 1).[34] Apparently, after all, the states were not meant to disappear but keep residual powers: The powers not delegated to the World Government shall be reserved 'to the several states or nations or unions thereof' (Art 2), residual powers are thus designated to the very agencies whose abolition was announced in the preamble.

The sovereignty of the Federal Republic consequently resides 'in the people of the world' and is not shared with component units (Art 3). The Federal Convention consists of delegates elected directly 'by the people of all states and nations'. Interestingly, the Federal Convention is a unicameral parliament despite of the fact that all federations of the time provided for a second chamber representing the federal units. Still, the drafters avoided a blunt majoritarian democracy and divided the Federal Convention into nine Electoral Colleges designed 'according to the nine Societies of kindred nations and cultures, or Regions' (Art 5).

These regions, oscillating between unnamed civilisation doctrines, historical coincidences, and a few democratic options, are the following:

- *Europe*: Europe and its islands outside the Russian area, together with the United Kingdom if the latter so decides, and with such overseas English-or French-or Cape Dutch-speaking communities of the British Commonwealth of Nations or the French Union as decide to associate;
- *Atlantis*: the USA, with the United Kingdom if the latter so decides, and such kindred communities of British, or Franco-British, or Dutch-British, or Irish civilization and lineage as decide to associate;
- *Eurasia*: Russia, European and Asiatic, with such East-Baltic or South-Danubian nations as associate with Russia;
- *Afrasia*: the Near and Middle East, with the states of North Africa, and Pakistan if the latter so decides;
- *Africa*: south of the Sahara, with or without the South African Union as the latter may decide;
- *India*: with Pakistan if the latter so decides;
- *Asia Major*: China, Korea, Japan, with the associate archipelagos of the North-and Mid-Pacific;

34 Thereby 'throwing considerable fog over the question of what units make up the federation' (Garrett [n 23] 566).

- *Austrasia*: Indochina and Indonesia, with Pakistan if the latter so decides, and with such other Mid- and South-Pacific lands and islands as decide to associate; and
- *Columbia*: the Western Hemisphere south of the United States.

The most important role of these somewhat surprising regions seems to be serving as Electoral College to elect the world legislators called World Council (Art 6) and to nominate by secret ballot three candidates for the office of President of the World Republic (Art 5).

Borgese and other committee members had high hopes that the division into these nine different regions would eliminate the deadly bi-polar character of post-war international politics. The proposed design of regional federalism was nevertheless one of the major causes of criticism. In a review of the draft constitution, Brodwell stated that the proposal could only function '[i]f we were working in a vacuum'.[35] In his opinion, it was challenging enough to bring the existing nation states to an international cooperation in which they must surrender sovereign powers to a global entity let alone new regions. He was convinced that '[w]e must build with the material we have, or we shall not build at all'.[36] Indeed, the coming together of units into a federation appears to be an unfeasible project if the units requested to delegate power must first be brought to disappearance and absorbed into artificial regions.

Nevertheless, the drafters were not wrong to consider an intermediate tier of coordination operating between the global and the national tier. While it was either overambitious or naïve to redesign the map from a professor's desk, it was appropriate to envisage several great regions interacting with their components and global institutions. The ongoing trend to strengthen regional organizations dealing with trade and politics, such as the Council of Europe, the European Union, the African Union, the Association of Southeast Asian Nations, the Union of South American Nations, and the Arab League, illustrate the relevant role that regional blocks play in the field of global governance.

## 5 Constitutionalising Social Liberalism

The different members of the Committee held opposing visions of the world order. Some advocated for universalist approaches, other preferred more pluralist views. The need of the eleven drafters to compromise let to ambivalent

35 Percy Bordwell, 'Preliminary Draft of a World Constitution by Robert M. Hutchins and G. A. Borgese, Review' (1949) 16 The University of Chicago Law Review 386, 387.

36 ibid.

principles in the areas of sovereignty, global representation, and human rights as well.[37]

The draft sets out with a chapter on rights and duties establishing 'Rights of Man' as well as a 'context of social duty and service' which the Republic of the World shall strive to see universally written and enforced by positive law. The drafters focus first on human duties and only then on human rights. In the view of the drafters, the world federation should neither be inhabited by global citizens capriciously using their rights and freedoms until stopped by law nor by *homines oeconomici* thoughtlessly optimising their benefits. In stark contrast to such image of humanity, the draft obliges 'everyone everywhere' to serve with word and deed and with productive labour 'the spiritual and physical advancement the living and of those to come, as the common cause of all generations of men, to do unto others as he would like others to do unto him, and to abstain from violence' (Art A). In referring to future generations, the drafters testify to a far-sightedness that even utopians later lacked. Their interest in sustainable approaches protecting the planet for the future is also evidenced by the fact that the four elements of life – earth, water, air, energy – are declared common property of mankind by the draft which must be owned and managed as a 'common good' (Art C).

According to the draft, social and economic human rights are core.[38] It is the right of everyone everywhere to maintain for himself and his fellowmen, to be free from the bondage of poverty and from the servitude and exploitation of labour, to freely assemble and associate in any creed or party or craft 'within the pluralistic unity and purpose the World Republic', and to protect individuals and groups against subjugation and tyrannical rule, racial or national, doctrinal or cultural and to enjoy any other rights and freedoms as are inherent in inalienable claims to life, liberty, and the dignity of the human person (Art B).[39] The drafters also invoked the concept of pluralism and proposed as a way of its realisation a right of self-determination for minorities and dissenters. Such a right would serve as a counterbalance to the majority principle. The draft, however, failed to specify who constitutes a minority, what the right to self-determination implies, and how dissenters could possibly claim and implement such right.[40]

---

37 Rosenboim (n 21) 170.

38 Early commentators in the USA promptly expressed their disapproval. See Garrett (n 23) 565: 'this draft puts first emphasis on economic and social 'freedoms', which is really a rather drastic redefinition of freedom in its constitutional context'.

39 ibid, 'two clauses of distressing generality'.

40 Garrett, distressed again, ibid: "Self-determination' has acquired a familiar Wilsonean meaning which it is the whole purpose of this constitution to deny or modify'; other

It is in this field that the drafters seem to have worked too isolated from other actors attempting to codify universal law. In 1946, the Economic and Social Council of the newly founded United Nations had established the Commission on Human Rights and mandated the commissioner to draft an international bill of human rights. In 1947, the Commission had established a special *Universal Declaration of Human Rights Drafting Committee*, chaired by Eleanor Roosevelt. In its 30 Articles, the Universal Declaration of Human Rights set out the fundamental rights and freedoms of the individual and affirmed their universal character as inherent, inalienable, and applicable to all human beings. In comparison, the Committee to Frame a World Constitution produced an anorexic catalogue of human rights, which already lacked standing alongside the Universal Declaration of Human Rights in the year of its publication.

For instance, in the last part of the draft about World Law, where further global rights are guaranteed, the draft states that no law shall be made or held valid in the World Republic or any of its component units which curtails the freedom of communication and information, of speech, of the press and of expression by whatever it means, of peaceful assembly or, of travel (Art 28 para 6). Other important freedom rights, such as freedom of conscience and religion, or the freedom of trade unions, are missing.[41] The prohibition of torture and inhuman treatment, the right to private and family life, to asylum and to property, guaranteed by the Universal Declaration of Human Rights, are also non-existent in the draft.[42] In contrast to some selected freedom rights to which there shall be no limit nowhere, the margin of national discretion in the field of socio-economic rights is barely limited, despite the first chapter's emphasis on freedom from poverty and hardship. Old age pensions, unemployment relief, insurance against sickness or accident, just terms of leisure, and protection of maternity and infancy shall be provided 'according to the varying circumstances of times and places as the local law may direct' (Art 30 para 1).

Remarkably, however, the drafters provided for global solidarity and redistribution: '[c]ommunities and states unable to provide adequate social security

---

voices expressing the opposite, such as Gertrude Hooker, stated: 'All that is novel about the Preliminary Draft [of a World Constitution] is the courage and clarity with which it faces historical reality', cited in: Joseph Preston Baratta, *The Politics of World Federation: From World Federalism to Global Governance* (Praeger Publishing 2004).

41 In contrast, freedom of thought, conscience and religion is protected in the UDHR separately in Art 18. In addition, freedom of expression and information (Art 19) and freedom of assembly and association (Art 20) are each set out in more detail in separate articles.

42 In contrast, the draft prohibits the death penalty (Art 29).

and relief shall be assisted by the Federal Treasury, whose grants or privileged loans shall be administered under federal supervision' (Art 30 para 2). Such global implementation duty, not provided for in the Universal Declaration, provoked harsh criticism. Garrett, an early commentator of the draft, claimed that global solidarity did not exist – and would not suffice even if it existed: 'Surely there are not enough incomes or undistributed profits in all the world, even if taxed at a 100 per cent, to guarantee 'just terms of leisure' to 450,000,000 Chinese'.[43] Garrett criticised the draft world constitution primarily from this pragmatic and economic perspective: It should not be made a constitutional duty of the World Republic 'to impoverish the United States' and to oblige all western states 'to pour their wealth down into a bottomless pit of providing social security for over two billion people' who live barely above starvation.[44] The draft constitution also guarantees each child from the age of six to twelve a right to education at public expense and again obliges the Federal Treasury to assist communities and states unable to fulfil this obligation (Art 30). Garrett did not explicitly comment on this provision, but no great imagination is needed to guess what he would have made of it.

For the drafters, however, it was crucial for world peace to not merely collectively deal with the global threat of an atomic war but to create a world order based on justice and solidarity. They were driven by the aim of establishing a global system able to provide for a world recovering from war, a world in which colonies fought for independence and development, and workers and their families for economic and social rights.[45]

A provision in the final chapter further illustrates this ambition. It states that no law shall be made or held valid in the World Republic or in any of its units which discriminates based on race, nation, sex, cast, creed, or doctrine (Art 28 para 1). It is a far-reaching guarantee of non-discrimination, particularly in its application to nationality. The provision also invalidates any preferential agreement or coalition of vested interests which hinders the equal access of all states and nations to raw materials and sources of energy (Art 28 para 2).

The drafters were aware of the risk of proposing an America-centred world constitution impregnated by American views and biases. To 'find a way out from the ideological conflict between totalitarian communism and rugged individualism',[46] the committee postulated a 'regulated economy' and 'liberal

43 Garrett (n 23) 566.

44 ibid.

45 Baratta (n 40) 317.

46 ibid.

socialism'.[47] This spirit of tamed markets permeates the entire draft. It is the reason not to guarantee a human right to property but to guarantee a fair access to and distribution of resources (Art 28 para 2). Accordingly, earth, water, air, and energy are common property of humanity. Their management and use – whether it be assigned to private or corporate, national or regional actors – shall 'be subordinated in each and all cases to the inherent interest of the common good' (Point C). Culbertson, arguably the most scathing critic of the draft, described the approach as downright Marxist.[48] This assessment was probably fuelled by the constitutional possibility of the world government to carry out expropriations whenever business actors acquire the position of a transnational monopolist.[49]

Soon after the war, all ambitions to internationally guarantee individual rights and freedoms were paralysed by the dividing effects of the cold war. The comprehensive universal human rights declaration was not translated into an international treaty binding on all but into two international covenants, both associated with an ideological block, and both equipped with an insufficient machinery to establish minimum standards to all. The developments of the new era, beginning after the fall of the Berlin wall, illustrate that the Committee was not wrong on insisting on social approaches to universal rights and freedoms. Like the Universal Declaration of 1948, the Millennium Declaration of 2000 emphasizes on freedom and equality as fundamental values. While the Universal Declaration states that all human beings 'are born free and equal in dignity and rights' (Art 1), the Millennium Declaration expresses a different understanding of both values. Men and women 'have the right to live their lives and raise their children in dignity, free from hunger and from the fear of violence, oppression or injustice'. Taking such approach, most people are born unfree and unequal, and it is therefore a duty to free people and fulfil the promises of equality. In contrast to the Universal Declaration, the Millenium declaration also mentions solidarity, tolerance, respect for nature, and shared responsibility as fundamental principles for the 21st century. The Millenium Declaration thus illustrates that the drafters of the world constitution had many reasonable ideas – just as relevant at the time of drafting as they are

47 Giuseppe Antonio Borgese, 'Introduction to Constitution 111 (Constitutio Major), 3 January 1947 [Doc. 112]', cited in Baratta (n 40) 317.

48 Culbertson (n 24) 477.

49 Art 32: 'All property or business whose management and use have acquired the extension and character of a federal public service, or whereon restrictive trade practices have conferred the character and power of a transnational monopoly, shall become the property of the Federal Government upon payment of a just price as determined by law'.

today – but met and continue to be met by a world wanting to hear little about common responsibilities.

## 6 The Distribution of Competences and the Weakness of Self-Rule

The powers granted to the world government by the draft are – even tough not unusual for a federal government[50] – not of modest scale. The world government has primary responsibility for overseeing the adherence to the constitution and enacting binding laws applicable to both communities and individuals. Secondary federal responsibilities relate to maintaining peace, settling conflicts among component units, overseeing the alteration of borders (which seem to continue to exist and be important) as well as the making of new states. Third, the world government has the competence to intervene in cases of intrastate violence and violation of law which affect world peace and justice. It possesses armed forces and exercises control over the weaponry of 'domestic militias'. Fourth, the world government sets and collects federal taxes, administers a World Bank, issues money, controls credits and regulates commerce, transport, and communication of federal interest. It fifth supervises the movement of peoples, grants federal passports, and sixth and lastly, administers the territory designated as Federal Districts (Art 1). The residual competence remains with the members of the Federal World Republic. 'States or nations or unions thereof' hence, within the limits of the federal constitution, remain free to use all powers not delegated to the World Government (Art 2).

The drafters of the constitution make it clear that the universal rights, the division of powers, and other norms of the constitution – including the basic principles and the preamble – are justiciable but hesitate to establish a neutral arbiter to adjudicate conflicts between the World Republic and its units. The draft provides for comprehensive legal remedies foreseeing concrete and abstract review: Individuals, groups, and communities (but apparently not member states) have the right to appeal against the unjust application of the law and against an unjust law itself. They must first exhaust domestic remedies but may then appeal to the Superior and the Grand Tribunal, and in doing so rely on the counsel and support of the Tribune of the People. If the federal judiciary finds that a law or statute is evidently in conflict with the guarantees of the federal constitution or irreparably in contradiction with the basic principles and intents of the World Republic, the Supreme Court has the power to

50 See eg Palermo and Kössler (n 3) 139ff.

declare it null and void (Art 33). It is unclear whether the units of the World Republic can appeal against global laws which contradict the distribution of powers or violate the principles or rules of the world constitution. The drafters either not envisaged such scenario or thought it wise to start all procedures at the level of member state jurisdictions.

Garrett blamed the federal constitution for being 'unitary in substance'.[51] His critic is not justified by the vertical division of powers but abundantly sourced by other (federal) weaknesses of the draft. Analysed from a comparative federalism perspective, the list of central competences (although vague and confusingly drafted) is not extraordinary. Most of the responsibilities given to world government are attributed to the federal tier in national federal systems (only external relations – no longer necessary or possible – are missing on the list). In most of the policy fields listed, some unity seems indeed required as states acting on their own (and even states cooperating regionally) are not able to fulfil the task or are likely to produce high spillover effects disadvantaging other states. In stark contrast to the UN Charter focusing on international conflicts and prohibiting interventions in domestic affairs, the draft constitution allows the world government to intervene in units in cases of intrastate conflicts and civil wars affecting peace and justice. While such intervening powers evidently would have needed more procedural and substantive constraints, they are necessary to guarantee peace to all and to take the universality of human rights seriously. Their absence in the current global governance system leaves individuals and communities to the cruelty of totalitarian regimes and deadly conflict and remains an observer when so-called universal values are trampled. Such ineffectiveness also compromises legitimacy.

The competences of the World Government are far-reaching but explicitly listed. Federal scholarship would surely have allowed to improve the draft. It would, for instance, have been crucial to clarify the type of competences the federal government is vested with. The draft should have made it clear, for example, that most (if not all) of the federal competences are concurrent, not exclusive. The absence of a clear guarantee of self-rule and acceptance of the diversity is aggravated by the fact that there is also considerable ambiguity regarding the role of the units within the federal institutions and their impact on the making of the shared rule and the design of unity.

51 Garret (n 23) 566.

## 7 The Design of the Federal Institutions and the Confusion about the Shared Rule

According to the draft, the government of the world is composed of a Federal Convention, a President, a Council and Special Bodies, a Grand Tribunal, a Supreme Court, and a Tribune of the People as well as a Chamber of Guardians (Art 3). The drafters visibly struggled to come up with global institutions which are federal and democratic at the same time and to find a fair representation of the different nation states within a democratic global republic. The main problem were the tremendous differences between the existing states in terms of their size, wealth, and population. For example, if the criteria for a member seat would have been population size and the small country of Iceland with about 350,000 inhabitants were to receive at least one vote, China at that time would have received 3,500 votes. All criteria using an arithmetic progression to weight the votes necessarily resulted in the most populous state being represented hundreds of times more than the least populated. Other criteria, such as a country's industrial production, was also considered flawed, as it would not be democratic and give the United States and the Soviet Union more than half the votes.[52]

At the outset, the pluralist approach found more support in the Committee. Representatives of this position advocated for a double assembly, with a federal chamber representing the states on one hand and a world assembly directly elected by the world population on the other. Their pluralist approach was considered reformist rather than revolutionary and labelled – not federalist – but 'minimalist'. Over time however, Borgese's universalist approach became more popular in the Committee. According to his political vision, the individual should be the starting point for building the world state rather than a national citizen – or the existing nation states. He held the majoritarian view that all people of the world should be represented as equals in the world state, and that the vote of all individuals, irrespective of their nationality, should have the same weight. Accordingly, Borgese refused to refer to states in the electoral system but wanted to strengthen the global spirit by inventing new regions and constituencies. The complex structure of Borgese's approach, eventually pursued by the Committee, was seen as a 'maximalist'. It is indeed a rather unitary approach.[53]

52 Analysis by Garrett ibid 640.

53 Rosenboim (n 21) 181ff.

Intentionally, the constitutional design of the world state created little overlap and interaction between the two levels of politics, eg, national governments had no influence on electoral procedures. Thus, the ambition was not to transform a fragmented system of states loosely held together by confederal arrangements into a binding federal system, but rather to first redivide the world into new units which then simultaneously delegate their powers to the World Republic. For this reason (also), the universalist approach was at the beginning met with fierce resistance even within the Committee. Despite the opposition, this system was incorporated into the final draft after July 1947.[54] It is regrettable that the views of Borgese had such a dominant influence on the draft. His ideas might be appealing intellectually. From a practical perspective it seems obvious, however, that newly designed regions holding no power can neither delegate nor share power. The real challenge would have been to design a federal system that all states would, willingly or not, join by a sovereign act, to think of compelling incentives to encourage such behavior, not least by establishing constitutional mechanisms ensuring the continued existence of states in a system of self-and shared rule.

According to the draft, there is a *Federal Convention* which is directly elected 'by the people of all states and nations', meeting once a year. The navigating of the drafters between the equality of states and the equality of citizens, however, did not lead to the obvious compromise of a bi-cameral legislative. There is just one chamber, and the delegates vote as individuals, not as representatives of their states or nations (Art 4). As for its composition, some consideration was given to the small states (but not the tiny ones). Each of the existing states with more than 100,000 inhabitants elects one delegate.[55] In addition, there is one additional delegate per million of people. The Committee considered this solution to be sufficiently democratic and acceptable to the United States and other western countries.[56] Wrongly so. The composition rules, which appear

---

54 ibid 182.

55 A state with a population below 100,000 shall be aggregated for federal electoral purposes to the electoral unit closest to its borders (Art 4).

56 See eg Culbertson (n 24) 479: 'The United States, the biggest have-nation in the world, will thus be completely disarmed by a World Government in which the biggest have-not-nations, such as China or India, are predominant, since the voice of America in the World Government shall be permanently restricted to one-ninth of the total voices'. And, with a racist undertone, ibid 481: 'It is true that the life and dignity of any human is a sacred trust of society. It is not true that China with its 400,000,000 is ten times more valuable and important than France with its 40,000,000. It is not true that 150,000,000 Americans who have created the greatest democracy of all times should sit humbly in the back rows of the world arena and surrender their sovereignties to a billion proliferating Asiatics. If the population concept of humanity were true, then the only just solution would be the

much later in a similar form in the second chamber of the Ethiopian parliament, offer no guarantees to small states and enable some big players to dominate parliamentary matters.

The functions of the Federal Convention are largely electoral.[57] Each Electoral College nominates lists of candidates for the *World Council* which will be in permanent session (Art 12). The Federal Convention then elects nine Councilmen from each list (at least three of them but not more than six must be from their ranks) for an electoral period of three years renewable (Art 7).[58] The Federal Council also elects, on nominations by international organisations, eighteen additional members regardless of their origin.[59] The indirectly elected *World Council* with its total of 99 members (Art 6) has the primary powers of a legislative: it initiates and enacts legislation for the World Republic (Art 7) and passes its budget (Art 13). It is, in fact, the unicameral legislature of the World Republic.[60] International organizations are apparently not planned to be integrated into the new governance structure. Their right to nominate additional members to the parliament of the World Republic remains nevertheless the only coordination mechanism the draft provides for.

The nine Electoral Colleges of the Convention also nominate up to three candidates for the office of *President* of the World Republic. Out of this list, the Federal Convention then elects the president with a two-thirds majority for a non-renewable period of six years (Art 5). No two successive Presidents shall originate from the same region (Art 10). The drafters of the World Constitution took inspiration from the US constitution when they provided that the executive power, including the right to initiate power in federal legislation, was vested in the President (Art 10), that the President could veto any legislation of the Council, and that the Council could overrule such veto by a two-thirds majority (Art 14).

The drafters must have looked into the German constitution before they agreed that the President appoints a *Chancellor*, who is to be the political leader of the world state, responsible to both the President and the Council (Art 11).[61] In case of a conflict between the two authorities, the Chancellor is

---

one proposed by the University of Chicago Committee. This is a solution of a world ant-hill state, whose sole function is regimented breeding, repeated with cosmical boredom untold millions of times through millions of years'.

57 Bordwell (n 35) 388.

58 Garrett (n 23) 640, is surely right when he claims that 'a Councilman so elected will have great difficulty finding his constituents'.

59 See ibid 566 for comments.

60 See Bordwell (n 35) 388.

61 ibid 387.

expected to side with the Council as the dominant political force of the World Republic.[62]

The World Council and the president are mandated by the constitution to establish the following *Special Bodies* with consultative or preparatory powers (Art 8):

- a House of Nationalities and States, with representatives from each, for the safeguarding of local institutions and autonomies and the protection of minorities;
- a Syndical or functional Senate, for the representation of syndicates and unions or occupational associations and any other corporate interests of transnational significance, as well as for mediation or arbitration in non-justiciable issues among such syndicates or unions or other corporate interests;
- an Institute of Science, Education and Culture.

Here, the pluralist approach supported by certain committee members has left some traces. Nationalities and states are represented to uphold the interest – not of the autonomous constituent units of the world federation which remain blurred – but to safeguard the 'local' (and apparently not the national) institutions and autonomies. Just like the functional Senate, the House of Nationalities and States is not designed as House or Chamber of parliament but as a special body with mere consultative powers.

The World Government is also mandated to establish a *Planning Agency*, composed of twenty-one independent members appointed by the president (subject to vetoes by two-thirds of the Council) for a fixed period of twelve years. The Planning Agency prepares programs and budgets for expenditures, both for current needs and for long-range improvements (Art 9).

The supreme judiciary power of the World Republic is vested in a *Grand Tribunal* of sixty Justices, with the President of the World Republic as Chief Justice and Chairman, and the Chairman of the Council as Vice-Chairman *ex officio*. The President as Chief Justice appoints the Justices of the Grand Tribunal for a period of 15 years (non-renewable), subject to vetoes by the Council by a two-thirds majority. The task of the Grand Tribunal is to settle disputes between the world government and the nation-states, disputes between the world government and individuals, international disputes, constitutional issues, and interpretation of the world laws.[63]

---

62 ibid.

63 Baratta (n 40) 316.

Twelve of the sixty Justices are assigned to each of the five benches of the Grand Tribunal (Art 18). The benches illustrate the wide powers the world judiciary was meant to assume:

- the First Bench deals with constitutional issues between the primary organs and powers of the World Government;
- the Second Bench deals with conflicts between the World Government and any of its component units, whether single states or unions thereof or Regions, as well as with issues and conflicts of component units of the World Republic among themselves;
- the Third Bench deals with conflicts between the World Government and individual citizens, corporations, and associations of citizens;
- the Fourth Bench deals with conflicts among component units, whether single states or unions of states or Regions, and individual citizens, corporations, or associations of citizens when the issues affect the interpretation or enactment of federal law;
- the Fifth Bench deals with conflicts, when they affect the interpretation and enactment of federal law, among individual citizens, corporations, or any other associations.

The *Supreme Court* serves as an appeal court.[64] It is composed of seven members: five representing each Bench of the Grand Tribunal, with the Chief Justice as their Chairman and the Chairman of the Council as their Vice-Chairman *ex officio* (Art 19). No two members of the Supreme Court shall originate from the same region. The representatives of the Benches in the Supreme Court are elected by secret vote of the Grand Tribunal. Regions which have not been represented in the Supreme Court for two successive six-year terms have mandatory precedence in the elections for the third term (Art 19). The Grand Tribunal, with the approval of the Supreme Court, can establish Lower Federal Courts and a Federal Appellate Court in each region (Art 22).

In addition, there is also an elected Tribunal of the People 'as a spokesman for the minorities' and people's defender. His mandate is to defend the rights of individuals and groups against violation or neglect by the World Government or any of its component units, to further and demand, 'as a World Attorney before the World Republic', and the observance of the letter and spirit of the Constitution (Art 27). The Tribune, or its appointed Deputy, has the privilege of the floor before the Grand Tribunal and the Supreme Court; but no vote in either (Art 26). He has no power except vehement oratory.

64 ibid.

A special body, *The Chamber of Guardians*, is provided for the control and direction of the armed forces of the Federal Republic of the World. The World Council and the Grand Tribunal elect the six members of the Chamber of Guardians every three years (Art 35). The Committee to frame a World Constitution wanted to avoid, on the one hand, placing the federal armed forces under the exclusive authority of the President, as this would create a constant danger of dictatorship, and, on the other hand, putting them under the authority of the World Council alone, which would, they presumed, tend to be dominated by the Council members from the wealthier and more advanced regions.[65]

Even if the Committee had to put up with heavy criticism of the proposed constitution, they were acknowledged to have at least made some promising departures and stimulated serious thoughts about a possible world government.[66] However, even the hope for such debates were disappointed. One reason for the frustrating disregard of the proposal might be found in the events that transpired over the three years that passed between the formation of the Committee in 1945 and the publication of the preliminary draft in 1948.

## 8 Arms Racing Instead of Federalizing

The Committee was formed in 1945, a moment when the world was in deep shock. The outrage of the global war was deeply etched in the collective memory of humankind, and the need for improved cooperation widely recognised. The fear of the atomic bomb seemed to allow no other option than to join together in a global organization to prevent the self-destruction of the world. Advocating at the forefront for a new world government were the physicists, feeling partly responsible for the weapon they had created. Many of them were upset by the reluctance of political leaders to establish legitimate global institutions able to effectively ensure peace. Albert Einstein approved of the Committee to Frame a World Constitution and in October 1945 co-signed a letter to the New York Times, among others with Justice Owen J Roberts, Senator J William Fulbright, Mortimer J Adler, and founder of the American Veterans Committee Charles Bolté, stating that: 'The [UN] Charter is a tragic illusion unless we are ready to take the further steps necessary to organize peace.[…] We must aim at a Federal Constitution of the world, a working world-wide

65 Review by Dean (n 25) 657.
66 See eg ibid 658; Garret (n 23) 640.

legal order, if we hope to prevent an atomic war.'[67] Out of fear of a third world war, Einstein founded the Emergency Committee of the Atomic Scientists in the spring of 1946. The aim of this committee was to raise funds to influence policy in the interests of the great atomic science movement.[68]

The plan faltered as the funds accumulated at a sluggish pace, falling significantly short of the desired target. Additionally, a growing discord emerged among scientists regarding the most effective means of conveying the perils of nuclear warfare to the public. Some argued that the scientists' own narratives of horror might inadvertently fuel public hysteria, exacerbating apprehensions about Russia and rendering international cooperation on nuclear weapon control unattainable. In these important months, when scientists were trying to establish new forms of international cooperation and control of nuclear weapons, the governments in the West and the East were already engaged in a race of nuclear armament. Scientists felt thus forced to choose between supporting their own country's defence and advocating for joint solutions to global threats. The hardening of the cold war fronts generated a schism among the scientists and robbed them of the shared objective they had previously collaboratively pursued. Even though part of the group saw in this very impotence the purpose of advancing international cooperation, regaining momentum, and pleading for a world government at the Lake Geneva Conference in Wisconsin in the summer of 1947, it was ultimately too late. The United States had already adopted a policy of containing Soviet expansion, and the conflict between the Western and Eastern blocs appeared to be cementing.[69] Probably its ultimate death blow came from Edward Teller's decision to abandon the dream of world government for building the H-bomb.[70]

Given these events, it becomes less astonishing that the release of the initial draft of a world constitution in 1948 was met with some criticism and more indifference. Disheartened physicists had either disengaged from politics, lost their optimism, or were already involved in the development of the next generation of bombs, while American policy focused on racing communism for its position of world leadership. In this regard, the well-intentioned efforts of Hutchins, Borgese, and co to eliminate American bias and bridge the ideological gap between totalitarian communism and rugged individualism, while

---

67 Cited in Baratta (n 40) 303.

68 ibid 304.

69 ibid 307ff.

70 ibid 304ff, 307ff, 310.

combining a regulated economy with social liberalism in a synthesis of East and West, truly appear to have fallen short of comprehending reality.[71]

## 9 Conclusions

The Committee to Draft a World Constitution worked for good reasons and with high ambitions on a constitution few people bothered to have a look at. The great vision, however, hit the ground of reality hard. The devastating failure of the scholarly attempt to federalise the world can be attributed to numerous factors, some linked to political context, others related to the drafting process itself, still others linked to the substance of the constitutional draft. As in all federalising processes, the procedural and substantive flaws cannot easily be separated as the shortcomings of the process impact on its outcome. Both factors, which mutually reinforced each other when the draft of the world constitution was made, reduced the legitimacy and effectivity of the grand plan. The method, the famous world federalist Gandhi persistently claimed, is more important than the end. If he had been a member of the drafting committee, he surely would have insisted on improving it.

The fact that a few well-intentioned academics of the Global North made the draft limited the chances of success. The lack of expertise in federalism, and constitutionalism more broadly, prevented the draft from being academically sound. Working behind closed doors, even before politicians were requested to make difficult compromises, further reduced the legitimacy of the process. Power cannot be effectively shared without involving those who hold it. Dealing with powerholders is not an easy task, especially when power is to be divided, shared, and constrained, but it is unavoidable. Ivory tower actors easily surpass themselves when asked to analyse and categorise power sharing arrangements, producing them is outside of their reach. Far away from the rough places where power operates, scholars run the risk of producing a 'mist of noble generalities and quasi poetic allusions' which, as a vicious commentator notes, are either bizarre or extraordinarily naïve – or both.[72]

Substantively, the draft constitution contains several shortcomings. The first concern that clearly stands out is the undecidedness over the very nature of the federal units. Most members of the drafting committee and their families

---

71 See ibid 317.

72 Culbertson (n 24) 474. Culbertson even claimed that he had never read anything 'so childish and at the same time so ferocious; so grimly utopian and yet so ominous as this Federal Constitution for the World State'.

had suffered from nationalism in its violent and brutal forms and wanted to build a world state to constrain the dangers they associated with the nation state. As refugees of Nazism and fascism, they had lost all trust in states and saw the World Republic as a means to do away with them, once and for all. From a federal perspective (and not only), the abolition of nation-states entails fundamental problems that the drafters either failed to recognize or failed to find a solution for. After all, federations without federal units cannot exist, and if they should still be made, they cannot survive. Federations without powerful decentralized hubs, persistently defending their right to autonomy, and their right to participate when decisions are made at the centre, are dysfunctional. Power has the tendency to accumulate, not to be divided and shared. To guarantee horizontal power-sharing, power must therefore be stopped and constrained by (other) power. The same is true for vertical power sharing. The draft of the committee, however, is federal by name only and imbued by a unitary spirit. The drafters hesitated to position federal units as powerful regional centres serving their constituencies, guaranteeing the diversity, and counterbalancing the powers of the world institutions. Consequently, the existing states, their interests and their diversity were looming heavily. This weight of reality does not go well with the light approach of the drafters to accommodate it. Some diversity and rotation principles, as provided for in the draft, do not suffice to provide relevant unity while taking diversity seriously.

It was far-fetched to expect political leaders to accept such new and unpredictable global institutions. It was also unreasonable to expect citizens placing their trust in creatively invented entities, such as the Federal Convention, the World Council, the Grand Tribunal and accepting that their national representatives would only sit in advisory bodies, such as the House of Nationalities and States. The authors of the draft neither succeeded in mapping out global institutions that could operate both federally and democratically, nor in drawing clear guarantees for regional self-governance and autonomy.

Critics of the draft were not mistaken when they stated that the members of the committee totally misconceived the real political, economic, social, and cultural forces in the world of the presence and the future. Garret, for example, felt that the division into world regions, by which the committee hoped to break down the fronts between the East and the West, were too far from any political (or other) reality to have any chance of being implemented.[73] Of course, he was right. How should electoral districts like Atlantis, Eurasia, Afrasia or Austrasia possibly organise elections and hold their representatives

73 Garrett (n 23) 640.

accountable? And how should elected world parliamentarians find their constituencies and defend their interests?

Culbertson was amongst those pointing out a circumstantial fact: the nation-state constitutes an 'all pervading reality of the political structure in the world', an all-compelling living force, politically, economically, militarily, culturally, and psychosocially. He rightly concluded that it was as utopian as it was blinded trying to abolish the states or drastically reduce their sovereignty 'by waving a magic wand'.[74] The making of the nation-state, he claimed (and his premonition proofed to be accurate), remained a creative and uncomplete endeavour and stood for the right of people to be sovereign and free.[75] He strongly believed that lasting world peace was possible but must be guaranteed by an effective World Court applying international law, not by dwarf-like attempts to diminish states.[76] From a federal perspective one cannot but agree with him and Bordwell claiming that we must build (a federation) 'with the material we have, or we shall not build at all'.[77] It was indeed quite clear that a World Republic could not do without the compelling living force of states. The drafters and their critics, however, neglected the fact that federations are not meant to do away with their units. They exist to guarantee the existence and autonomy of their constituent units, to accept their diversity, and to provide for mechanisms to jointly create and implement some limited unity.

The failure of the draft must also be reflected against the political reality in 1948. The development of a world federation takes times, especially when the era of international cooperation is still in its infancy. During its work, the committee only saw two possible options for the future: binding international regulation of nuclear weapons or the Earth's self-destruction. It oversaw a third option which pushed itself into the political foreground while intellectuals racked their brains at desks: engaging in an arms race and attaining military dominance over adversaries, or at last, a balance of terror that neither side dares to seriously shake. Three years after the committee's enthusiastic initiation, when the draft was eventually published, the divisions between East and West had already solidified to a point where the idea of being governed by a single world government, not to mention under the abolishment of national sovereignty, had become more than inconceivable.

---

74 Culbertson (n 24) 476.

75 ibid 475: 'To try to abolish nationalism is like abolishing love: to abolish love, one must abolish women [and probably men, too]; and to abolish nationalism, one must abolish nations'.

76 ibid 476.

77 Bordwell (n 35) 387.

In view of the events of recent years, namely the recent pandemic, the climate crisis, migration and the wars in Syria, Ethiopia, and the Ukraine, we again seem to be at a turning point in history, where the magnitude of the problems to urgently tackle surpasses the means and powers of states. Some of the issues at hand might be addressed on a regional scale, but some require global rules which are applied to all. However, such coordination, urgently required to safeguard common interests of humanity, seems to be receding into an ever further distance in the presence of state failure, state capture, and autocratic regimes busy saving their own skins (and bank accounts) even at the prize of threatening peace and trampling justice.

It is not too far-fetched to say that global warming and its consequences confront the peoples of today with problems as monumental as the control of nuclear weapons and global peace were in 1945. As emissions are notoriously not static, and their effects often felt most where they are least caused, global solutions constitute a necessity. Federal systems fail to deliver when they neglect the principle of subsidiarity, and cause governance defects when burdening entities with tasks outside of their reach. Once again, there are overwhelming arguments to say that world government is necessary, and therefore must be possible. In contrast to 1945, the climate crisis cannot be 'resolved' through an arms race and the making of two blocks which keep each other in check, thereby creating a precarious and costly stability. While the peoples of the world clearly need more coordination, and the victims of brutal violations of universal rights and freedoms more protection, states do not federate but rather drift apart. Global institutions are currently not progressing but receding.[78]

Especially in this time overshadowed by suffering and gloomy prospects, it seemed important to recall the ambitions of earlier times. Hutchins was right when he claimed that university meant universality and that, when there was no future, it was up to universities to create one.[79] The drafters of the proposal of 1948 accurately stated that debates about a world government were surrounded by great uncertainty and discussions between scholars, diplomats, and politicians trapped in clouds for lack of specific common points of reference.

78 Take, for example, the World Trade Organisation Arbitration Tribunal, which has been completely undermined by the United States blocking of the appointment of new judges. Another illustrative instance is the obstruction faced by the World Health Organisation team when attempting to access China for the purpose of investigating the origins of the coronavirus.

79 Borgese and McKeon (n 18).

'Most of those who are opposed to world government, and most of those who support it, have no clear idea of what they are opposing or supporting.'[80]

Realities are hard to change, and yet they often do. A precondition of such change is that ideas are aired, debated, and improved. Visions can turn into strategies, and strategies evolve into politics, plans, tactics, and finally deals. Garrett, commenting on the draft, expressed the hope that the proposal to establish a world constitution would stimulate other speculative people who have their feet a little bit deeper in the mud to take up the same problem. We share this hope and, with this contribution, aspire to motivate scholars and other actors to not give into fatalism but make another, better, 'proposal to history'.[81]

## Bibliography

Army Information School, *Pamphlet No 4, Pillars of Peace. Documents Pertaining to American Interest in Establishing a Lasting World Peace. January 1941-February 1946* (Book Department, Army Information School, Carlisle Barracks, Pa 1946).

Baratta JP, *The Politics of World Federation: From World Federalism to Global Governance* (Praeger Publishing 2004).

Belser EM, 'The White Man's Burden: Arbeit und Menschenrechte in der globalisierten Welt' (Habilitation thesis, Universität Freiburg 2007).

Belser EM, 'Rosika Schwimmer - Erinnerungen an eine Frau ohne Grenzen und ohne Heimat' in Belser EM, Pichonnaz P and Stöckli H (eds), *Le droit sans frontières – Recht ohne Grenzen – Law without Borders* (Stämpfli 2022).

Billion JF, 'The World Federalist Movements from 1945 to 1954 and European Integration' (1991) 33 The Federalist 28.

Bordwell P, 'Preliminary Draft of a World Constitution by Robert M. Hutchins and G. A. Borgese, Review' (1949) 16 The University of Chicago Law Review 386.

Borgese GA, 'Introduction to Constitution 111 (Constitutio Major), 3 January 1947 [Doc. 112]' (1951) 5 Common Cause 640.

Borgese GA and McKeon RP, 'BorgeseMcKeon Memorandum to Hutchins (September 16, 1945)' CFWC, box 46, document 2.

Burgess M, *In Search of the Federal Spirit: New Theoretical and Empirical Perspectives in Comparative Federalism* (Oxford University Press 2012).

80 Robert Maynard Hutchins, 'The State of the University' (Report, Chicago, November 1946) 8f found in Common Cause (n 19) 11.

81 Committee to Frame a World Constitution (n 17) VII.

Bußjäger P, *Föderale Systeme. Über Entstehung, Scheitern und Erfolg von Föderalismus* (Jan Sramek Verlag 2017).

Cousins N, *Modern Man Is Obsolete* (Viking 1945).

Cousins N, Norman Cousins to Giuseppe Antonio Borgese (6 January 1948) CFWC, box 35.

Culbertson E, 'The Preliminary Draft of a World Constitution, by the Committee to Frame a World Constitution' (1949) 24 Indiana Law Journal 474.

Dean WT Jr, 'Preliminary Draft of a World Constitution by Robert M. Hutchins, G. A. Borgese, Mortimer J. Adler, Stringfellow Barr, Albert Guérard, Harold A. Innis, Erich Kahler, Wilber G. Katz, Charles H. McIlwain, Robert Redfield, Rexford G. Tugwell' (1949) 35 American Bar Association Journal 656.

Franck TM (ed), *Why Federations Fail: An Inquiry into the Requisites for Successful Federations* (New York University Press 1968).

Gandhi M, 'Quit India' in Prabhu RK and Rao UR (eds), *Quit India* (Padma Publications Ltd 1942).

Garrett R, 'A World Constitution: Analysis of the Draft by the Hutchins Committee' (1948) 34 American Bar Association Journal 563.

Hutchins RM, 'Hutchins' Radio Discussion (with R. Gustavos and R. Ogburn) on "Atomic Force: Its Meaning for Mankind" (August 18, 1945)' CFWC, box 46, document 1.

Hutchins RM, 'The State of the University' (Report, Chicago, November 1946).

Keil S and Belser EM (eds), *Federalism and Internal Conflicts* (Palgrave Macmillan 2019–2023).

Keil S and Kropp S (eds), *Emerging Federal Structures in the Post-Cold War Era* (Palgrave Macmillan 2022).

Mann T, *Deutsche Hörer!, Radiosendungen nach Deutschland aus den Jahren 1940 bis 1945* (Fischer Verlag 1987).

Mann T, *Brief über den Entwurf einer Welt-Verfassung* (Fischer Verlag 2011).

Palermo F and Kössler K, *Comparative Federalism: Constitutional Arrangement and Case Law* (Bloomsbury Publishing 2017).

Palmer M, 'Arab Republic: An Assessment of Its Failure' (1966) 20 Middle East Journal 50.

Riker WH, 'Federalism' in Goodin RE, Pettit P and Pogge T (eds), *A Companion to Contemporary Political Philosophy* (2nd edn, Blackwell Publishing Ltd 1993).

Rosenboim O, *The Emergence of Globalism: Visions of World Order in Britain and the United States, 1939–1950* (Princeton University Press 2017).

Schlup M, 'Emperor Haile Selassie, God of the Rastafarians' (*Nationalmuseum Schweiz*, 28 January 2022) <https://blog.nationalmuseum.ch/en/2022/01/emperor-haile-selassie-god-of-the-rastafarians/> accessed 20 September 2023.

Steytler N and de Visser J, "Fragile Federations' and the Dynamics of Devolution' in Palermo F and Alber E (eds), *Federalism as Decision-Making, Changes in Structures, Procedures and Policies* (Brill/Nijhoff 2015).

The Committee to Frame a World Constitution, *Preliminary Draft of a World Constitution* (University of Chicago Press 1948).

Threlkeld M, '"Chaos, War, or a New World Order?" A Radical Plan for Peace and World Government in the 1930s' (2018) 43 Peace & Change 473.

Wallace E, 'The West Indies Federation: Decline and Fall' (1962) 17 International Journal 269.

Watts RL, 'Federalism, Federal Political Systems, and Federations' (1998) 1 Annual Review of Political Science 117.

CHAPTER 2

# Economic and Fiscal Factors in the Development of Federal Constitutions

## *Lessons from the History of the German Reich and the European Union*

*Gisela Färber*

## 1 Introduction

Economic integration has played an important role as starting point for the establishment of bigger territorial entities. Furthermore, the rules of intergovernmental financial affairs not only provide a 'neutral' setting of revenues for the layers of government, but also involve aspects of political control among the governments and play an important role in the process of building federations. The roots of German federalism as well as of the European Union are quite similar regarding their economic starting points which were continually completed through common legal rules, the establishment of institutions and the centralization of further powers. The history of distribution of European financial powers shows similar patterns as those of the German Empire before the First World War; the latter were highly centralized in the 1920s.

This paper compares the historical driving factors of German federalism and the European Union regarding economic factors and the distribution of fiscal powers. Both are examples of aggregative 'federations'. This raises the question what we can learn for the challenges, risks and future of the European Union. This paper focuses especially on financial autonomy and the intergovernmental fiscal relations necessary for the governments of a federal system to fulfil their assigned tasks.

The paper therefore starts with a brief summary of the arguments in favour of economic integration of markets and the normative basics of intergovernmental fiscal relations. The following review of the German federalizing process in the 19th century that resulted in the establishment of the *Deutsches Reich*, or 'German Empire', (1871–1919) and of the establishment of the European Union more recently, focuses on the integration of markets and fiscal federalism, what provided the foundation for the development of legal rules and institutions. Finally, a comparison of these two cases shall provide insights into the further development of the EU.

© GISELA FÄRBER, 2024 | DOI:10.1163/9789004528581_004

## 2 The Integration of Markets as Starting Point of Common Political 'Arrangements': Some Theoretical Arguments

The economic theory of (market) integration has been well established and was the basis for the establishment of the European Economic Union in the late 1950s.[1] The theory of fiscal federalism has been a more recent development.[2] Although both are influenced by empirical analysis of historical developments, they are both based on the principles of normative economic theory.

### 2.1 *Advantages of the Integration of Markets, Currency Unions, and the Centralisation of Competences*

The economic theory of integration is an enhancement of the theory of economic trade.[3] In the 18th century, Ricardo developed the theory of comparative advantage whereby international exchange of goods[4] creates mutual economic benefit because it leads to an efficient use of production factors and achieves economies of scale.

During the 20th century – influenced by the continuing process of the European integration – further elements were added into a broader theory of economic integration, which on the one hand started from the decline of costs of national borders and on the other hand discussed the advantages and problems of the development of common institutions. However, there are more advantages of economic integration:[5]

- Free migration of labour force and capital provides further benefits from their most productive assignment. Limited capacities of immovable or natural production factors no longer restrict national economic growth.
- Common infrastructure and transnational standards lower production costs for all producers and open up broader markets.
- A common currency reduces transaction costs within the integrated market area and creates greater transparency for a more intensive competition.

---

1 See Alfred Müller-Armack, *Wirtschaftsordnung und Wirtschaftspolitik. Studien und Konzepte zur sozialen Marktwirtschaft und zur europäischen Integration* (Verlag Rombach 1966).

2 See Richard A. Musgrave, *The Theory of Fiscal Finance: A Study in Public Economy* (McGraw-Hill 1959).

3 See Peter Zweifel and Robert Heller, *Internationaler Handel: Theorie und Empirie* (2nd edn, Physica-Verlag 1992) 345.

4 See David Ricardo, *The Principles of Political Economy and Taxation* (John Murray 1817).

5 See Jürgen E. Blank, Hartmut Clausen and Holger Wacker, *Internationale ökonomische Integration: Von der Freihandelszone zur Wirtschafts-und Währungsunion* (Vahlen 1998).

- Common law, uniform rules of behaviour and standards of economic accountancy generate a stable economic frame for all economic trans-border activities.
- New institutions and rules not only lead to centralized political decisions, but also create legitimacy and new common identities.

There is no special order or sequence for the introduction of the various integration measures during the process of integration. However, there should be a consequent logic among them, and a balance between, on the one hand, economic instruments implemented and, on the other hand, legal and institutional developments.

### 2.2 *Assignment of Fiscal Authority and Intergovernmental Fiscal Equalization*

A special field of economic integration within the public sector deals with the intergovernmental financial relations. The basic ideas come from the theory of fiscal federalism, which is concerned with the distribution of financial powers – notably, service provision, expenditure and revenues among the levels of government and intergovernmental transfer payments/fiscal equalization. The closer jurisdictions are connected, the more important common fiscal rules and transfer payments get. These not only achieve distributional goals, but are very often also constructed to compensate for imbalances of economic capacities and the suboptimal distribution of revenues.[6]

However, there are some fundamental issues that play an important role for the growing economic integration of markets and of formerly independent countries:

- Each level of government needs own revenues to cover the expenditures necessary to fulfil its assigned tasks.
- That autonomy includes the decision on (marginal) expenditures and tax rates.
- The implicit or explicit fiscal equalization should be constructed in a way that it is able to:
  - compensate for deficiencies in the assignment of tax revenues,
  - internalize (cross-border) external effects, and
  - achieve distributional goals (at least to a certain degree).

6 See, eg, Richard A. Musgrave, 'Who Should Tax, Where and What?' in Charles E. McLure (ed), *Tax Assignment in Federal Countries* (Centre for Research on Federal Financial Relations 1983) 2 and Teresa Ter-Minassian, 'Intergovernmental Fiscal Relations in a Macroeconomic Perspective' in Teresa Ter-Minassian (ed), *Fiscal Federalism in Theory and Practice* (International Monetary Fund 1997).

Theory assumes full authority of government tiers, that a new supra-state level type of government can only achieve after many years of integration. The broad variety of fiscal constitutions in federal countries around the world shows, however, that the 'integration' of intergovernmental financial relations can be reached in many ways of which each has to follow its own logic and should correspond with other details of the economic and institutional integration. The different economic capacities of the states to be integrated might have a fundamental influence on the distribution of financial competences to the new centre and the restrictions to be established for the former independent and now 'integrated' member states.

It is rather new, that a stable currency union requires convergence and decline of public sector deficits.[7] The former arguments against excessive public debt dealt with the principle of solidarity among the members of a currency union that should exclude a bail-out. The latter is more likely in formally established currency unions and fully integrated capital markets because the member states have lost their 'automatic balance' of trade deficits via changes of exchange rates within the currency markets. The recent experience in the so-called 'Euro debt crisis' 2010–2012 has additionally shown the vulnerability of the whole currency union regarding market speculation against small member states that are heavily in debt.

## 3 The Genesis of the German *Reich*

The history of the establishment of a German nation state under the label of the German *Reich* in the 19th century is one of a continuing economic integration during which more and more common institutions were built up and rules were harmonized. This process was neither stable nor coordinated but took place in three fundamental steps. These steps were accompanied by democratization and the implementation of constitutions. Even wars were waged among later 'partners' in the new national state.[8] These three steps are named after the new supra-state institutions:

7 See Paul De Grauwe, *Economics of Monetary Union* (4th edn, Oxford University Press 2000).

8 See Werner Frotscher and Bodo Pieroth, *Verfassungsgeschichte* (12th edn, Beck 2013); Heinrich August Winkler, *Der lange Weg nach Westen*, vol 2 (Beck 2001); Thomas Nipperdey, *Deutsche Geschichte 1800–1866. Bürgerwelt und starker Staat* (Beck 1983); Thomas Nipperdey, *Deutsche Geschichte 1866–1918*, vol 1 (Beck 1990); Thomas Nipperdey, *Deutsche Geschichte 1866–1918*, vol 2 (Beck 1992).

- the German Confederation (1815–1866),
- the North-German Federation (1867–1870), and
- the (second) German *Reich* (1871–1919).

### 3.1 *The German Confederation*

The main goals of the German Confederation[9] were internal and external security. It had its impetus in the Napoleonic wars, during which many German states had lost their independence or 'survived' as more or less voluntary allies of the French. Most of the very small independent German states closed ranks and established a joint institution in order to improve their military power.

The Federal Convention was introduced as a central decision-making body. Members were the governments of the States. The number of votes of the States in the Federal Convention followed the size of their population. The law of the Confederation overrode State law, and joint military entities were founded among the partners.

It took about 20 years to foster economic integration by starting a customs union (*Deutscher Zollverein*) which was introduced step by step from 1834 onwards. The customs union was initiated by Prussia, which took the leadership. Prussia's great Germanic rival, Austria, was suspicious regarding the customs union. Austria had lost the Imperial Crown across all German states in 1806 when Napoleon made himself the Emperor; however, the Austrian Emperor still reigned across a vast territory including the South of Germany. Prussia was the emerging state with regard to economic and military power and had increased its territory at the Vienna Congress in 1815. During the Napoleonic occupation, Prussia had undertaken important economic and administrative reforms.[10] These reforms put the country on top of the upcoming so-called industrial revolution.

The introduction of a customs union from 1834 onwards was accompanied by other measures of integration.[11] One of the most important factors for the increasing proceeding of the industrial revolution across Germany was the building of an inter-state railway network that not only lowered transportation costs but also offered more continuous transportation routes for the

9 See for details Thomas Nipperdey, *Deutsche Geschichte 1800–1866. Bürgerwelt und starker Staat* (Sonderdruck, Beck 1998).

10 The so-called 'Stein-Hardenberg' reforms, see Hans-Ulrich Wehler, *Deutsche Gesellschaftsgeschichte 1700 – 1815*, vol 1 (Beck 1987); Elisabeth Fehrenbach, *Vom Ancien Regime zum Wiener Kongress* (4th edn, Oldenbourg 2001).

11 See Knut Borchart, *Grundriß der deutschen Wirtschaftsgeschichte* (Vandenhoeck & Ruprecht 1978).

economy. People from poor agricultural regions migrated to more prosperous areas where their labour force was much needed in the growing industries. Many people living in poor regions emigrated abroad; thus, there were fewer people to feed, particularly during the frequent hunger crises. Meanwhile, the emigrants had the chance to gain a decent source of income in the growing industries or in foreign countries.[12]

The migration of workforce to the growing cities and the increase of income there also led to the development of a new and expanding self-assured middle class. Their members fostered the new ideas of separation of powers and the implementation of a 'formal' constitution. In 1848, they initiated the so-called 'March revolution'. The 'March revolution' was successful in various German states, eg by enlarging the power of the existing Parliaments, gaining freedom of the press and abolishing still existing peasant bondage. Finally, a first all-German Parliament, the National Assembly, was founded at the *Paulskirche* in Frankfurt. The National Assembly appointed the first national government for Germany and elaborated, passed and published the first German Constitution, but failed to agree on it with the reigning heads of the member states. However, upcoming riots and street disorders on the one hand and the growing antagonism of Prussia and Austria on the other hand marked the end of all achievements of the First German Empire in 1849. In the following two years, Prussia tried to establish a German state that should be allied with Austria under its leadership, while Austria tried to implement a 'Greater-Austria'. In 1850, the conflicts were resolved by re-establishing the former rules of the German Confederation.

The Confederation continued until 1866/67 and discussed reforms without results. It ended after the so-called 'German war' between Prussia and Austria in 1866, in which Prussia was victorious. At that time, a majority of States (almost all South German states, eg the kingdoms of Bavaria, Baden, Württemberg as well as Saxony and Hannover) were allies of Austria and only very few (eg, Mecklenburg-Schwerin and Oldenburg) were connected to Prussia. Only a few minor States were 'neutral'.

### 3.2 *The North German Federation*

In 1867, Prussia founded the North German Federation, located north of the river *Main*, as a genuine federation. It can be seen as the pre-stage of

12 Although life did not improve for everyone due to the extremly bad working and living conditions in the industries (see eg Karl Marx, 'Das Kapital – Kritik der politischen Ökonomie, vol 1' in Institut für Marxismus-Leninismus [ed], *Marx-Engels-Werke*, vol 23 [Dietz Verlag 1962]; Friedrich Engels, *Die Lage der arbeitenden Klasse in England* [Verlag Otto Wigand 1845]).

the German *Reich* with a constitution and legislative bodies in form of the Prussian Parliament for the narrower Prussia and of the *Reichstag* for the supra-state level; the member states were represented in a Second Chamber by a *Bundesrat* (not a *Reichstag*!). The member states were still responsible for the administration of federal laws. At the same time, Prussia continued the economic integration by establishing a 'Customs Federation' with a Customs Parliament responsible for a common commercial law, uniform measurements and weights, and a new industrial code.

During the period of the North German Federation, industrialization continued. Especially the production of coal and steel was growing and needed the expansion of the railway network. Smaller railway enterprises were nationalized, which made the establishment of a common transport infrastructure easier. The North German Confederation also continued the policies of centralization of economic standards and institutions.[13] The *Reichstag* passed laws on a citizenship and passports, free movement of persons, a General Commercial Code, laws for a General Draft Order and Economic Cooperatives, a Trade, Commerce and Industry Act, a law for the protection of intellectual property and introduced a common postal service with a uniform pay scale.

Nevertheless, this more integrated area did not convince South German states to join the Federation. However, they worked together on economic integration within the Custom Federation. It was only with the German–French War in 1870, to which the South German states were obliged to contribute troops due to military treaties with Prussia from 1866,[14] that these States were formally included into the Federation by the so-called 'November treaties'.

### 3.3 *The German* Reich *or* Kaiserreich *1871–1918*

The German *Reich* – also named *Kaiserreich* to distinguish it from the later 'Third *Reich*' – was founded on 1 January 1871. On that date a new constitution entered into force. Additionally to his title as Prussia's Head of State, the Prussian King became German Emperor and presided the new federation. Furthermore, he was the head of the military forces of the *Reich*. A bicameral parliament was established: the *Reichstag* (Imperial Assembly) was composed of elected (male) members. Most of them came from Prussia because more than two thirds of the population of Germany lived there at that time.[15] The

13 See Hans-Ulrich Wehler, *Deutsche Gesellschaftsgeschichte*, vol 3 (Beck 1995) 309.

14 See Klaus-Jürgen Bremm, *70/71 – Preußens Triumph über da Kaiserreich Frankreich und die Folgen* (wbg Theiss 2019).

15 See Sean Mueller and Alan Fenna, 'Dual versus Administrative Federalism: Origins and Evolution of Two Models' (2022) 52 Publius 525.

member states were represented in the *Bundesrat* (the Federal Council) where the number of votes depended on the size of the State ranging from three to six. This weighting guaranteed that Prussia and its allies always held the majority of votes. The *Reich* also had a common national border.

Executive power was centred in the position of the *Reichskanzler* (Imperial Chancellor).[16] At the beginning, there was no intention to establish a central administration at the federal level, continuing the practice of the North German Federation. However, the Prussian Chancellor Otto von Bismarck hugely shaped the role of the Imperial Chancellor. He had run Prussia as Minister President from 1862 and then held both offices from 1871 until 1890 – with a very short interruption in 1873. There was less federal administration during this time. It was mostly subordinate to the Prussian ministries and administrations. Instead of ministries, Bismarck implemented Secretaries of State under his control, who headed agencies, among them agencies for the administration of railways, postal services, judiciary and treasury, external and internal affairs, and the German colonies.

The process of economic integration was continued and intensified from 1871 onwards.[17] The end of the internal state borders and the abolition of all remaining (now internal) customs reduced the formerly still existing border costs and opened further opportunities for economics of scale as well as for bigger markets.

In 1871, a currency union[18] was implemented which became compulsory in 1873. The *Reichsmark* became the only currency in November 1876; all other currencies – except the simple '*Taler*' which was valid until 1907, the Austrian '2-*Taler*'-piece valid until 1900 and the Bavarian '*Heller*' valid until 1924 – were no longer accepted. Later, from 1910 onwards, the gold-based currency was complemented by banknotes issued by the Central Bank and, until 1914, by 'private note issuing banks' of the States.

Common measures and weights were in force, patent and property rights protected. The completion and standardization of infrastructure were as important:[19]

16 See Michael Kotulla, *Deutsches Verfassungsrecht 1806–1918. Eine Dokumentensammlung nebst Einführungen*, vol 1 (Springer 2006) 279.

17 See eg Hans-Werner Hahn, *Die industrielle Revolution in Deutschland* (2nd edn, Oldenbourg 2005).

18 See Johannes Beermann, 'Zur Einführung der Mark im Dezember 1871' *Börsen-Zeitung* (Frankfurt am Main, 3 December 2021) <https://www.bundesbank.de/de/presse/gastbeitraege/zur-einfuehrung-der-mark-im-dezember-1871-782816> accessed 3 February 2023.

19 See Hans-Peter Ullmann, *Das Deutsche Kaiserreich 1871–1918* (Suhrkamp Verlag 1995).

- The States started to purchase existing private railway enterprises and to establish an inter-connected railway network across Germany which again promoted further industrialization, migration of workers and transport of foodstuffs from the countryside to the growing cities. However, until 1920 the States did not want to have a single German Railway Enterprise (*Deutsche Reichsbahn*) because railways were profitable enterprises at that time.
- The legal system was unified: common civil and criminal laws were introduced; a Federal Court was introduced as highest instance in civil and criminal matters in addition to the harmonized system of courts and justice of the States.
- Bismarck introduced Germany-wide social insurance schemes: social health insurance in 1883, social accident insurance in 1884 and social pension insurance in 1889. Participation was compulsory for all blue-collar male and female workers and the schemes were financed by employer and employee contributions. They were run by a so-called 'self-administration' which was controlled by representatives of employers and employees. This marked the foundation of Germany's 'corporatist' welfare state and was the forerunner of social insurance schemes around the world.

All these economic and social reforms fostered the ongoing industrialization and increased the interdependence of the German economy. Growing urbanization required more labour force emigrating from the rural areas and a higher volume of foodstuffs to nourish them. Productivity increased in all sectors. While the industrial sector was growing, the agricultural one was shrinking. The population increased from 41 million in 1871 to 65 million in 1910.[20]

This rapid economic development was accompanied by changes in public sector economics.[21] After the German–French war, the economy consolidated from the excessive war expenditures. However, and probably influenced by social ideas – eg from Adolph Wagner and other economists[22] – public sector economic and social intervention increased. An indication for this

20 See Bundeszentrale für politische Bildung, *Bevölkerungsentwicklung* (10 August 2020) <https://www.bpb.de/kurz-knapp/zahlen-und-fakten/soziale-situation-in-deutschland/61532/bevoelkerungsentwicklung/> accessed 6 February 2023.

21 See Eckart Schremmer, *Steuern und Staatsfinanzen während der Industrialisierung. England, Frankreich, Preußen und das Deutsche Reich 1800 bis 1914* (Springer 1994).

22 See Ralf Stremmel, Florian Tennstedt and Gisela Fleckenstein (eds), *Quellensammlung zur Geschichte der deutschen Sozialpolitik 1867 bis 1914. I. Abteilung: Von der Reichsgründungszeit bis zur Kaiserlichen Sozialbotschaft (1867 – 1881)*, vol 8 (wbg 2006).

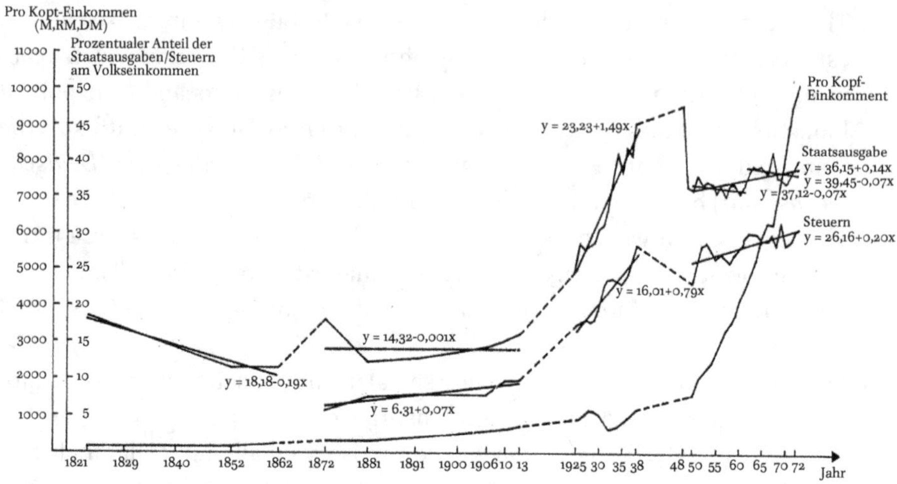


FIGURE 2.1 Economic growth and public sector development in Germany 1821–1972
Reproduced from Horst Claus Recktenwald, 'Umfang und Struktur der öffentlichen Ausgaben in säkularer Entwicklung' in Fritz Neumark (ed), *Handbuch der Finanzwissenschaft*, vol 1 (3rd edn, Mohr 1977) 721.

development was a growing share of public expenditures and tax revenues in relation to national income (see Figure 2.1).

For a long time, the new federation was underfunded, because the member states refused to assign further tax powers to the new central government. They only conceded the revenues from customs and a few excise and transactional taxes (tobacco, sugar, salt, beer, spirits and a note tax) to the Federation. The administration of these taxes took place at the State level; the collected revenues were transferred to the central government budget. The States covered expenditures that exceeded the proper *Reich* tax revenues through specific assessments (*Matrikularbeiträge*) which needed an annual approval by the States. By this mean, they kept control over the expenditures of central government.[23]

In 1875, Bismarck introduced protective tariffs in order to generate higher revenues for central government. As a reaction, the States[24] negotiated the

23 See Julia Cholet, *Der Etat des Deutschen Reiches in der Bismarckzeit* (Berliner Wissenschaftsverlag 2012) 102.

24 See Stefan Fisch, 'Von der Föderation der Fürsten zum Bundesrat des Grundgesetzes. Zur Rolle der Länder im deutschen Föderalismus von 1848 bis heute' in Hans Herbert von Arnim, Gisela Färber and Stefan Fisch (eds), *Föderalismus – Hält er noch, was er verspricht? Seine Vergangenheit, Gegenwart und Zukunft, auch im Lichte ausländischer Erfahrungen* (Duncker & Humblot 2000) 29.

TABLE 2.1 Tax revenues of the *Reich* and the States in Germany 1872–1908[a]

| | Tax and custom revenues of the *Reich* | Tax revenues of the States | Total tax and custom revenues |
|---|---|---|---|
| | **Billion *Reichsmark*** | | |
| 1872 | 169.1 | n.a. | n.a. |
| 1881 | 422.3 | 379.3 | 801.6 |
| 1891 | 821.5 | 448.3 | 1269.8 |
| 1901 | 1057.8 | 574.4 | 1632.2 |
| 1906 | 1205.4 | 677.6 | 1883.0 |
| 1907 | 1351.4 | 718.9 | 2070.3 |
| 1908 | 1411.4 | 770.2 | 2181.6 |

a Jürgen Sensch, 'Die Struktur der kassenmäßigen Steuereinnahmen im Deutschen Reich und in der Bundesrepublik Deutschland, 1872 bis 2009' (GESIS *Data Archive*, 2013) <https://search.gesis.org/research_data/ZA8530?doi=10.4232/1.11725> accessed 3 February 2023.

so-called 'Franckenstein Clause' in 1879. This clause redistributed custom revenues exceeding 130 million *Reichsmark* to the States as lump-sum distributions based on the number of inhabitants from 1883. The States did not pay any assessments between 1883 and 1893. However, the *Reich* had some revenues from its own state-owned enterprises, notably the Post Office and the Railway administration, later a State printing firm and the State bank. Economic development of activities that were taxed by the central government partially covered growing expenditures. Furthermore, expenditures were covered by an increasing public debt.

In 1881, the tax revenues of the central government exceeded those of the States (see Table 2.1). At that time, the latter levied direct taxes, particularly general and specific income taxes, but also taxes on real estate and rents, some excise taxes, taxes on inheritances and a general sales tax. In Prussia, under a new government after the retirement of Bismarck, the Minister of Finance, Johannes von Miquel, reformed the income tax in 1891/93 to create what is today regarded as the first modern income tax.[25] This reform also transferred the real estate tax and the trade tax from State to local governments. Other States followed the Prussian example. However, the tax rates of the State taxes were low, and the increase in tax revenues remained behind that of the central government.

The central government got under pressure due to increasing tax deficits and therefore had to find new tax sources for the *Reich*. After the harmonization of civil law on inheritances in 1900, the Central government introduced a decent inheritance tax, which came into force in addition to the inheritance taxes of the States (Prussia, for example, levied an inheritance tax since 1783) and later established the first shared tax. In the following, other excise taxes were introduced. The First World War led to the introduction of a wealth tax in 1913, which was declared to be a 'contribution' to military forces. In 1916, a stamp duty with a tax rate of 1% was the starting point to a central government general sales tax introduced in 1918, shortly before the end of the First World War.

However, this increase in the *Reich* tax revenues was not sufficient to cover growing central government expenditures. From 1893 onwards, the States had to pay assessments, again according to the number of their inhabitants. Deficits had to be covered by borrowing. Public debt of the States, however, was much higher than public debt of the Federation because the States had accumulated more debt before entering the *Reich*.

Only the Bavarian constitution restricted borrowing materially. In the other States, borrowing was solely allowed to cover 'extraordinary needs' and required the approval of the Parliament since the early 19th century. The Constitution of the North German Federation and of the *Reich* followed that tradition and adopted these regulations into Art 73 of the Constitution of the *Reich*.

The amount of central government public debt in relation to total public sector debt increased from zero to almost 20% in 1910 and reached about 3.5 times the amount of the *Reich* tax revenues (see Table 2.3). However, the situation of the States was even worse due to their lower level of tax revenues. Despite Miquel's tax reforms in 1906 and the transfer of specific tax sources to local governments, they experienced the highest increase of public debt in the first decade of the 20th century.

The *Kaiserreich* ended with Germany's defeat in the First World War. A further centralization of tax powers and the introduction of a fiscal equalization

25 See Wilfried Loth, *Das Kaiserreich. Obrigkeitsstaat und politische Mobilisierung* (Deutscher Taschenbuch Verlag 1996) 94.

TABLE 2.2 Own revenues of German central government[a]

| **Billion *Reichsmark*** | **1872** | **1888/89** | **1912** |
|---|---|---|---|
| *Revenues from Enterprises* | | | |
| Post Office | 14.1 | 31.7 | 112.8 |
| Railway Administration | 5.3 | 20.3 | 33.8 |
| State Printing Firm | | 1.4 | 3.2 |
| State Banks | | 1.1 | 15.3 |
| *Customs and Excise Taxes* | | | |
| Customs | 94.9 | 283.1 | 703.5 |
| Tobacco Tax | 1.3 | 10.8 | 11.3 |
| Tax on Cigarettes | | | 33.5 |
| Sugar Tax | 4.1 | 9.5 | 157.6 |
| Salt Tax | 24.6 | 41.3 | 59.7 |
| Tax on Alcohol | 33.5 | 99.7 | 203.5 |
| Tax on Breweries | 12.7 | 22.0 | 124.8 |
| Tax on Vinegar Acid | | | 0.8 |
| Sparkling Wine Tax | | | 10.7 |
| Excise Duty on Lamps | | | 13.3 |
| Excise Duty on Matches | | | 19.6 |
| *Stamp Duties on ...* | | | |
| Playing Cards | | 1.2 | 1.9 |
| Exchanges | 5.1 | 6.6 | 18.6 |
| Stock Market Gains and Lotteries | | 27.2 | 128.3 |
| Freight Papers | | | 17.4 |
| Motor Vehicles | | | 3.4 |
| Train Tickets | | | 22.3 |
| Author's Fees | | | 5.9 |
| Sales | | | 39.2 |
| Cheques | | | 3.1 |
| *Others* | | | |
| Tax on Inheritances | | | 44.0 |
| Tax on Value Growth | | | 18.0 |
| Others | | | 2.8 |
| *Total* | 176.1 | 502.1 | 1.643.3 |

a Theodor Karl von Eheberg, 'Finanzen und Steuern' in Siegfried Körte and others (eds), *Deutschland unter Kaiser Wilhelm II.*, vol 1 (Reimar Hobbing 1914).

TABLE 2.3 Public debt of the *Reich* and the member states (including local debt) 1860–1913[a]

| | *Reich* | | States | | Local governments | | Total |
|---|---|---|---|---|---|---|---|
| | *Reichsmark* | % of total | *Reichsmark* | % of total | *Reichsmark* | % of total | *Reichsmark* |
| 1872 | 38 | 2.8% | 1318 | 97.2% | n.a. | - | 4497 |
| 1880 | 268 | 4.3% | 5244 | 84.1% | 722 | 11.6% | 6234 |
| 1890 | 1318 | 11.0% | 9230 | 77.2% | 1401 | 11.7% | 11949 |
| 1900 | 2396 | 14.7% | 10797 | 66.3% | 3098 | 19.0% | 16291 |
| 1913 | 4918 | 15.1% | 16840 | 51.7% | 10800 | 33.2% | 32558 |

a Richard Tilly, *Kapital, Staat und sozialer Protest in der deutschen Industrialisierung* (Vandenhoeck & Ruprecht 1980) 87; Roland Sturm, *Staatsverschuldung. Ursachen. Wirkungen und Grenzen staatlicher Verschuldungspolitik* (Leske und Budrich 1993) 28; own calculations.

scheme took place from 1920[26] onwards and probably was – among other reasons like the ideas of public finance theory during the last three decades of the 19th century – a result of the war costs and the huge payments of reparations. The assignment of fiscal powers to the *Reich* remained incomplete because the States wanted to maintain control over the new centre. This was a sharp contrast to the dominance of Prussia among the States and its direct influence on the federal political and administrative actions, which may have been the most important reason for the loss of peace in 1914.

## 4 From the European Economic Community to the European Union

Although the European Economic Community was founded twelve years after the end of the Second World War,[27] it seems to have been the result of that experience, as the (national) powers to lead a war (steel production and coal

26 See Wolfgang Renzsch, 'Länderfinanzausgleich' (*Historisches Lexikon Bayern*, 2 May 2011) <https://www.historisches-lexikon-bayerns.de/Lexikon/Länderfinanzausgleich#Finanzausgleich_im_Bismarckreich> accessed 5 February 2023.

27 See Wilfried Loth, *Der Weg nach Europa. Geschichte der europäischen Integration 1939–1957* (Vandenhoeck & Ruprecht 1996).

mining, nuclear powers and agricultural policy) were transferred to a supranational level and hereby into the common responsibility of the six founding member states, all of them warring parties on opposite sides. Although peace was not explicitly stated as an objective of the European Economic Community, the concentration on economic advantages might have helped to generate solutions among the partners who had been 'eternal' enemies for centuries.

The idea of creating a common market among the six started with a step-by-step introduction of the four fundamental elements of economic integration:[28]

- the abolition of internal restrictions of trade and customs,
- free movement of services, people (labour) and capital,
- common external trade policies, and
- the creation of European institutions which at first were the European Council (of the member governments) and the European Commission (as executive organ).

Later, starting in the 1970s, European economic integration was 'enlarged' and 'deepened':[29]

- Enlargement of the European Economic Community and the later European Union has increased the number of member states from six to twenty-seven.
- In 1979, the European Parliament was established as third pillar of power representing the voters of the member states.
- During the years, European regulations for economic integration developed in order to deepen the internal market. In 1986, the *Single European Act* was set up, guaranteeing the 'four free movements' for goods, services, labour and capital, which had not been fully realized until then.
- The currency union constituted the next step of economic integration. In the 1992 *Maastricht Treaty*, the member states signed a plan of economic convergence that was deemed necessary to establish a stable currency union. In 1998, it was decided which countries would be part of the currency union. This decision was taken based on six indicators representing monetary and fiscal stability. An internal exchange rate was introduced. On 1 January 2002, the Euro replaced the national currencies of the participating countries. Meanwhile, 20 of the 27 EU member states are members of the Euro group.

---

28 See Zweifel and Heller (n 3) 346.

29 See Guido Thiemeyer, *Europäische Integration. Motive, Prozesse, Strukturen* (Böhlau 2010).

- The EU is involved in many national policy fields. Within the economic one, the EU holds exclusive (related to the external borders of the European market) or shared (regulation of the functions of the internal market and related fields, eg social, joint foreign, security and defence policies) powers. Furthermore, the EU has taken over a variety of 'supporting powers' in further policy fields like culture, tourism, health and education.

The assignment of fiscal powers to European institutions started in much the same way as it did in the German *Reich*. Right from the beginning, the Union had the right of an own budget[30] funded by customs and agricultural duties as well as assessments from the member states. From the 1970s, it has received 1% of the member states VAT tax base and additional GDP related tax resources from the member states as decent revenues. The budget not only needs the approval of the European Council, but also of the European Parliament, which very often tries to negotiate expenditures that the member states are not willing to supply.[31]

The EU has to deliver a balanced budget, the European treaties formally do not permit borrowing. However, in response to the refusal of the member states to concede higher assessments or even proper tax revenues to the European level – which was continuing during the recent period of crisis – the EU Commission has developed new instruments and institutions dealing with European public debt:

- In order to save the Euro, which had gotten under pressure as a result of the over-indebtedness of some smaller (South) European countries, the Euro member states first established the *European Financial Stability Facility* (EFSF) in 2010. In 2012, the EFSF was amended by the permanent *European Stability Mechanism* (ESM) in order to guarantee that member states and the common currency will not be affected by damaging capital market speculation. 'The EFSF and ESM have disbursed €295 billion to five countries. Both institutions helped preserve the integrity of the euro. They proved that a cash-for-reforms approach works, and that countries emerge fitter and more dynamic after economic and structural.'[32]

30 See Commission Directorate-General for Budget, *European Union public finance* (4th edn, Publications Office 2008).

31 See Antje Draheim, *Probleme der finanzpolitischen Willensbildung in Europa – Eine kritische Analyse der europäischen Haushalts-und Finanzverfassung* (Peter Lang International Academic Publishers 2004).

32 European Stability Mechanism, *History* <https://www.esm.europa.eu/about-us/history> accessed 7 February 2023.

- In 2012, following the experiences of the European debt crisis, the *Treaty on Stability, Coordination and Governance in the Economic and Monetary Union*, briefly: the Fiscal Stability Treaty, set up tighter regulations for public debt of member states on the base of the Fiscal Compact.[33] From that point, member states lost an important part of their budgetary sovereignty related to public debt.
- The EU does not have an explicit fiscal equalization scheme. However, an implicit fiscal equalization derives from the transfer payments of the European Budget, particularly from the special EU funds, which indicate wealthier member states as net payers and the 'poorer' ones as net recipients.[34]
- Recently, the COVID-19-crisis caused huge deficits in member state budgets and prompted the decision to establish a €750 billion COVID-fund financed by common loans of the EU, which are guaranteed by the member states.[35]

The war of Russia against Ukraine caused new European expenditures. These will probably be covered by additional EU borrowing and just cover up ongoing discussion in several fields related to the European financial structure: starting with discussions about the fiscal compact to be softened, eg for the 60% debt/GDP ratio, the debate on a European minimum tax rate for enterprise profits is continuing. The project of a common European (basic) unemployment insurance will not be realized soon. All these discussions on centralization of further powers, which is very expensive, will probably (finally) lead to proper European tax powers as they did in the German *Reich*.

33 See Commission, 'Report from the Commission presented under Article 8 of the Treaty on Stability, Coordination and Governance in the Economic and Monetary Union' COM (2017) 1201 final <https://economy-finance.ec.europa.eu/system/files/2017-02/c20171201_en.pdf> accessed 8 February 2023.

34 Bundeszentrale für Politische Bildung, *Nettozahler und Nettoempfänger in der EU* (25 March 2022) <https://www.bpb.de/kurz-knapp/zahlen-und-fakten/europa/70580/nettozahler-und-nettoempfaenger-in-der-eu/> accessed 8 February 2023.

35 Commission, *Recovery Plan for Europe* <https://commission.europa.eu/strategy-and-policy/recovery-plan-europe_en> accessed 8 February 2023; critical arguments in Bundesrechnungshof, *Bericht nach § 99 BHO zu den möglichen Auswirkungen der gemeinschaftlichen Kreditaufnahme der Mitgliedstaaten der Europäischen Union auf den Bundeshaushalt* (*Wiederaufbaufonds*) (11 March 2021) <https://www.bundesrechnungshof.de/SharedDocs/Downloads/DE/Berichte/2021/eu-wiederaufbaufonds-volltext.pdf?__blob=publicationFile&v=1> accessed 8 February 2023.

## 5 Lessons to Be Learned for the Future Development of the EU?

The comparison of the beginning of German federalism and the European Union shows that economic integration was a crucial factor for creating a new political entity from a group of formerly independent states. The comparison also shows that establishing institutions simultaneously promoted economic integration sometimes even prior to political integration like the *Deutsche Zollverein* and the European Economic Union. Both integration processes were led by the same economic measures: customs union, construction of common infrastructure and transportation networks, harmonization of weights and measures as well as economically relevant law and finally, a currency union. Economic integration was even fostered by and among former rivalling countries. This was the case for both *Deutsches Reich* and European Union.

The development of intergovernmental financial relations including a new level of government occurred almost identically in the *Reich* and the EU. The member states only conceded a few proper revenues to the federation/union, as were revenues from customs and a few special taxes close to centralized tasks. They covered the gap between expenditures and revenues by transfers from their budgets and tried to keep control on the new supra-state budget. The *Reich* was in an insofar more advantageous position as it received the income from a variety of excise taxes and taxes on 'trans-border' transactions which are still revenues of the member states in the EU. For both institutions, the underfunding with decent revenues led to increasing financial deficits that were covered by public debt and marked the beginning of a further centralisation of fiscal powers.

These similarities between the role of economic integration in the formation of the German *Reich* and the European Union and regarding the assignment of fiscal powers to the new institutions leads to further questions about the future of Europe. Some conclusions can be drawn:

- Economic integration, particularly the 'abolition' of border restrictions, is crucial factor for the federalization of independent neighbouring states but not the only one.
- The often included goal of external and internal security is not independent from economic factors. The most recent experiences of the Russian war against Ukraine teach that economic and financial solidarity among the members of the federation can help dealing with external threats and implementing effective sanctions against countries violating international peace by waging aggressive wars.
- There was no event during the history of the German *Reich* corresponding to the recent British secession from EU, the 'Brexit'. The German loss

of territory was a result of the Second World War, giving the Eastern parts to Poland and running two divided German states for 40 years. Germany has experienced the integration of the East German economy from 1990 onwards after the (re-)unification of both parts. The United Kingdom, however, has until now not met the expectations that their economic relations within the EU could be replaced by other international relations and its greater openness to international markets. Brexit seems to turn out as an expensive 'experiment' for which the British economy and the British working population has to pay for in the end.

Another range of questions arises regarding the common experience of both federalization processes according to which the member state governments keep control over the 'new' central level by 'their' second chamber (*Bundesrat*, European Council). Meanwhile, after a sharp centralization of all fiscal powers in the Weimar Republic and the Third *Reich*, Germany has developed a fiscal constitution with shared tax revenues across its three levels of government and a strong fiscal equalization scheme under a centralized legislation of the *Bund*. This path should not be repeated for the supra-national level; it corresponds neither with theoretical perspectives nor with the political reality of EU member states, which show a much higher economic (and cultural) divergence than the German States ever did. However, the actual distribution of fiscal powers might be too restrictive regarding the fiscal accountability of the European Union across all decision-making institutions. The lack of own tax sources has led and will in the future probably lead to the establishment of non-transparent shadow budgets and foster 'illegal' behaviour in order to create additional funding. It generates high incentives for unsustainable borrowing that will later burden citizens and the economy of the member states.

One last experience has to be mentioned, considering that a substantial centralization of taxation powers to the German *Reich* only happened after the latter had accumulated a tremendous amount of debt during the First World War starting from 4.9 billion *Reichsmark* in early 1914 going up more than 30 times to 159.1 Billion *Reichsmark* in 1919. As Peacock and Wiseman worked out, public spending has inevitably been increased during periods of crisis and war against taxpayers' interests.[36] This obviously coincides with a process of centralization of fiscal powers. The actual pressure derives from the increase in public debt and the needed interest payments and redemptions. Therefore, the breakthrough of permitting borrowing to the European Commission

36 Alan T. Peacock and Jack Wiseman, *The Growth of Public Expenditure in the United Kingdom* (Princeton University Press 1961).

regarding 'crisis expenditures' may be the starting point for adding more pressure on the member states to assign some of their tax sources to the EU, maybe the – actually national – corporate income tax and/or the tax on capital gains and interest incomes, which often levy transnational tax bases. It is not sure that all national governments foresee these developments as an unavoidable consequence of their political compromises.

## Acknowledgments

The author is very grateful to Alan Fenna for helpful comments and improvements of my poor English!

## Bibliography

Beermann J, 'Zur Einführung der Mark im Dezember 1871' *Börsen-Zeitung* (Frankfurt am Main, 3 December 2021) <https://www.bundesbank.de/de/presse/gastbeitraege/zur-einfuehrung-der-mark-im-dezember-1871-782816> accessed 3 February 2023.

Blank JE, Clausen H and Wacker H, *Internationale ökonomische Integration: Von der Freihandelszone zur Wirtschafts-und Währungsunion* (Vahlen 1998).

Borchart K, *Grundriß der deutschen Wirtschaftsgeschichte* (Vandenhoeck & Ruprecht 1978).

Bremm KJ, *70/71 – Preußens Triumph über da Kaiserreich Frankreich und die Folgen* (wbg Theiss 2019).

Bundesrechnungshof, *Bericht nach § 99 BHO zu den möglichen Auswirkungen der gemeinschaftlichen Kreditaufnahme der Mitgliedstaaten der Europäischen Union auf den Bundeshaushalt* (*Wiederaufbaufonds*) (11 March 2021) <https://www.bundesrechnungshof.de/SharedDocs/Downloads/DE/Berichte/2021/eu-wiederaufbaufonds-volltext.pdf?__blob=publicationFile&v=1> accessed 8 February 2023.

Bundeszentrale für politische Bildung, *Bevölkerungsentwicklung* (10 August 2020) <https://www.bpb.de/kurz-knapp/zahlen-und-fakten/soziale-situation-in-deutschland/61532/bevoelkerungsentwicklung/> accessed 6 February 2023.

Bundeszentrale für politische Bildung, *Nettozahler und Nettoempfänger in der EU* (25 March 2022) <https://www.bpb.de/kurz-knapp/zahlen-und-fakten/europa/70580/nettozahler-und-nettoempfaenger-in-der-eu/> accessed 8 February 2023.

Cholet J, *Der Etat des Deutschen Reiches in der Bismarckzeit* (Berliner Wissenschaftsverlag 2012).

Commission Directorate-General for Budget, *European Union public finance* (4th edn, Publications Office 2008).

Commission, 'Report from the Commission presented under Article 8 of the Treaty on Stability, Coordination and Governance in the Economic and Monetary Union' COM (2017) 1201 final <https://economy-finance.ec.europa.eu/system/files/2017-02/c20171201_en.pdf> accessed 8 February 2023.

Commission, *Recovery Plan for Europe* <https://commission.europa.eu/strategy-and-policy/recovery-plan-europe_en> accessed 8 February 2023.

De Grauwe P, *Economics of Monetary Union* (4th edn, Oxford University Press 2000).

Draheim A, *Probleme der finanzpolitischen Willensbildung in Europa – Eine kritische Analyse der europäischen Haushalts- und Finanzverfassung* (Peter Lang International Academic Publishers 2004).

Engels F, *Die Lage der arbeitenden Klasse in England* (Verlag Otto Wigand 1845).

European Stability Mechanism, *History* <https://www.esm.europa.eu/about-us/history> accessed 7 February 2023.

Fehrenbach E, *Vom Ancien Regime zum Wiener Kongress* (4th edn, Oldenbourg 2001).

Fisch S, 'Von der Föderation der Fürsten zum Bundesrat des Grundgesetzes. Zur Rolle der Länder im deutschen Föderalismus von 1848 bis heute' in von Arnim HH, Färber G and Fisch S (eds), *Föderalismus – Hält er noch, was er verspricht? Seine Vergangenheit, Gegenwart und Zukunft, auch im Lichte ausländischer Erfahrungen* (Duncker & Humblot 2000).

Frotscher W and Pieroth B, *Verfassungsgeschichte* (12th edn, Beck 2013).

Hahn HW, *Die industrielle Revolution in Deutschland* (2nd edn, Oldenbourg 2005).

Kotulla M, *Deutsches Verfassungsrecht 1806–1918. Eine Dokumentensammlung nebst Einführungen*, vol 1 (Springer 2006).

Loth W, *Das Kaiserreich. Obrigkeitsstaat und politische Mobilisierung* (Deutscher Taschenbuch Verlag 1996).

Loth W, *Der Weg nach Europa. Geschichte der europäischen Integration 1939–1957* (Vandenhoeck & Ruprecht 1996).

Marx K, 'Das Kapital – Kritik der politischen Ökonomie, vol 1' in Institut für Marxismus-Leninismus (ed), *Marx-Engels-Werke*, vol 23 (Dietz Verlag 1962).

Mueller S and Fenna A, 'Dual versus Administrative Federalism: Origins and Evolution of Two Models' (2022) 52 Publius 525.

Müller-Armack A, *Wirtschaftsordnung und Wirtschaftspolitik. Studien und Konzepte zur sozialen Marktwirtschaft und zur europäischen Integration* (Verlag Rombach 1966).

Musgrave RA, *The Theory of Fiscal Finance: A Study in Public Economy* (McGraw-Hill 1959).

Musgrave RA, 'Who Should Tax, Where and What?' in McLure CE (ed), *Tax Assignment in Federal Countries* (Centre for Research on Federal Financial Relations 1983).

Nipperdey T, *Deutsche Geschichte 1800–1866. Bürgerwelt und starker Staat* (Beck 1983).

Nipperdey T, *Deutsche Geschichte 1866–1918*, vol 1 (Beck 1990).

Nipperdey T, *Deutsche Geschichte 1866–1918*, vol 2 (Beck 1992).

Nipperdey T, *Deutsche Geschichte 1800–1866. Bürgerwelt und starker Staat* (Sonderdruck, Beck 1998).

Peacock AT and Wiseman J, *The Growth of Public Expenditure in the United Kingdom* (Princeton University Press 1961).

Recktenwald HC, 'Umfang und Struktur der öffentlichen Ausgaben in säkularer Entwicklung' in Neumark F (ed), *Handbuch der Finanzwissenschaft*, vol 1 (3rd edn, Mohr 1977).

Renzsch W, 'Länderfinanzausgleich' (*Historisches Lexikon Bayern*, 2 May 2011) <https://www.historisches-lexikon-bayerns.de/Lexikon/Länderfinanzausgleich#Finanzausgleich_im_Bismarckreich> accessed 5 February 2023.

Ricardo D, *The Principles of Political Economy and Taxation* (John Murray 1817).

Schremmer E, *Steuern und Staatsfinanzen während der Industrialisierung. England, Frankreich, Preußen und das Deutsche Reich 1800 bis 1914* (Springer 1994).

Sensch J, 'Die Struktur der kassenmäßigen Steuereinnahmen im Deutschen Reich und in der Bundesrepublik Deutschland, 1872 bis 2009' (*GESIS Data Archive*, 2013) <https://search.gesis.org/research_data/ZA8530?doi=10.4232/1.11725> accessed 3 February 2023.

Stremmel R, Tennstedt F and Fleckenstein G (eds), *Quellensammlung zur Geschichte der deutschen Sozialpolitik 1867 bis 1914. I. Abteilung: Von der Reichsgründungszeit bis zur Kaiserlichen Sozialbotschaft (1867 – 1881)*, vol 8 (wbg 2006).

Sturm R, *Staatsverschuldung. Ursachen. Wirkungen und Grenzen staatlicher Verschuldungspolitik* (Leske und Budrich 1993).

Ter-Minassian T, 'Intergovernmental Fiscal Relations in a Macroeconomic Perspective' in Ter-Minassian T (ed), *Fiscal Federalism in Theory and Practice* (International Monetary Fund 1997).

Thiemeyer G, *Europäische Integration. Motive, Prozesse, Strukturen* (Böhlau 2010).

Tilly R, *Kapital, Staat und sozialer Protest in der deutschen Industrialisierung* (Vandenhoeck & Ruprecht 1980).

Ullmann HP, *Das Deutsche Kaiserreich 1871–1918* (Suhrkamp Verlag 1995).

Von Eheberg TK, 'Finanzen und Steuern' in Körte S and others (eds), *Deutschland unter Kaiser Wilhelm II.*, vol 1 (Reimar Hobbing 1914).

Wehler HU, *Deutsche Gesellschaftsgeschichte 1700–1815*, vol 1 (Beck 1987).

Wehler HU, *Deutsche Gesellschaftsgeschichte*, vol 3 (Beck 1995).

Winkler HA, *Der lange Weg nach Westen*, vol 2 (Beck 2001).

Zweifel P and Heller R, *Internationaler Handel: Theorie und Empirie* (2nd edn, Physica-Verlag 1992).

CHAPTER 3

# Aggregative and Devolutionary Federalism Revisited

## *The Impact of Founding Processes on Federal Systems*

*Karl Kössler*

## 1 Introduction

It has become popular in studies of federal systems to classify such systems with a view to their initial formation processes. In particular, Alfred Stepan's classical differentiation of 'coming-together', 'holding-together' and 'putting-together' federalism[1] has had an enormous appeal for many. As useful as these distinctions are for purposes of classification, they sometimes seem to be applied with excessive confidence in their explanatory potential. Put differently, the fact that they appear to be clear-cut categories invites scholars of federalism to jump to conclusions, perhaps erroneous ones, about the actual effects of the formation of a federal system on the latter's institutional features. Therefore, it seems time to revisit what we really know about these classifications and their impact.

Against this background, my chapter starts with a brief conceptual history of categorizations based on the formation process in both law and political science (Section 2). It then attempts to analyze from a critical perspective what is clear and what is not regarding these categorizations. I identify an unmistakable trend towards 'holding-together' federalism and point to the problem that some of the most common formation-based classifications actually do not refer to the dynamics of the founding process but to its (coercive vs voluntary) nature (Section 3). The core part of the chapter explores the effects that the dynamics of formative processes have on three key elements of the distribution of powers between the national and subnational levels of government, that are the issues of asymmetrical, exclusive and broad general powers (Section 4). Section 5 concludes.

---

1 Alfred C. Stepan, 'Federalism and Democracy: Beyond the U.S. Model' (1999) 10 (4) Journal of Democracy 19, 21f.

© KARL KÖSSLER, 2024 | DOI:10.1163/9789004528581_005

## 2 A Brief Conceptual History of Federal Formation Processes

There can be little doubt that the traditional view was that federal systems are based on an initial compact. According to this interpretation, entities, which were both historically and legally sovereign, would join forces and come together to establish a federal government. In this very moment of a 'federal big bang' their original sovereignty would be transformed into autonomy as a result of the primacy of the (new) federal constitution.[2] From a legal perspective, this transformation is reflected in the so-called homogeneity clauses in federal constitutions, such as Art 4 para 4 of the US Constitution (the Republican Clause), Art 28 of the German Basic Law, etc.[3] In some cases, the 'federal big bang' has even resulted in federalism becoming entrenched and protected against constitutional amendments. In fact, several constitutions declared the initial compact to be indissoluble. At the founding of the Australian federal system in 1900, for example, constitution-makers deemed it fit to emphasize that the people of the colonies 'have agreed to unite in one indissoluble Federal Commonwealth'. Even if a formation process involving an initial compact therefore has certain legal *implications* which seem likely to occur in such cases, any distinction of federal systems based on their origins is not legal *in nature* but rather historical. It is probably for this reason that such distinctions, made by both lawyers and political scientists, do not seem to diverge based on the specific perspectives of their respective disciplines. Instead, everyone looks at the phenomenon through a historical lens that focuses on the dynamics of the founding process.

A first effort to demonstrate that federal systems must not necessarily involve a 'federal big bang' was Carl Friedrich's in the mid-1960s. Friedrich acknowledged the existence of the classical 'integrating' kind of federalization, which is characterized by a centralizing dynamic of bringing together previously separate entities. Importantly, however, he claimed that there is another type, that is 'differentiating' federalization, whereby a unitary state recognizes distinct political communities in a decentralizing process.[4] With this definition, Friedrich anticipated almost six decades ago the distinction of

---

2 The term 'federal big bang' originates from European integration studies (Neil Walker, 'The shifting foundations of the European Union Constitution' [2012] University of Edinburgh School of Law Research Paper Series 18/2012).

3 Francesco Palermo and Karl Kössler, *Comparative Federalism: Constitutional Arrangements and Case Law* (Hart Publishing 2017) 133–136.

4 Carl J. Friedrich, 'New Tendencies in Federal Theory and Practice' (1965) 14 Jahrbuch des Öffentlichen Rechts 1.

'aggregative' and 'devolutionary' federal systems, which is today very popular and widespread in studies of federalism. While my chapter uses this newer terminology, and thus a different one than Friedrich, it follows his above-mentioned definition. In Friedrich's view, 'integrating' federalization may well involve different degrees of 'separateness' of the entities concerned, as they could either be completely independent or – like in the case of the United States – parts of a confederation. In a similar vein, it has been argued more recently that units of 'aggregative' federal systems can be entities that were either fully independent or enjoyed 'a high degree of autonomy before their aggregation into the new federal structure' because they were like 'Canada, Australia and Malaysia, dominions and colonies enjoying autonomy and self-government within the former British Empire'.[5]

It then took until 1990 for the first lawyer to make considerations like Friedrich's. Perhaps unsurprisingly, given his legal background, Koen Lenaerts thereby focused on (legislative) powers. In his view, 'integrative federalism' brings together 'previously independent or confederally related component entities' in such a way that the 'goal of establishing an effective central government with direct operation on the people inside its sphere of powers is pursued under respect of the powers of the component entities'. While this is about the (partial) *retention* of powers, 'devolutionary federalism' is about the *redistribution* of powers 'of a previously unitary State among its component entities; these entities obtain an autonomous status within their fields of responsibility'.[6]

Today's arguably most popular classification of federal systems according to founding process was coined a little more than two decades ago by Alfred Stepan. His declared aim was to move 'beyond Rikerian federalism'[7] because the latter had passed off characteristics of the US model as features of federalism more generally and thus created a 'misleading picture of federalism'.[8] These characteristics are that federal systems are 'constitutionally symmetrical', 'demos-constraining' and the result of a process of pooling sovereignty for collective security and economic motives, something that Stepan called 'coming-together' federalism. The latter follows from Riker's classical definition of federalism as a 'constitutional bargain' between future national and subnational government leaders to aggregate territory, increase tax revenue

5 Palermo and Kössler (n 3) 45f.

6 Koen Lenaerts, 'Constitutionalism and the many faces of federalism' (1990) 38 American Journal of Comparative Law 205, 206.

7 Alfred C. Stepan, *Arguing Comparative Politics* (Oxford University Press 2001) 315.

8 Stepan (n 1) 20.

and facilitate army recruitment for an act of aggression or for defense against an external threat.[9] Stepan argued that 'coming-together' federalism would utterly fail to grasp the reality of how more recent federal countries like India, Spain or Belgium came into being. He characterized these as examples of 'holding-together' federalism,[10] as in these cases leaders of 'political systems with strong unitary features' came to the conclusion that the only way 'to hold their countries together in a democracy would be to devolve power constitutionally and turn their threatened polities into federations'.[11] Beyond that, Stepan invented – with a view to the Soviet Union – a third category, that of 'putting-together' federalism, which involves a 'heavily coercive effort by a nondemocratic centralizing power to put together a multinational state, some of the components of which had previously been independent states'.[12] In conclusion, Stepan's classificatory work regarding federal systems based on their formation processes is remarkable, above all, because of its deliberate and explicit contradistinction from the Rikerian tradition and its threefold terminological distinction that came to be widely recognized and used since the turn of the century.

Another more recent conceptualization is that of Ronald Watts.[13] While he continued to espouse, like his predecessors, the distinction between aggregative and devolutionary processes (finding the latter typical of the 20th century), Watts identified a third pattern, that is cases in which a combination of *both* processes was at play. He found such cases especially among federations in the context of colonialism, a subject that he had already studied in-depth.[14] After all, Canada involved both a devolution of power to two new provinces carved out of the unitary Province of Canada (Ontario and Quebec) and an aggregation of two separate colonies (New Brunswick and Nova Scotia) in 1867 and later still other provinces and territories. In fact, there is yet another peculiar devolutionary element which is absent from Watts' view on Canada through the additional level of the British Empire. After all, the founding of the federal

9 William H. Riker, *Federalism: Origin, Operation, Significance* (Little, Brown & Company 1964) 1.

10 Stepan (n 1) 21f.

11 ibid.

12 ibid 22.

13 Ronald L. Watts, 'Comparing Federal Political Systems' in Alain-G. Gagnon, Soeren Keil and Sean Mueller (eds), *Understanding Federalism and Federation: Essays in Honour of Michael Burgess* (Ashgate Publishing 2015) 24f.

14 Ronald L. Watts, *New Federations: Experiments in the Commonwealth* (Clarendon Press 1966).

system involved at its core a devolution of imperial power from London.[15] In India, the devolutionary element was the transfer of power to newly founded states which had previously been provinces of British India, while the aggregative element was the integration of the nearly 600 princely states. As the latter process occurred with various degrees of coercion,[16] the country might be called a case of 'putting-together' federalism in some sense, even if India in 1950, of course, may not be described as a 'nondemocratic centralizing power', as Stepan defined this category.

## 3 Aggregative and Devolutionary Federalism Revisited

### 3.1 *What Is Clear? A Shift towards Devolutionary Federalism*

One thing that seems to be rather evident and widely accepted is an unmistakable trend towards devolutionary federalism. It is contested though when the turning point from the predominance of aggregative formation processes to that of devolutionary ones actually occurred. Stepan went back particularly far in history and even claimed that after the French Revolution 'no sovereign democratic nation-states have ever "come together" in an enduring federation'.[17] One might wonder whether this assertion has (negative) implications for the European Union, even if the EU crucially differs from an average federal system in many respects, not least regarding the freedom of constituent parts to exit the union.[18]

According to another perspective provided by Thomas Fleiner, the transition to devolutionary federalism happened much later. He regarded 'first generation' federations,[19] that is those established before the 20th century, as a distinct category because, in his view, the Industrial Revolution marked a watershed and had a profound impact on the formation of federal systems. While aggregative founding processes would be typical of the first generation,

15 Nicholas Aroney, 'Formation, Representation and Amendment in Federal Constitutions' (2006) 54 The American Journal of Comparative Law 277, 319.

16 See section 3.2 below.

17 Stepan (n 1) 33.

18 Karl Kössler, 'Federal Constitutions and Secession: From "Perpetual Union" to a Right to Separate?' in Annegret Eppler, Charlie Jeffery and Stefan August Lütgenau (eds), *Qualified Autonomy and Federalism versus Secession in EU Member States* (Studien Verlag 2021).

19 In chronological order, the United States, Switzerland, Canada and Australia, which were formed prior to the 20th century transformation in the role of government: Thomas Fleiner-Gerster, 'Federalism in Australia and in Other Nations' in Greg Craven (ed), *Australian Federalism: Towards the Second Century* (Melbourne University Press 1992).

the devolutionary path to federalism would be characteristic of the second generation.[20]

Ultimately, also Watts made an assessment on this transition and opined that devolutionary federal systems have become prevalent over the last 60 years. It was during this time frame that the phenomenon of what he called 'emergent federations' developed. In contrast to the older 'mature federations', that is those that came into being up until the post-war constitutions of Germany (1949) and India (1950), they would have several typical features – a certain restlessness, as they are still in search for their equilibrium, an overall quite high degree of centralization and their devolutionary formation process.[21] To be sure, Watts' concept of 'emergent federations' may be criticized for the lack of homogeneity of the cases falling within this category, with some being democratic federations and others being democratic and federal merely on paper.[22] However, the relevant insight for the purpose of this paper is the strong trend towards devolutionary federalism since about 1960.

### 3.2 *What Is Unclear? The Problem of the False Third Category*

If we compare Stepan's 'putting-together' federalism with Watts' category of formation processes combining both aggregative and devolutionary dynamics it becomes clear that these potential third categories significantly differ from each other. As for 'putting-together' federalism, recognition of the new concept was widespread but not universal, as some critical issues were raised. Michael Burgess argued that by placing 'coming-together' and 'holding-together' federalism at the two ends of his 'democratic continuum', Stepan would have left his third category of nondemocratic 'putting-together' federalism 'completely out in the conceptual cold' with ultimately all three categories remaining 'theoretically incomplete and underdeveloped'.[23] But beyond this critique by Burgess there seems to be another reason why 'putting-together' federalism does not fit quite well with Stepan's other two categories. This is because its focus is entirely on the element of coercion, as is evident from its definition as a 'heavily coercive effort by a nondemocratic centralizing power to put together a multinational state'. This is to say that 'putting-together' federalism refers to the *nature* of the formation, coercive instead of voluntary, and – unlike Stepan's other two

20 Alan Fenna, 'What hope for comparative federalism?' in John Kincaid (ed), *A Research Agenda for Federalism Studies* (Edward Elgar 2019) 80.

21 Ronald L. Watts, *Comparing Federal Systems* (McGill-Queen's University Press 2008) 24f.

22 Palermo and Kössler (n 3) 45.

23 Michael Burgess, *In Search of the Federal Spirit. New Comparative Empirical and Theoretical Perspectives* (Oxford University Press 2013) 239.

categories – not on the *dynamics* of this process, aggregative or devolutionary. Another third category that is sometimes seen as variation to Stepan's is Nancy Bermeo's imposed or 'forced-together' federalism.[24] She argues that the formation of a federal system must be voluntary by recalling Daniel Elazar's 'sense of partnership',[25] if it is to stand a chance of survival. In her view, federal systems that collapsed or turned towards unitarism were actually those imposed by an outside power, typically in the context of (post)colonialism or (post)communism.[26] While Bermeo's focus is slightly different through the emphasis placed on outside actors and the enabling internal condition of system frailty, it is still quite similar to Stepan's 'putting-together' federalism insofar, as it also refers to the coercive nature of the formation process.

Given the fact that different combinations are conceivable between the *dynamics* of this process (aggregative vs devolutionary) and its *nature* (voluntary vs coercive), it becomes even more clear that the two need to be distinguished. While it is often assumed that aggregation and devolution are voluntary processes, they might in fact involve different degrees of coercion. In this regard, the founding of federal India is a good example. As pointed out by Watts,[27] a combination of both aggregative (concerning the princely states) and devolutionary (concerning the provinces of British India) dynamics was at play. But thereby it is key to bear in mind that the accession of the nearly 600 princely states, which had enjoyed a certain degree of internal autonomy in exchange for the acceptance of British suzerainty, was in several cases far from being based on a free decision. This follows from significant pressure exercised not only by the Indian Government, but – in the context of decolonization – also by Lord Mountbatten as Viceroy and then Governor-General of India, declaring that the British Crown would sever any ties with the princely states if they refused to join either India or Pakistan.[28] But several princes were still holding out. Maharaja Hari Singh, the Hindu ruler of predominantly

24 Nancy Bermeo, 'A New Look at Federalism: The Import of Institutions' (2022) 13 Journal of Democracy 96, 107f.

25 Daniel J. Elazar, *Exploring Federalism* (University of Alabama Press 1987) 67.

26 Federalism came into being in Czechoslovakia as a Soviet imposition in 1968 in order to marginalize liberalizing forces in the Czech part of the country, while Yugoslavia's Soviet-inspired constitution was approved by a constitutional assembly without any non-communist representation (Christopher Binns, 'Federalism, Nationalism and Socialism in Yugoslavia' in Murray Forsyth [ed], *Federalism and Nationalism* [Leicester University Press 1989] 122).

27 See section 2 above.

28 Ian Copland, *The Princes of India in the Endgame of Empire, 1917–1947* (Cambridge University Press 1997) 255.

Muslim Jammu and Kashmir, eventually realized the futility of early attempts at independence and turned to India after tribal forces from Pakistan had crossed the border.[29] In the case of Hyderabad, it was not only political pressure but an invasion of the Indian Armed Forces to overwhelm the Nizam ruler of this princely state, which secured its annexation to the Union.[30] Whereas little more than a decade earlier the reluctance of some princes to join a Union had still thwarted attempts by the 1935 Government of India Act to establish some sort of quasi-federalism, such a refusal was now no viable option anymore. In contrast to these states under suzerainty, the provinces of British India, that is the territories under direct colonial rule since 1858, did not even have a choice back in 1935. Their accession was not voluntary but compulsory. Against this background it is understandable that at independence the 17 provinces, accounting for 54% of the territory and 70% of the population, did even have less of a choice and were simply incorporated into India or Pakistan.

It is striking to compare this situation with the constitutional bargaining power of the prospective US states at the Philadelphia Convention (a classical example of aggregative federalism) or, for that matter, of Belgium's regions and communities during the country's six state reforms from 1970 to 2011 (a classical example of devolutionary federalism). While a *foedus* at the end of a bargaining process between the constituent entities is obvious at the founding of the United States, something that we might call an 'ex-post compact' has even been concluded with each of the Belgian state reforms on the path from unitarism to federalism.[31] Similar to Spain and the United Kingdom, in Belgium such reforms occurred *legally* within the framework of the national constitution and following devolutionary dynamics, but were *politically* a reaction to the initiative and pressure from subnational entities.[32]

In the Indian case, the constituent units had much less opportunities to shape federalism because the above-mentioned integration process, involving different degrees of coercion, was already completed and their bargaining power virtually non-existent at the time when BR Ambedkar, the Chairman of

29 Navnita Chadha Behera, *Demystifying Kashmir* (Brookings Institution Press 2006) 213.

30 Arun K. Thiruvengadam, *The Constitution of India: A Contextual Analysis* (Hart Publishing 2017) 30.

31 Karl Kössler, *Multinationaler Föderalismus in Theorie und Praxis: Kompetenz-und finanzverfassungsrechtliche Aspekte der territorialen Self-Rule in Kanada, Belgien und Spanien* (Nomos 2012) 112; Nicholas Aroney, 'Types of Federalism', *Max Planck Encyclopedia of Comparative Constitutional Law* (2016) para 13 <https://oxcon.ouplaw.com/display/10.1093/law-mpeccol/law-mpeccol-e294?prd=MPECCOL> accessed December 2022.

32 Aroney (n 31) para 13.

the Drafting Commission, presented the first draft constitution.[33] Federalism, it has been said, was therefore a 'gift bestowed upon Indian provinces and princely states'[34] and one that they could arguably hardly decline. It is therefore quite logical and telling that there were 'few champions of "states' rights" in the leadup to, or within, the Constituent Assembly'.[35] This is also reflected in the text which the assembly agreed upon. As Ambedkar put it, India was to be a federation, but unlike the United States not one built upon an original act of union by its constituent units. Instead, '[t]hough the country and the people may be divided into different States for convenience of administration the country is one integral whole, its people a single people living under a single *imperium* derived from a single source'.[36]

In conclusion, the early days of federal India demonstrate quite vividly not only a combination of aggregative and devolutionary dynamics of the founding process, but also a coercive-voluntary combination regarding this process. More precisely, it shows that there is no binary distinction of voluntary and coercive but rather a continuum between the two. The Indian example also makes clear that concerning the degree of compulsion considerable variation is possible between different categories of prospective subnational entities and even between cases within one single category, such as that of the princely states.

## 4 The Dynamics of Founding Processes and the Distribution of Powers

### 4.1 *Asymmetrical Powers*

Whether a federal system comes into being through aggregation or devolution or both appears to have several implications for the distribution of powers between the national and subnational levels of government. Devolutionary processes involve – by their very nature – a transfer of powers from the center to the peripheries. The fact that such decentralization often responds to different levels of pressure and calls from subnational entities for different

33 Mohit Bhattacharya, 'The Mind of the Founding Fathers' in Nirmal Mukarji and Balveer Arora (eds), *Federalism in India: Origins and Development* (Vikas 1992).

34 Thiruvengadam (n 30) 75.

35 ibid.

36 Parliament of India, *Constituent Assembly Debates*, vol VII (4 November 1948) 43 <https://www.constitutionofindia.net/constitution_assembly_debates/volume/7/1948-11-04> accessed December 2022.

competences typically entails two things that are interconnected: bilateral instruments of (re)distributing powers in terms of procedures and (constitutional) asymmetry in terms of outcomes. At this point, it is important to refer to a long-standing key distinction between 'constitutional asymmetries', that is legal differences concerning 'the status or legislative and executive powers',[37] and 'political asymmetries', that is differences among subnational entities regarding demographic, economic and political resources.

It is the asymmetries in terms of powers which are interesting for the purpose of this chapter. A glaring example of such differences are those that emerged from the establishment of the Russian Federation in 1991–1993. President Yeltsin's weak political position and the challenge posed by secessionism in several parts of the country led him to famously declare in 1990 that – in exchange for basic loyalty – subnational governments would be allowed to 'take as much sovereignty as they can stomach'.[38] From this statement it was not a long way to what has been described as 'contract federalism' which eventually involved a 'war of laws and sovereignties'.[39] This refers to a situation from 1994 to 1998 in which the central government concluded bilateral agreements with most of the 89 federal subjects. Unsurprisingly, bilateralism as procedure entailed asymmetry as quite natural outcome. It has been argued that this process in the 1990s has given rise to a three-tiered model of federalism with some subnational entities remaining heavily dependent on the central government, others enjoying 'conventional federal-state relations' and still others, like Bashkortostan and Tatarstan, 'operating in a confederal relationship with the centre'.[40] Altogether, this resulted in intergovernmental relations that were perceived as extremely complex, if not chaotic. Some even argued that Russia's 'contract federalism' of those years 'pushed the concept of asymmetrical federalism to its reductio ad absurdum'.[41] Others similarly opined that this was not federalism but 'segmented regionalism', defined as a

37 Watts (n 21) 125–130.

38 Quoted in James Hughes, 'Managing Secession Potential in the Russian Federation' in James Hughes and Gwendolyn Sasse (eds), *Ethnicity and Territory in the Former Soviet Union: Regions in Conflict* (Routledge 2002) 55.

39 Cameron Ross, 'Russia's Multinational Federation: From Constitutional to Contract Federalism and the 'War of Laws and Sovereignties'' in Michael Burgess and John Pinder (eds), *Multinational Federations* (Routledge 2007).

40 Michael Burgess, 'The Paradox of Diversity – Asymmetrical Federalism in Comparative Perspective' in Francesco Palermo, Carolin Zwilling and Karl Kössler (eds), *Asymmetries in Constitutional Law, Recent Developments in Federal and Regional Systems* (Europäische Akademie Bozen/Accademia Europea Bolzano 2009) 27.

41 ibid.

constellation 'in which subnational systems exploit the weakness of national integrative mechanisms (notably the presidency, Parliament, the ministerial system, the courts and the Constitution)',[42] resulting in legal fragmentation or even inconsistency, in obstacles to the national market and a lack of coherence of Russia as an international actor.[43]

Another main example of devolutionary federalism entailing bilateralism and eventually asymmetry is Spain. After all, the autonomy statutes of the country's autonomous communities are negotiated bilaterally between the respective region and the national government before they are approved by the regional legislature and then by the Spanish parliament as an organic law (Art 147 para 3 of the Constitution). While the details of the procedures applied actually vary from region to region and in four regions feature a mandatory regional referendum as an additional requirement, they all do have in common a clear reliance on bilateralism. The very fact that the distribution of powers was deconstitutionalized and thus not regulated in a multilateral legal framework but in bilaterally agreed autonomy statutes contained the seeds from which asymmetry could grow. According to some observers, it grew at least in a first phase from 1978 to 1981 in a quite chaotic way,[44] albeit certainly much less so than Russian federalism in the 1990s.

Whereas devolutionary federalism kind of naturally breeds bilateralism and asymmetry because the national government makes different concessions to different subnational demands, it is important to recognize that this is anything else but a one-way street. Indeed, when political actors have come to see asymmetry as overly complex or utterly chaotic, processes of resymmetrization have often ensued. In the Spanish case, the country's main national parties[45] responded to the political instability in the wake of an attempted coup d'état in 1981 with a series of agreements (*acuerdos autonómicos*) that eventually gave rise to the adoption of the 1982 Organic Law on the Harmonisation of the Autonomy Process (LOAPA – *Ley Orgánica de Armonización del Proceso*

42 Richard Sakwa, 'Devolution and Asymmetry in Russia' in Ferran Requejo and Klaus Jürgen Nagel (eds), *Federalism Beyond Federations. Asymmetry and Processes of Resymmetrisation in Europe* (Routledge 2016) 158.

43 ibid 160.

44 Luis Medina Alcoz, 'The Spanish Approach to Asymmetric Federalism' in Francesco Palermo, Carolin Zwilling and Karl Kössler (eds), *Asymmetries in Constitutional Law, Recent Developments in Federal and Regional Systems* (Europäische Akademie Bozen/ Accademia Europea Bolzano 2009) 49ff, 57; José Juan González Encinar, 'Ein asymmetrischer Bundesstaat' in Dieter Nohlen and José Juan Gonzáles Encinar (eds), *Der Staat der autonomen Gemeinschaften in Spanien* (Leske + Budrich 1992) 223.

45 *Partido Socialista Obrero Español* (PSOE) and *Unión del Centro Democrático y Social* (UCD).

*Autonómico*). As the law's name reveals, uniformity was the rationale behind it. This was to be achieved by limiting regional competences and subjecting regional laws to the approval of the national government. The Constitutional Court, however, invalidated large parts of the LOAPA because it exceeded the limits of the national parliament's power to adopt harmonization laws under Art 150 para 3 of the Constitution.[46] Moreover, and this is crucial, it also emphasized that homogeneity must always be balanced with heterogeneity so that some degree of asymmetry would be a characteristic feature of the Spanish state of the autonomies. Nonetheless, however, the partial invalidation did have some chilling effect on the decentralization process and contributed to the distribution of powers becoming not as asymmetrical as some had hoped and others had feared.[47] While it is undeniable and widely recognized that in the Spanish case the pendulum has from time to time swung back to uniformity, some argue that 'two opposing processes have always co-existed' and trace them through all periods since the adoption of the Constitution of 1978. Arguably, devolutionary federalism 'has always been accompanied by a hidden process of reactive de-federalization that has continually eroded self-government through recentralization (i.e. reinforcement of the powers of the federation) and resymmetrization (i.e. placing all nationalities and regions on the same footing)'.[48] These developments have occurred much to the chagrin of Catalan and Basque nationalists. In their view, they are evidence that the national government reneged on the constitutional compromise of 1978 because constitutional asymmetries 'should be characteristic of the territorial organization of Spain as a de facto multinational State'.[49]

In the case of Russia, the countertrend towards recentralization and resymmetrization was even stronger. From the time when Putin assumed responsibility for intergovernmental relations in 1998, no new bilateral treaties were

---

46 STC 76/1983. See also Juan José Solazábal, 'Spain: A Federation in the Making?' in Joachim J. Hesse and Vincent Wright (eds), *Federalizing Europe? The Costs, Benefits and Preconditions of Federal Political Systems* (Oxford University Press 1996) 245ff, 252.

47 Robert Agranoff, 'Intergovernmental Relations and Management of Asymmetry in Federal Spain' in Robert Agranoff (ed), *Accommodating Diversity. Asymmetry in Federal States* (Nomos 1999) 94ff, 108.

48 Ramon Maiz, Francisco Caamaño and Miguel Azpitarte, 'The Hidden Counterpoint of Spanish Federalism: Recentralization and Resymmetrization in Spain (1978–2008)' (2010) 20 Regional & Federal Studies 63, 65.

49 Pau Bossacoma Busquets and Marc Sanjaume-Calvet, 'Asymmetry as a Device for Equal Recognition and Reasonable Accommodation of Majority and Minority Nations. A Country Study on Constitutional Asymmetry in Spain' in Patricia Popelier and Maja Sahadžić (eds), *Constitutional Asymmetry in Multinational Federalism. Federalism and Internal Conflicts* (Palgrave Macmillan 2019) 457.

concluded and a law in 2003 stipulated that all existing ones would lapse, unless they were renewed in compliance with national legislation (which they were not). Furthermore, the Law on Regions of 1999 established that all new federal and regional legislation would need to conform with this law and a Presidential Decree issued one year later grouped the federal subjects into seven federal districts headed by presidential envoys. It has been argued that all these measures aimed at countering supposedly excessive asymmetry were based on three motivations, that is the *rationalization* of hitherto fragmented governance, a pursuit of the *values* of state integrity and universality of constitutional norms and, ultimately, the consolidation of the *power* of President Putin's regime.[50] It is evident that such a trajectory like that of Russia, which has been characterized as a journey 'from wild federalism to weak asymmetry'[51] bears a certain risk, namely 'that the baby of federalism is thrown out with the bathwater of segmented regionalism'.[52] This is arguably what has occurred over the last two decades, since '[i]n Russia the spirit of federalism was signally lacking from below *and* from above'.[53]

### 4.2 *Exclusive Powers*

Another feature of the distribution of powers that is often linked to the formation of federal systems is the issue of exclusive competences, that is those that are attributed to only one level of government without the possibility for others to intervene. As Lenaerts' argument goes, for example, devolutionary federalism would give rise to exclusivity due to a specific feature of intergovernmental relations in such cases: '[G]iven the basic distrust between the central government and the component entities – a constitutional undertone which contrasts sharply with the model of integrative federalism – the relationship between the powers' spheres tends to be mutually exclusive.'[54] A comparison between two of the clearest cases of devolutionary federalism demonstrates, however, that a general pattern is hard to establish.

A link between such a formation process and a penchant for exclusive powers may hold true in the case of Belgium with which Lenaerts is, as he stems from

50 Sakwa (n 42) 166–170.

51 Elena A. Kremyanskaya, 'Constitutional Asymmetry in Russia: Issues and Developments. A Country Study of Constitutional Asymmetry in the Russian Federation' in Patricia Popelier and Maja Sahadžić (eds), *Constitutional Asymmetry in Multinational Federalism. Federalism and Internal Conflicts* (Palgrave Macmillan 2019) 408ff.

52 Sakwa (n 42) 159.

53 ibid.

54 Lenaerts (n 6) 238.

that country, particular familiar. Indeed, it is certainly true that the Belgian distribution of powers, which follows from both the Constitution and the Special Act of 1980 on Institutional Reform,[55] has sought to accomplish exclusivity. But this ambition was as much the result of several other reasons as of the country's devolutionary path to federalism. Among these reasons was, importantly, the need to deal with the inherent complexity of a system with two types of subnational entities (three regions and three communities) which have different sets of competences and overlapping territorial jurisdictions. Exclusivity seemed to be a way to avoid making an already complicated constellation of intergovernmental relations even more complicated. There can be little doubt that Belgium has preserved exclusive powers in a more efficient manner than most federal systems and that this has a lot to do with the case law of the country's Constitutional Court.[56] To be sure, the Court had to acknowledge that the complex task of allocating competences makes de facto concurrency in certain cases unavoidable.[57] Introducing a 'double aspect' doctrine,[58] it recognized, for instance, that the issue of a complementary Flemish care insurance can come under the community power regarding aid to persons and at the same time under the federal competence for social security.[59] But even in case of such de facto concurrency, the Belgian Constitutional Court did not resort – unlike the written constitutions or constitutional courts of other federal countries – to a rule of federal paramountcy. Instead, if national and subnational laws on the same issue cannot be applied cumulatively, the judges determine whose exclusive competence has the closest link with the matter concerned, something that not only reinforced the self-government of communities and regions but also, to the extent possible, exclusivity as a principle.[60]

---

55 A special act has to be adopted under the rules of Art 4 para 3 of the Constitution as 'a law passed by a majority of the votes cast in each linguistic group in each House, on condition that a majority of the members of each group is present and provided that the total number of votes in favour that are cast in the two linguistic groups is equal to at least two thirds of the votes cast'. The Belgian parliament features a Dutch-and a French-speaking language group with relevance under some procedures.

56 Karl Kössler, 'The Role of Constitutional Judges in Protecting Territorial Self-Government' in Ferran Requejo and Marc Sanjaume-Calvet (eds), *Defensive Federalism: Protecting Territorial Minorities from the 'Tyranny of the Majority'* (Routledge 2022) 157f.

57 Belgian Constitutional Court 166/2003.

58 Patrick Peeters and Jens Mosselmans, 'The Constitutional Court of Belgium: Safeguard of the Autonomy of the Communities and Regions' in Nicholas Aroney and John Kincaid (eds), *Courts in Federal Countries: Federalists or Unitarists?* (University of Toronto Press 2017) 69ff and 97. Belgian Constitutional Court 168/2011.

59 Belgian Constitutional Court 33/2001 and 51/2006.

60 Peeters and Mosselmans (n 58) 69ff, 97 and 102.

Compared to Belgium, another classical case of devolutionary federalism provides a counterexample regarding the role of exclusive powers. Spain's distribution of competences is clearly dominated by concurrencies. A superficial reading of the country's Constitution might suggest otherwise because Art 149 confers to the national government 'exclusive competence' with regard to 32 subject matters. This provision is complemented by Art 148, containing a list of responsibilities which the autonomous communities may take over. On this constitutional basis, concrete details are then worked out, as mentioned above, bilaterally in the autonomy statutes. However, this first impression is misleading because 'exclusive competence' in Art 149 only means a real legislative monopoly of the national government concerning some of the subject matters listed by the provision (eg labor law).[61] With regard to other issues its power only extends to basic legislation (eg environmental protection) or the regulation of single aspects of broader policy fields (eg air traffic regarding infrastructure). Another reason why exclusivity is in fact not so much a characteristic of the distribution of powers in Spain has to do with how its deconstitutionalization, that is its regulation in the autonomy statutes, has been interpreted by the Constitutional Court. To be sure, autonomous communities, above all Catalonia, vigorously attempted to demarcate regional competences as precisely as possible for the sake of making them exclusive and thus safe against national government interference during the era of statute reforms 2006–2011. In hindsight, however, this strategy known as *blindaje* (armour plating)[62] was offset to some extent by a strong response of the Constitutional Court. The judges recognized that the statutes may describe the content of regional competences based on Art 147 para 2d of the Constitution. Yet, it was not for the statutes to exactly determine the scope of these competences in relation to national powers because only the Court could make a 'genuine and unchallengeable interpretation of the principles and categories in the Constitution'.[63]

It therefore follows that Belgium and Spain have been influenced by the contemporary trend towards concurrency of national and subnational powers, even if in the former case to a much lesser extent. This trend is due to an increasing complexity of governance problems which requires the involvement

61 Enric Argullol and Xavier Bernadí, 'Kingdom of Spain' in Akhtar Majeed, Ronald L. Watts and Douglas M. Brown (eds), *Distribution of Powers and Responsibilities in Federal Countries* (McGill-Queen's University Press 2006) 248.

62 Francisco Balaguer Castejón, 'Cuestiones competenciales de los actuales procesos de reforma de los Estatutos de Autonomía' (2006) 1 Revista General de Derecho Constitucional 37, 42.

63 STC 31/2010.

of multiple actors.[64] Times have definitely changed since Kenneth Wheare could still claim in the immediate aftermath of World War II that '[t]he ideal distribution of powers between governments in a federation is the one in which each government is able to act independently within its own watertight sphere of responsibility'.[65] Exclusive spheres of powers have become more and more substituted by intergovernmental cooperation and concurrent competences. In fact, 70 years after Wheare's statement, conclusions from comparative research suggest that 'concurrency of powers is an integral feature, if not the cornerstone, of the distribution of powers'.[66] In light of such a changed context, it is therefore hardly surprising that the argument of a devolutionary formation process leading to exclusive spheres of competences needs to be put in perspective.

### 4.3 *Broad General Powers*

A third argument regarding the impact of founding processes on the distribution of powers concerns the legal technique of how competences are allocated to the national or subnational government levels. As the line of reasoning goes, aggregative federalism would give rise to a residual clause allowing subnational entities to still retain *broad general* powers, which are only marginally delimited by *specific listed* powers of the national government.[67] This is regarded as some sort of compensation for subnational entities, as they traded their original sovereignty as independent states or members of a confederation for autonomy within a federal state. In short, residual competence is a relic of this historic sovereignty. Moreover, it might also be seen as still reflecting the logic of confederations,[68] which have often preceded aggregative federal systems, namely that the members of such a union of independent states keep all prerogatives that are not explicitly delegated. As Art 2 of the short-lived

---

64 Karl Kössler and Yonatan T. Fessha, 'Federalism and the Courts' in Javier Cremades and Cristina Hermida (eds), *Encyclopedia of Contemporary Constitutionalism* (Springer 2022) 8.

65 Kenneth C. Wheare, *Federal government* (Oxford University Press 1947) 14. Wheare's terminology goes back to the 'watertight compartments', first mentioned in Canadian jurisprudence in *Canada* (AG) *v Ontario* (AG) [1937] AC 326, 354 (JCPC).

66 Nico Steytler, 'Concurrency of powers: The zebra in the room' in Nico Steytler (ed), *Concurrent powers in federal systems: Meaning, making, managing* (Brill/Nijhoff 2017) 349.

67 Ronald L. Watts, 'Comparative Conclusions' in Akhtar Majeed and others (eds), *Distribution of Powers and Responsibilities in Federal Countries* (McGill-Queen's University Press 2006) 324; Anna Gamper, 'A "Global Theory of Federalism": The Nature and Challenges of a Federal State' (2005) 6 German Law Journal 1297, 1308f; Aroney (n 15) 297.

68 Murray Greensmith Forsyth, *Unions of States: The Theory and Practice of Confederation* (Leicester University Press 1981).

Articles of Confederation (1781–1789) put it: 'Each state retains its sovereignty, freedom, and independence, and every power, jurisdiction, and right, which is not by this confederation expressly delegated to the United States, in Congress assembled.'

Looking at written constitutions of federal systems, the argument of aggregative federalism leading to broad subnational residual powers seems to hold true. Indeed, a residual clause in favour of subnational governments exists, for example, in the United States and Australia, with the latter arguably being the 'purest case of an aggregative federation, having been formed in 1901 by voluntary and democratic union of the same six constituent units as make it up today'.[69] But also in the US case, the need for the 13 original states to accept the move from the above-mentioned Articles of Confederation to a more integrated union entailed a strong bargaining position for these 13 governments. Given these circumstances, it hardly comes as a surprise that they succeeded in retaining broad residual powers. In this light, it was certainly justified to call the original constellation of federal–state relations in the United States one of 'Enumerated Powers Federalism'[70] with limited national government authority.

However, this *original* constellation has been altered significantly over time. To be precise, these changes did not concern the legal technique of how powers are distributed, as the residual clause enshrined in the Tenth Amendment is still in place now as it was more than two centuries ago. It still determines that '[t]he powers not delegated to the United States by the Constitution, nor prohibited by it to the States, are reserved to the States respectively, or to the people'. What did change, however, is the relative scope of the (subnational) powers under this clause, on the one hand, and the (national) powers based on enumeration, on the other. It is indeed a widely shared fallacy that a residual clause in favor of subnational governments would kind of *naturally* translate, as the above-mentioned initial idea suggested, into broad general powers. In reality, however, the practical significance and scope of this clause may be hollowed out dramatically by an extensive judicial interpretation of listed federal powers. This is precisely what has happened in a number of countries. As a result, the residual clause is sometimes 'a principle more relevant for systematic purposes than in practice',[71] these purposes being to ensure that the

69 Alan Fenna, 'The Pleasant Greyness of Australian Federalism' (*50 Shades of Federalism*, 2018) <http://50shadesoffederalism.com/case-studies/the-pleasant-greyness-of-australian-federalism/> accessed December 2022.

70 Randy E. Barnett, 'Three Federalisms' (2008) 39 Loyola University Chicago Law Journal 285, 286f.

71 Palermo and Kössler (n 3) 140.

distribution of powers is complete and covers unforeseen issues which may possibly arise over time.

It would actually seem reasonable to hypothesize that in aggregative federal systems 'given the history of independent constituent units, the delegated power to the centre will be interpreted restrictively'.[72] However, the opposite has been true for both the United States and Australia. In the latter case, the High Court had originally championed a reserved powers doctrine, which was based on an interpretation of Australia's founding in 1901 as a compact between the new federal government and the former colonies. Only several years later, however, the Court initiated a shift away from this doctrine which had involved a restrictive interpretation of federal specific powers with a view to the residual powers of the states under Section 107 of the Constitution. Eventually, the doctrine was abandoned entirely with the seminal judgment in the *Engineers case* of 1920,[73] which has been widely accused of having undermined Australian federalism by interpreting the constitution 'in a manner widely at variance with the intentions and expectations of its founders'.[74]

In the US case the hollowing out of the states' residual powers by judicial fiat has been an even longer process than in Australia. A very broad interpretation of listed national competences at the expense of the above-mentioned Tenth Amendment has concerned several provisions. Very early jurisprudence of the US Supreme Court significantly expanded the power of Congress 'to make all Laws which shall be necessary and proper for carrying into execution the foregoing powers' (Art I, section 8, clause 18 of the Constitution). Following a seminal judgment as early as in 1819,[75] this so-called Necessary and Proper Clause gives Congress a lot of flexibility in defining what actually is 'necessary' for the implementation of federal powers. The fact that not a single federal law based on this provision was judged *not* 'necessary' by the Court made it known as 'Elastic Clause' or 'Sweeping Clause'. Some minor limits to this provision have only been introduced more recently. Federal legislation might be judged unconstitutional because it is not 'proper' in the sense of this clause.[76] Another enumerated federal power whose scope has been extended immensely is the

72 Steytler (n 66) 346.

73 *Amalgamated Society of Engineers v Adelaide Steamship Co Ltd* (1920) 28 CLR 129 ('Engineers').

74 Nicholas Aroney and James Allan, 'An Uncommon Court: How the High Court of Australia Has Undermined Australian Federalism' (2008) 30 Sydney Law Review 245.

75 *McCulloch v Maryland* 17 US (4 Wheat) 316 (1819).

76 *Printz v United States* 521 US 898 (1997); *National Federation of Independent Business v Sebelius* 567 US 519 (2012).

Commerce Clause (Art I, section 8, clause 3 of the Constitution). The US Supreme Court interpreted this provision as granting Congress the authority to regulate many social or economic activities on the basis that they were regarded as having potential effects on interstate commerce. After a long period of failing to strike down a single federal law as violating the Commerce Clause (1937–1995), some invalidations since then[77] have not changed the general trend.[78] While the Court has thus espoused a broad interpretation of key listed powers of Congress, it has reduced the scope of the above-mentioned Tenth Amendment. Indeed, after it had acknowledged in one single judgment of the 1970s that reserved state powers under this provision pose limits to the federal legislature,[79] it overruled this view not even a decade later.[80] Thus, the New Deal, court's famous characterization of the Tenth Amendment as a mere 'truism',[81] was never really challenged and reversed. Following this view, the Court's task is simply to ascertain the scope of federal power. Whatever happens to be left to the states in this process is seen as a mere 'residue'.[82] This marks a noticeable terminological change from the wording of the Tenth Amendment itself which speaks of powers 'reserved' to the states.

In the aggregative federal systems of both Australia and the United States, certain conditions have been conducive to the judicial expansion of enumerated federal competences and simultaneous reduction of subnational general powers. A first factor is the broad formulation of the heads of powers which is typical of these two countries (and other older federal systems). In comparison, more detailed distributions of power are more often found in newer federal constitutions, such as those of Belgium, Switzerland in 1999 and Germany, in the latter case especially after the amendments of 2006.[83] To be sure, the vague wording referring to broad areas has the clear advantage of avoiding an overload of the constitution with too much detail. A possible disadvantage

77 *United States v Lopez* 514 US 549 (1995); *United States v Morrison* 529 US 598 (2000).

78 Ilya Somin, 'The Supreme Court of the United States: Promoting Centralization More Than State Autonomy' in Nicholas Aroney and John Kincaid (eds), *Courts in Federal Countries: Federalists or Unitarists?* (University of Toronto Press 2017) 460f.

79 *National League of Cities v Usery* 426 US 833 (1976).

80 *Garcia v San Antonio Metropolitan Transit Authority* 469 US 528 (1985).

81 *United States v Darby* 312 US 100, 124 (1941).

82 In *United States v Darby* 312 US 100, 124 (1941), Justice Stone declared the following: 'From the beginning and for many years the [Tenth] [A]mendment has been construed as not depriving the national government of authority to resort to all means for the exercise of a granted power which are appropriate and plainly adapted to the permitted end'.

83 Thomas O. Hueglin and Alan Fenna, *Comparative Federalism: A Systematic Inquiry* (2nd edn, Broadview Press 2015) 43.

is, however, that a specific law may fall within one or another of these broad areas, which evidently increases the likelihood and frequency of national–subnational disputes about competences. If these conflicts are then not solved amicably through intergovernmental relations, they end up with the constitutional court, which may then act as an agent of centralization.[84] A second factor facilitating the judicial expansion of national enumerated powers is a situation in which they are not countered by listed powers of subnational entities, which are well-defined and well-protected. In such cases, 'there is no a priori agreement on their core competences that would be beyond federal reach'[85] so that the expansion of federal power is potentially boundless. It is therefore hardly surprising that federal systems, in which only national competences are listed, are marked by a tendency towards centralization.[86]

## 5 Conclusions

While much has been taken for granted regarding the effect of the formation of federal systems on their actual effects on these systems' institutional elements, this chapter suggests that a more cautious approach is in order. Since Friedrich and other political scientists, as well as lawyers have pointed to devolutionary federalism as the 'other' founding process besides the older aggregative federalism, several assumptions have governed the academic discourse which have never been tested and validated. To be sure, much more comprehensive empirical research is needed in this regard. But the evidence examined in this chapter, which analyzed such assumptions regarding the distribution of powers, allows us to glean some preliminary insights.

After its brief overview of conceptual history, the chapter's first focus has been on the certainties and uncertainties with which this history leaves us. Among the things that are clear is without doubt the unambiguous trend towards devolutionary federalism. In this regard, the only controversial point is when exactly the tide has turned and given way to a marginalization of aggregative federalism that had been characteristic of older federal systems. According to some, this occurred only 60 years ago, while this watershed had come for others with the turn of the 20th century and still others as early as with the French Revolution (which apparently disregards Australia's

84 Palermo and Kössler (n 3) 140f.

85 Steytler (n 66) 346.

86 Arun Sagar, 'Constitutional Interpretation in Federations and its Impact on the Federal Balance' (2011) 3 Perspectives on Federalism 1, 12f.

aggregative founding process in 1901). Much more interesting than the obvious trend towards devolutionary federalism is what is not clear after the chapter's overview of conceptual history, namely what I've called 'the problem of the false third category'. As pointed out, Stepan's 'putting-together' federalism actually refers to the coercive (vs voluntary) *nature* of the founding process. It therefore differs fundamentally from the categories of aggregative and devolutionary federalism (or 'coming-together' and 'holding-together' federalism, as he called them) which relate to the *dynamics* of this process. That nature and dynamics need to be distinguished was illustrated by the fact that different combinations of the two are possible. The United States combined aggregative federalism and Belgium devolutionary federalism with a formation process that was rather voluntary in nature. In comparison, as the chapter has shown, the founding of India was characterized by both aggregative and devolutionary dynamics, as well as a both voluntary and coercive nature. The latter depends a lot on the concrete state that one looks at, as some of them were integrated with a considerable degree of coercion. This is a strong reminder of the need to caution against any kind of purism. Indeed, aggregative and devolutionary federalism certainly remain a 'neat and useful distinction, but neater than things are in the real world'.[87]

The chapter's second focus has been on presumed effects of the formation of federal systems on the distribution of powers. According to one presumption, devolutionary federalism leads to asymmetrical powers of subnational entities because decentralization of authority in these cases is usually a reaction to pressure from some of these entities and most often effected through bilateral procedures. As demonstrated using the examples of Russian 'contract federalism' (1994–1998) and Spain's initial drive towards asymmetry with the first autonomy statutes in the context of the Constitution of 1978, this argument is certainly quite persuasive. These two examples also show, however, that this effect can be rather short-lived, as asymmetry is certainly not something set in stone. Quite the contrary, the impression that differentiation became excessive, overly complex or even chaotic led relevant political actors in both countries to initiate a trend towards resymmetrization. Such an impression is arguably more justified for Russia in the 1990s, where several dysfunctionalities have been identified of a system of differentiated powers with, on the one hand, some subnational entities dependent on the central government and, on the other hand, single republics enjoying a confederal relationship with Moscow. Even though asymmetry's track record in Spain is certainly

87 Fenna (n 20) 80.

not as negative, a development towards more uniformity occurred there too, starting with the LOAPA of 1982. A very real risk is then that resymmetrization goes hand in hand with (excessive) recentralization. This is something that occurred without doubt in Russia in the wake of Putin's reforms from 1998, but especially from the perspective of Catalan and Basque nationalists also in Spain. In any case, evidence from both countries has shown that devolutionary federalism's penchant for asymmetry certainly does not amount to a one-way street towards differentiation.

The main argument regarding exclusive powers is that such powers are more typical of devolutionary federalism as a result of basic distrust characterizing national–subnational relations in case of such a founding dynamics. Yet, the case studies of Belgium and Spain provide a different picture. Even if the Belgian federal system has managed, not least due to its Constitutional Court, to uphold the principle of exclusivity to the extent possible, for a number of reasons, it has not been able to totally elude the global trend towards concurrency of national and subnational powers and intergovernmental cooperation. But it is surely true that Spain has much more given in to this trend with, again, the country's Constitutional Court playing a key role. It has done so both through its interpretation of only prima facie 'exclusive' national powers and its curbing of regional powers listed in some of the statutes reformed 2006–2011.

A third argument holds that aggregative federalism would lead to subnational entities retaining broad general powers based on their residual clause, something seen as a result of their strong bargaining position at the founding and as compensation for relinquishing their original sovereignty as independent states or parts of a confederation. To be sure, the two classical aggregative federal systems analyzed in this chapter, that is the United States and Australia, both do have a residual clause in favor of the states. However, if we move beyond this formal perspective and consider the actual scope of subnational powers that these clauses ensure (in relation to national enumerated powers), a different picture emerges. It is interesting to see again the crucial role of constitutional interpretation. While Australia's High Court started to hollow out residual powers of the states in a marked shift of its jurisprudence only a few years into its existence, the US Supreme Court has followed a similar pattern by significantly expanding listed national powers at the expense of the Tenth Amendment. It has been pointed out that in both cases two enabling factors of such massive changes of the distribution of powers by judicial fiat have been the broad formulation of the heads of powers and the absence of a (complementary) list of explicitly mentioned state competences.

This widespread fallacy that a residual clause in favor of subnational governments would inevitably grant them broad general powers, is a clear reminder that things are not always as they appear at first sight. The same holds true for another point raised in this chapter, that is the 'the problem of the false third category'. In this case, it seems even more important to avoid confusion by clearly distinguishing the (voluntary–coercive) nature of the (aggregative–devolutionary) formation process from its dynamics. This is because the former arguably has a strong impact on whether federalism fails or succeeds. In fact, as Burgess aptly remarked concerning the implications of Bosnia-Herzegovina and Iraq for other recent aspiring federal systems '[i]t is dangerous to attempt to superimpose constitutional structures and political institutions – incorporating Western liberal democratic assumptions, ideas, and ideologies – upon communities' which can turn out to be even 'more detrimental to peace, order, and stability than are the dangers of civil war and secession, or even the complete disintegration of an existing state'.[88] If, conversely, the formation of new federal systems shall be voluntary rather than coercive in nature, a crucial precondition must be fulfilled: 'policy makers will need to be convinced that federalism really does have the beneficial effects'[89] which scholars ascribe to it.

## Bibliography

Agranoff R, 'Intergovernmental Relations and Management of Asymmetry in Federal Spain' in Agranoff R (ed), *Accommodating Diversity. Asymmetry in Federal States* (Nomos 1999).

Alcoz LM, 'The Spanish Approach to Asymmetric Federalism' in Palermo F, Zwilling C and Kössler K (eds), *Asymmetries in Constitutional Law, Recent Developments in Federal and Regional Systems* (Europäische Akademie Bozen/Accademia Europea Bolzano 2009).

Argullol E and Bernadí X, 'Kingdom of Spain' in Majeed A, Watts RL and Brown DM (eds), *Distribution of Powers and Responsibilities in Federal Countries* (McGill-Queen's University Press 2006).

Aroney N, 'Formation, Representation and Amendment in Federal Constitutions' (2006) 54 The American Journal of Comparative Law 277.

88 Burgess (n 23) 247.

89 Nancy Bermeo, 'The Merits of Federalism' in Ugo Amoretti and Nancy Bermeo (eds), *Federalism and Territorial Cleavages* (Johns Hopkins Press 2004) 474.

Aroney N, 'Types of Federalism', *Max Planck Encyclopedia of Comparative Constitutional Law* (2016) <https://oxcon.ouplaw.com/display/10.1093/law-mpeccol/law-mpeccol-e294?prd=MPECCOL> accessed December 2022.

Aroney N and James A, 'An Uncommon Court: How the High Court of Australia Has Undermined Australian Federalism' (2008) 30 Sydney Law Review 245.

Balaguer Castejón F, 'Cuestiones competenciales de los actuales procesos de reforma de los Estatutos de Autonomía' (2006) 1 Revista General de Derecho Constitucional 37.

Barnett RE, 'Three Federalisms' (2008) 39 Loyola University Chicago Law Journal 285.

Behera NC, *Demystifying Kashmir* (Brookings Institution Press 2006).

Bermeo N, 'The Merits of Federalism' in Amoretti U and Bermeo N (eds), *Federalism and Territorial Cleavages* (Johns Hopkins Press 2004).

Bermeo N, 'A New Look at Federalism: The Import of Institutions' (2022) 13 Journal of Democracy 96.

Bhattacharya M, 'The Mind of the Founding Fathers' in Mukarji N and Arora B (eds), *Federalism in India: Origins and Development* (Vikas 1992).

Binns C, 'Federalism, Nationalism and Socialism in Yugoslavia' in Forsyth M (ed), *Federalism and Nationalism* (Leicester University Press 1989).

Bossacoma Busquets P and Sanjaume-Calvet M, 'Asymmetry as a Device for Equal Recognition and Reasonable Accommodation of Majority and Minority Nations. A Country Study on Constitutional Asymmetry in Spain' in Popelier P and Sahadžić M (eds), *Constitutional Asymmetry in Multinational Federalism. Federalism and Internal Conflicts* (Palgrave Macmillan 2019).

Burgess M, 'The Paradox of Diversity – Asymmetrical Federalism in Comparative Perspective' in Palermo F, Zwilling C and Kössler K (eds), *Asymmetries in Constitutional Law, Recent Developments in Federal and Regional Systems* (Europäische Akademie Bozen/Accademia Europea Bolzano 2009).

Burgess M, *In Search of the Federal Spirit. New Comparative Empirical and Theoretical Perspectives* (Oxford University Press 2013).

Copland I, *The Princes of India in the Endgame of Empire, 1917–1947* (Cambridge University Press 1997).

Elazar DJ, *Exploring Federalism* (University of Alabama Press 1987).

Fenna A, 'The Pleasant Greyness of Australian Federalism' (*50 Shades of Federalism*, 2018) <http://50shadesoffederalism.com/case-studies/the-pleasant-greyness-of-australian-federalism/> accessed December 2022.

Fenna A, 'What hope for comparative federalism?' in Kincaid J (ed), *A Research Agenda for Federalism Studies* (Edward Elgar 2019).

Fleiner-Gerster T, 'Federalism in Australia and in Other Nations' in Craven G (ed), *Australian Federalism: Towards the Second Century* (Melbourne University Press 1992).

Friedrich CJ, 'New Tendencies in Federal Theory and Practice' (1965) 14 Jahrbuch des Öffentlichen Rechts 1.

Gamper A, 'A "Global Theory of Federalism": The Nature and Challenges of a Federal State' (2005) 6 German Law Journal 1297.

Gonzáles Encinar JJ, 'Ein asymmetrischer Bundesstaat' in Nohlen D and Gonzáles Encinar JJ (eds), *Der Staat der autonomen Gemeinschaften in Spanien* (Leske + Budrich 1992).

Greensmith Forsyth M, *Unions of States: The Theory and Practice of Confederation* (Leicester University Press 1981).

Hueglin TO and Fenna A, *Comparative Federalism: A Systematic Inquiry* (2nd edn, Broadview Press 2015).

Hughes J, 'Managing Secession Potential in the Russian Federation' in Hughes J and Sasse G (eds), *Ethnicity and Territory in the Former Soviet Union: Regions in Conflict* (Routledge 2002).

Kössler K, *Multinationaler Föderalismus in Theorie und Praxis: Kompetenz-und finanzverfassungsrechtliche Aspekte der territorialen Self-Rule in Kanada, Belgien und Spanien* (Nomos 2012).

Kössler K, 'Federal Constitutions and Secession: From "Perpetual Union" to a Right to Separate?' in Eppler A, Jeffery C and Lütgenau SA (eds), *Qualified Autonomy and Federalism versus Secession in EU Member States* (Studien Verlag 2021).

Kössler K, 'The Role of Constitutional Judges in Protecting Territorial Self-Government' in Requejo F and Sanjaume-Calvet M (eds), *Defensive Federalism: Protecting Territorial Minorities from the 'Tyranny of the Majority'* (Routledge 2022).

Kössler K and Fessha YT, 'Federalism and the Courts' in Cremades J and Hermida C (eds), *Encyclopedia of Contemporary Constitutionalism* (Springer 2022).

Kremyanskaya EA, 'Constitutional Asymmetry in Russia: Issues and Developments. A Country Study of Constitutional Asymmetry in the Russian Federation' in Popelier P and Sahadžić M (eds), *Constitutional Asymmetry in Multinational Federalism. Federalism and Internal Conflicts* (Palgrave Macmillan 2019).

Lenaerts K, 'Constitutionalism and the many faces of federalism' (1990) 38 American Journal of Comparative Law 205.

Maiz R, Caamaño F and Azpitarte M, 'The Hidden Counterpoint of Spanish Federalism: Recentralization and Resymmetrization in Spain (1978–2008)' (2010) 20 Regional & Federal Studies 63.

Palermo F and Kössler K, *Comparative Federalism: Constitutional Arrangements and Case Law* (Hart Publishing 2018).

Parliament of India, *Constituent Assembly Debates*, vol VII (4 November 1948) <https://www.constitutionofindia.net/constitution_assembly_debates/volume/7/1948-11-04> accessed December 2022.

Peeters P and Mosselmans J, 'The Constitutional Court of Belgium: Safeguard of the Autonomy of the Communities and Regions' in Aroney N and Kincaid J (eds), *Courts in Federal Countries: Federalists or Unitarists?* (University of Toronto Press 2017).

Riker WH, *Federalism: Origin, Operation, Significance* (Little, Brown & Company 1964).

Ross C, 'Russia's Multinational Federation: From Constitutional to Contract Federalism and the 'War of Laws and Sovereignties'' in Burgess M and Pinder J (eds), *Multinational Federations* (Routledge 2007).

Sagar A, 'Constitutional Interpretation in Federations and its Impact on the Federal Balance' (2011) 3 Perspectives on Federalism 1.

Sakwa R, 'Devolution and Asymmetry in Russia' in Requejo F and Nagel KJ (eds), *Federalism Beyond Federations. Asymmetry and Processes of Resymmetrisation in Europe* (Routledge 2016).

Solazábal JJ, 'Spain: A Federation in the Making?' in Hesse JJ and Wright V (eds), *Federalizing Europe? The Costs, Benefits and Preconditions of Federal Political Systems* (Oxford University Press 1996).

Somin I, 'The Supreme Court of the United States: Promoting Centralization More Than State Autonomy' in Aroney N and Kincaid J (eds), *Courts in Federal Countries: Federalists or Unitarists?* (University of Toronto Press 2017).

Stepan AC, 'Federalism and Democracy: Beyond the U.S. Model' (1999) 10 (4) Journal of Democracy 19.

Stepan AC, *Arguing Comparative Politics* (Oxford University Press 2001).

Steytler N, 'Concurrency of powers: The zebra in the room' in Steytler N (ed), *Concurrent Powers in Federal Systems: Meaning, making, managing* (Brill/Nijhoff 2017).

Thiruvengadam AK, *The Constitution of India: A Contextual Analysis* (Hart Publishing 2017).

Walker N, 'The shifting foundations of the European Union Constitution' (2012) University of Edinburgh School of Law Research Paper Series 18/2012.

Watts RL, *New Federations: Experiments in the Commonwealth* (Clarendon Press 1966).

Watts RL, 'Comparative Conclusions' in Majeed A and others (eds), *Distribution of Powers and Responsibilities in Federal Countries* (McGill-Queen's University Press 2006).

Watts RL, *Comparing Federal Systems* (McGill-Queen's University Press 2008).

Watts RL, 'Comparing Federal Political Systems' in Gagnon AG, Keil S and Mueller S (eds), *Understanding Federalism and Federation: Essays in Honour of Michael Burgess* (Ashgate Publishing 2015).

Wheare K, *Federal government* (Oxford University Press 1947).

## *Table of Cases*

*Amalgamated Society of Engineers v Adelaide Steamship Co Ltd* (1920) 28 CLR 129 ('Engineers')

Belgian Constitutional Court 166/2003
Belgian Constitutional Court 168/2011
Belgian Constitutional Court 33/2001
Belgian Constitutional Court 51/2006
*Canada* (AG) *v Ontario* (AG) [1937] AC 326 (JCPC)
*Garcia v San Antonio Metropolitan Transit Authority* 469 US 528 (1985)
*McCulloch v Maryland* 17 US (4 Wheat) 316 (1819)
*National Federation of Independent Business v Sebelius* 567 US 519 (2012)
*National League of Cities v Usery* 426 US 833 (1976)
*Printz v United States* 521 US 898 (1997)
Spain, STC 31/2010
Spain, STC 76/1983
*United States v Darby* 312 US 100 (1941)
*United States v Lopez* 514 US 549 (1995)
*United States v Morrison* 529 US 598 (2000)

CHAPTER 4

# Federal Dynamics and Stability

## *The Quest for the Most Optimal Structure of Political Systems*

*Patricia Popelier*

## 1 Introduction

Federal scholars have been concerned with the question of federal dynamics and stability, or the 'success or failure' of federal systems. Determining the mechanisms to enhance the stability of such systems has been called 'the most challenging task in research on federal systems'.[1] Even the notion of stability of federal systems seems obvious at first glance, but is difficult to grasp on closer inspection – an ‚ill-defined and poorly measured concept'.[2]

Nonetheless, studies have already revealed the most important conditions that explain the success or failure of federal systems.

Some of them are of institutional nature. For example, having more than two constituent entities is considered a recipe for success, because it allows for varying alliances, whereas dyadic systems encourage conflicts.[3] Also, constitutional symmetry – all territorial entities have equal status, competences and fiscal powers[4] – is recommended because constitutional asymmetry implies

1 Simon Hug, 'Federal Stability in Unequal Societies' (2005) 16 Constitutional Political Economy 113, 114.

2 Mikhail Filippov, Peter C. Ordeshook and Olga Shvetsova, *Designing Federalism* (Cambridge University Press 2004) 12. See also Maja Sahadžić, *Asymmetry, Multinationalism and Constitutional Law* (Palgrave Macmillan 2019) 130–133.

3 Ivo D. Duchacek, 'Dyadic Federations and Confederations' (1988) 18 Publius 5, 10; Daniel J. Elazar, *Exploring Federalism* (University of Alabama Press 1987, Edn 1991) 244; John Pinder, 'Multinational Federations' in Michael Burgess and John Pinder (eds), *Multinational Federalism* (Routledge 2007) 8; Ronald L. Watts, *Comparing Federal Systems* (McGill-Queen's University Press 2008) 184.

4 Francesco Palermo, 'Asymmetries in Constitutional Law – An Introduction' in Francesco Palermo, Carolin Zwilling and Karl Kössler (eds), *Asymmetries in Constitutional Law, Recent Developments in Federal and Regional Systems* (Europäische Akademie Bozen/Accademia Europea Bolzano 2009); Patricia Popelier and Maja Sahadžić, 'Linking Constitutional Asymmetry with Multinationalism' in Patricia Popelier and Maja Sahadžić (eds), *Constitutional Asymmetry in Multinational Federalism* (Palgrave Macmillan 2019) 6; Sahadžić (n 2) 16ff.

© PATRICIA POPELIER, 2024 | DOI:10.1163/9789004528581_006

inequality and leads to complexity and rivalry.[5] This suggests that institutional design matters: it influences the dynamics of federal systems. We come back to this in Section 5.

For now, we concentrate on the non-institutional conditions. The reason is that institutional conditions are features of the institutional design, ie an institutional solution for the governance of a society with specific characteristics. In other words: non-institutional factors are the starting point, the features of a society for which an institutional shape is chosen. For example, political (a) symmetry may explain constitutional (a)symmetry.[6] Only in second order may these institutional features, in turn, impact on federal dynamics.

Amongst the non-institutional conditions, political symmetry stands out as one of the most important ingredients for success. Political symmetry means the absence of variations in the size of population, territory, wealth, economic geography, identity or political landscape.[7] No federal system is perfectly political symmetrical, but asymmetries are said to become problematic where the differences are too substantial and especially when a clear dominance of one region occurs.[8] Income differences in particular appear to be an important determinant for secession demands in richer regions.[9] Also, differences in identity are considered highly problematic. Instead, a homogeneous society – or at least a non-multinational society – is ideal for the creation of a sense of belonging, and thus for social cohesion.[10]

The conclusion seems to be that the most successful federal systems are the ones that most closely resemble a unitary state. This is unsatisfactory, because

---

5 Rainer Bauböck, 'United in Misunderstanding? Asymmetry in Multinational Federations' (2002) ICE Working Paper Series 26; Angustias Hombrado, 'Learning to catch the wave? Regional demands for constitutional change in contexts of asymmetrical arrangements' (2011) 21 Regional & Federal Studies 479.

6 For a more nuanced conclusion Patricia Popelier and Maja Sahadžić, 'Conclusion. A Country Studies-Based Deliberation on Constitutional Asymmetry in Multi-tiered Multinational Systems' in Patricia Popelier and Maja Sahadžić (eds), *Constitutional Asymmetry in Multinational Federalism* (Palgrave Macmillan 2019) 489–492.

7 Popelier and Sahadžić (n 4) 5.

8 Elazar (n 3) 170, 244; Charles D. Tarlton, 'Symmetry and Asymmetry as Elements of Federalism: A Theoretical Speculation' in John Kincaid (ed), *Federalism*, vol II (Sage Publications 2011) 311; Watts (n 3) 181.

9 Hug (n 1) 113–124.

10 Elazar (n 3) 169; Jan Erk, 'Austria: A Federation without Federalism' (2004) 34 Publius 1, 2; James A. Gardner and Antoni A. Ninet, 'Sustainable decentralization: power, extraconstitutional influence and subnational symmetry in the United States and Spain' (2011) 59 The American Journal of Comparative Law 491, 498; John McGarry and Brendan O'Leary, 'Federation and managing nations' in Michael Burgess and John Pinder (eds), *Multinational Federalism* (Routledge 2007) 197f.

there is no urgent reason for a homogeneous and politically symmetrical society to opt for federal arrangements – unless it has a vast territory, in which case efficiency and pragmatic reasons call for some degree of decentralisation. In the end, it seems that the conditions that predict the stability of a federal system, are simply the pre-conditions for the success of any political system. They do not predict the continuation of the federal arrangement. On the contrary, federal systems that meet all the conditions tend to undergo centralisation processes. The question is, then, at which point they are still a federal system. If regionalized systems such as Italy or Spain are considered too centralist to be called a 'genuine' federation, then surely federalism proves unsuccessful in the case of a system like Austria, which has become so centralized that it is now called a 'centralistic federation' or a 'federation without federalism'.[11] This means that the condition of non-diversity predicts the continuity of the political system, but not how longlasting the federal arrangement is.

The insight that political symmetry, and homogeneity in particular, is a condition for the stability of federal systems is also unsatisfactory for the reason that nowadays, federal arrangements have become a particularly popular devise for multinational systems. Federal arrangements, then, are opted for despite the fact that the conditions for stability are not in place. Even more: often, these systems opt for federal arrangements precisely to accommodate ethnic diversity. In democratic environments this does not seem too problematic. In fact, Stepan points out that the most longstanding multinational democracies are all federal states.[12] In other environments, multinational systems are probably unstable irrespective of their structure. The more interesting question for multinational systems, then, is under which circumstances a system can be stable in the absence of these conditions; and whether federal arrangements can create these circumstances.

The key question is which structure is the most adequate for a given political system. This is the question that will guide this chapter. The chapter will argue that the question whether federal systems are stable in themselves, is misconceived. The issue of stability arises with respect to the political system rather than the structure that system adopts. Regarding political systems, the question expands to one of sustainability, not just stability according to this chapter. For (types of) federal systems, the question is rather one of transition.

This necessitates a clarification of what we understand by federal systems and types of federal systems or formal structures (Section 2). Building on that,

---

11 Erk (n 10).

12 Alfred Stepan, 'Federalism and Democracy: Beyond the U.S. Model' (1999) 10 Journal of Democracy 19, 19f.

we can then explore what we mean by stability (Section 3), and transition (Section 4). Finally, the paper will present propositions as to which structures are most adequate, and on how a system best moves towards another type of formal structure (Section 5).

We start with some preliminary notes on the desirability of stability.

The chapter is only concerned with the (federal) structure of a political system, and whether it allows that system to persist without too many internal threats and distractions. It does not deal with the form of state and the moral justification of the system's endurance. Hence, the question which structure best ensures the stability of a political system is relevant, irrespective of whether that system has a democratic or authoritarian regime.[13]

Also, this chapter does not imply that the continuation of a political system in itself has moral value. It is very well possible that the discontinuation of a political system is deemed the optimal outcome for an orderly governance of public affairs. Hence, the dissolution of Czechoslovakia was negotiated peacefully in 1993 and in literature, the effects of the partitition have been evaluated as predominantly positive in scholarship.[14]

## 2 On Types of Federal Systems

This paper's research question is which structure is the most adequate for a given political system and furthermore, what types of structures are available to organize a political system.

The most well-known typology is the trichotomy of unitary state, federation and confederation. Usually, these types are classified according to defining institutional features.[15] This is open to criticism, for several reasons.[16] For the purpose of this paper, what matters most is that the categories are too rigid, resulting in the creation of a new category of 'hybrids' – those structures that do not fully conform to the rigid set of features required to categorize as unitary, federal or confederal. This category contains the most diverse formal

13 Keith M. Dowding and Richard Kimber, 'The Meaning and Use of Political Stability' (1983) 11 European Journal of Political Research 229, 230.

14 Michal Illner, 'Czechoslovakia. A peaceful disintegration' in John Loughlin, John Kincaid and Wilfried Swenden (eds), *Handbook of Regionalism and Federalism* (Routledge 2013) 540.

15 Jean François Aubert, 'Essai sur le fédéralisme' (1963) 80 Revue Du Droit Public Et De La Science Politique 401, 403; Pinder (n 3) 2.

16 Patricia Popelier, *Dynamic Federalism* (Routledge 2021) 20–32.

structures, which makes it unfit for analytical purposes. This means that the trichotomy remains problematic, even if we were to stretch the definition of a federation to include those hybrids. If a category is so broad that it contains the most diverse structural types, then it is impossible to identify precisely which type exactly is most suitable for a political system. It is also impossible to notice at which point a system changes its structure in such a way, that the paradigms that determine its operation have fundamentally changed. This calls for a more nuanced categorisation.

A categorization of types of federal systems is necessarily linked with the core elements of federal systems. This necessitates a definition of federal systems that displays these elements. In previous work, I defined them as systems with territory-based tiers of government, in search of a balance between autonomy and cohesion.[17]

*Autonomy* is the ability of these tiers to organize themselves and make their own decisions (*self-rule*), to secure their interests in central decision-making (*shared rule*) and to organize themselves (*constituent autonomy*).

*Cohesion* refers to a commitment to living together peacefully, in mutual recognition and respect, and based on solidarity.[18] It is not centralization – ie the opposite of autonomy – but refers to a way of governing together with subnational entities, based on shared values and in pursuit of a common interest, but with respect for the specificities and needs of each entity in itself.

The federal *balance* between cohesion and regional autonomy points to any possible relation between any degree of cohesion (on a scale from the most integrated to the most disintegrated systems) and any degree of autonomy (on a scale from the most centralized to the most decentralized systems). What the optimal balance is for a particular political system, rests on a political decision, and is then incorporated in the institutional design of that system. As a political decision, however, it is perpetually contested: political, social and judicial actors may push to change this balance. Institutional mechanisms can even be incorporated in the institutional design to help change this balance. Change is therefore inherent to the operation of federal systems.[19]

Starting from this definition of federal systems, it is possible to distinguish nine types of federal systems, dependent on the federal balance that they incorporate. This is visualized in Table 4.1.

17 ibid 50–60.

18 Michael Burgess, *In Search of the Federal Spirit* (Oxford University Press 2012) 322; Sahadžic (n 2) 216.

19 See also Lawrence Anderson, 'Both Too Much and Too Little: Sources of Federal Instability in Canada' (2014) 44 American Review of Canadian Studies 15, 16.

TABLE 4.1 Types of federal systems

| | SUBNATIONAL AUTONOMY → | | |
|---|---|---|---|
| COHESION ↑ | **High – Low:** Integrationist MTS | **High – Medium:** Federation type 1 | **High – High:** Federation type 2 |
| | **Medium – Low:** Consociation-based MTS | **Medium – Medium:** Regionalized system | **Medium – High:** Confederation |
| | **Low – Low:** Deconcentrated unitary system | **Low – Medium:** Decentralized system | **Low – High:** Political association |

SOURCE: PATRICIA POPELIER, *DYNAMIC FEDERALISM* (ROUTLEDGE 2021) 74.

Positioning a political system in Table 4.1 requires a measurement of institutional cohesion and autonomy. For this purpose, indexes have been developed.[20] It would take us too far to discuss them in this paper. What matters is that it is possible to establish the federal balance of each political system and, on that basis, to determine what type of federal system it is.

The question that guides this paper – which structure is the most adequate for a given political system – refers to these types of federal systems. It is therefore a question of federal balance: which degree of institutional autonomy and which degree of institutional cohesion form the most optimal combination to sustain a particular political system?

## 3 On the Stability of Political Systems

Stability is a relational term that links the (un)stable object with the contingency that threatens it.[21] This points to three elements: the object of stability, the notion of stability, and threats.

### 3.1 *The Object of Stability*

In Section 1 it was held that the quest for a stable federal system is in fact a concern for a stable political system. In other words: the object of stability is the political system, not the federal structure. The research question was which structure is the most adequate for a given political system. A structure that fails to provide stability to a political system is clearly not the most optimal.

20 Popelier (n 16) 87–189.

21 Dowding and Kimber (n 13) 231.

### 3.2 *Stability*

Another question is what we mean by stability. In other words: when do we consider a political system to be stable?

It has been stated, that a stable political system is one that possesses the capacity to prevent its own forced non-survival.[22] In view of our research question, however, this definition is unsatisfactory. A structure by which a political system, while persisting, stumbles from crisis to crisis, can hardly be considered the most adequate one. Instead, the structure should enable an orderly governance of public affairs. Hence, a political system is unstable if it is under such pressure that it cannot handle public affairs in an orderly way, and instead must spend a disproportionate amount of political energy on dealing with this pressure. Obvious indicators of such disruption are violence or states of emergency. But they can also be non-violent. For example, a political crisis, when unsolvable disputes between political actors paralyze decision-making. Or if economic hardship makes it impossible to properly manage public affairs.

Distinction can be made between the stability and the sustainability of a political system – the one referring to the short term, the other to the long term.

A political system is *unstable* if its survival is under immediate threat, or if – and as long as – contingencies prevent the orderly handling of public affairs. For example, the tensions between the Ethiopian federal government and the Tigray Region indicated instability since they resulted in a civil war, leading to the destruction of civilian structure and a humanitarian crisis, and affecting other regions as well.[23] Hence, these tensions threatened the stability of Ethiopia, even if its existence in itself was not at stake.

The system is *unsustainable*, if contingencies threaten its survival or the orderly handling of affairs on the longer run.

In Russia, for example, a period of 'Wild Federalism' is sketched in which the President granted rights and privileges to sub-states through bilateral agreements in exchange for their political support. Each agreement in itself did not threaten the country's stability. Together, however, they created a dynamic that spiralled out of control towards the disintegration of the Russian Federation.[24]

Federal systems can be unstable but sustainable. Anderson refers to Canada in its early years: it was unstable because under real and persisting threats to

---

22 Dowding and Kimber (n 13) 238f.

23 Kjetil Tronvoll, 'The Anatomy of Ethiopian's Civil War' (2022) 121 Current History 163.

24 Elena A. Kremyanskaya, 'Constitutional Asymmetry in Russia: Issues and Developments. A Country Study on Constitutional Asymmetry in the Russian Federation' in Patricia Popelier and Maja Sahadžić (eds), *Constitutional Asymmetry in Multinational Federalism* (Palgrave Macmillan 2019) 403ff.

the territorial integrity, but sustainable because of the ‚willingness to negotiate, compromise, and make concessions'.[25]

However, if a system manages to overcome periods of instability, this does not necessarily mean that it is sustainable over time. An example is Belgium. Since 1970, six constitutional reforms (called 'state reforms') changed the structure of the political system to accommodate multinational conflicts between the Flemish and the francophone population. According to Art 1 of the constitution, Belgium is a federal system since 1994. If we apply Table 1, however, the system transformed from a unitary system to a regionalized system and then a confederation.[26] The dynamics display a shift towards even more regional autonomy, with hardly any regard for cohesion. Debates about a seventh state reform continue in that vein, with a proposal from the largest Flemish political party N-VA (Nieuw-Vlaamse Alliantie) for a loose structure that comes down to a political association.[27] Given these dynamics, it can be argued that the country has survived over time, but gradually its sustainability in the long run can be questioned. Signs of emerging instability are increasing difficulties to form a federal government after elections – even when faced with a serious health crisis that requires firm crisis governance.[28]

### 3.3 *Threats*

In turn, *threats* are those events that make it difficult for the system to survive or to handle public affairs in an orderly way. These threats indicate a seizure between the normal state of affairs and the breakdown of the system. Instability, then, is a transitional situation: the system is under threat, and it has difficulties overcoming that threat, but it has not (yet) been struck down by it. Hence, the falling apart of the system is only a possible result of instability – once broken down, it is not unstable anymore.

Distinction can be made between external and internal threats. External threats destabilize a country from the outside. For example a health crisis caused by a virus, or a war instigated by another country. Internal threats are inherent to the political system itself and the society it governs. This chapter is

---

25 Anderson (n 19) 21.

26 An application of the indexes on Belgium gives a score of medium cohesion and strong autonomy, pointing to a confederation. See Popelier (n 16) 84ff, 257–268.

27 N-VA, *Verandering voor vooruitgang* (2014) 5f <https://www.n-va.be/sites/default/files/generated/files/dossier/definitieve_congresbrochure.pdf> accessed 15 March 2023.

28 Elections were held in May 2019 but no federal government was formed when the corona crisis hit Belgium (hard) in February 2020. A weak resigning minority government had to be entrusted with the crisis management until a new government was finally sworn in on 1 October 2020.

concerned with internal threats, because they are the ones a given structure is meant to deal with.

Importantly, threats are not consensual, but forced.[29] However, in borderline cases the line between consensus and force may not be crystal-clear.

One example is a scenario in which nationalist parties do not use violence to gain autonomy or independence, but continuously undermine the efficient functioning of the central government as a political strategy to force negotiated constitutional reform. In that case, the acts undermine the efficient functioning and threaten the political system in a non-consensual way. In turn, the negotiated transition shows the robustness of the system, if this brings political rest and allows the system to concentrate again on the orderly handling of public affairs – this is further discussed in Section 5. If, however, the new structure accelerates dynamics towards a continuous increase of regional autonomy without concern for institutional cohesion, the transition in itself may threaten the sustainability of the system.

The question is whether secessionist movements in themselves pose a threat to the stability of a country. It has been argued that 'a state with an active and viable secessionist movement within it will not be deemed stable, nor will one that is subject to military usurpation of civil authority'.[30] One can read into this that instability exists if the survival of the country is threatened or if it cannot manage its public affairs in an orderly way through civil authority, and that secession movements are threats, ie indicators of instability.

Not all secessionist movements threaten the stability of a political system, even if they are active and viable. First, this depends on how they operate. Secessionist movements are threats if the means they use to force secession – violence, for example – prevent the political system from handling public affairs in an orderly way. Otherwise, much depends on what secession would result in for the political system.

Secession in itself does not necessarily make a system unstable. For example, the withdrawal of the UK has not destabilized the European Union. Secession can even restore stability where secessionist movements have destabilized the system. This is different if the seceding part is crucial for the continuity of the political system. For example, Slovak secession movements finally led to the dissolution of Czechoslovakia and the creation of two new states. Likewise,

29 Dowding and Kimber (n 13) 238f.

30 Filippov, Ordeshook and Shvetsova (n 2) 13.

the secession of Flanders would endanger the continuity of Belgium as a whole.[31] This is because the Flemings constitute the majority of the country, and the Flemish Region is the most wealthy one.

Secession movements also threaten the stability of the political system, if the country relies on the wealth created in the region that seeks independence. For this reason, independence movements in the Basque Country and Catalonia pose a threat to the stability of Spain, at least as long as economic activity is concentrated in these regions.[32]

## 4 On the Transition of Federal Systems

### 4.1 *The Notion of Transition*

In the previous section, stability was linked with the ability to handle public affairs in an orderly manner. The political system was identified as the object of stability because it produces the government that is mandated to handle public affairs. The federal structure is only a way to accommodate the government in that task. To obtain its goal, changes in the federal structure may be required. Nigeria, for example, has adjusted its federal structure several times in an attempt to accommodate group rivalries.[33]

The question whether a federal structure is stable, does not make much sense from that perspective. As Anderson puts it: change is endemic to federal systems and therefore something that has to be managed, not solved.[34] The real question is one of suitability, rather than stability: it is not a suitable structure for a particular political system if it does not enable that system to orderly handle public affairs.

The argument is illustrated by Palermo and Kössler where they discuss confederations (defined as a treaty-based association of sovereign states). They notice that past experiences raise the question 'as to whether confederations

---

31 Anna Mastromarino, 'Secessionist Claims in a Federal System: the Belgian Case' in Alberto Lopéz-Basaguren and Leire Escajedo San-Epifanio (eds), *Claims for Secession and Federalism* (Springer 2019) 222.

32 For an overview of economic development in the Spanish regions, see Pau Bossacoma Busquets and Marc Sanjaume-Calvet, 'Asymmetry as a Device for Equal Recognition and Reasonable Accommodations of Majority and Minority Nations. A Country Study on Constitutional Asymmetry in Spain' in Patricia Popelier and Maja Sahadžić (eds), *Constitutional Asymmetry in Multinational Federalism* (Palgrave Macmillan 2019) 434.

33 Aderonke Majekondumni, 'Federalism in Nigeria: the past, current peril and future hopes' (2015) 9 Journal of Policy and Development Studies 107.

34 Anderson (n 19) 16.

are doomed to fail'[35] – which would imply that they are inherently unstable – and then dismiss the proposition, arguing that 'first, no form of government is eternal (in spite of the terminology normally used by constitution drafters), and second, the "inevitable evolution" from a confederation into a federation tends to be rather common when federal states come together through ever deeper integration of previously sovereign entities, such as in the case of the United States or Switzerland'.[36] In other words: all structures are transitional – it does not matter whether they structure a political system for a long or a short time, as long as they are appropriate to that particular system at that moment in time.

If a type of structure is not or no longer suitable for a particular political system, it must be traded for another type of structure. This is the moment of transition: the process by which a political system shakes off one type of federal system and adopts another one. This points to more than a mere change in the federal structure. If changes do not alter the overall federal balance, there is no question of transition.

The transformation from one type to another type of federal structure may cause instability – for example if it diverts all political energy to institutional affairs, leaving public affairs ungoverned, with no certainty as to whether negotiations will succeed and relations will remain peaceful. If the transition is brought about by constitutional reform, at least some political energy will be absorbed by the process. This is only destabilizing if it prevents political actors from paying due attention to governing public affairs, and even then this may only be temporary. But in the longer term, the system may prove sustainable, because throughout these transformations, it persists and order is restored.

When a transition does not involve instability, it may not even be recognized as one. This is especially the case if the transition is one towards centralisation.[37] Changes to the institutional design can be made gradually, where one change by itself does not alter much, but the set of changes moves the system to a different federal balance. It is important to remain aware of such transitions, precisely because they change the federal balance, and therefore the paradigms in which the system operates. Over time, disintegrating dynamics created by these transitions may endanger the sustainability of the political system or centralizing dynamics may imperceptibly transform the system

35 Francesco Palermo and Karl Kössler, *Comparative Federalism: Constitutional Arrangements and Case Law* (Hart Publishing 2017) 37.
36 Palermo and Kössler (n 35) 37.
37 Anderson (n 19) 19.

in violation of an eternity clause that may require the political system to be organized as a federation.

This brings us to the issue of robustness.

## 4.2 *Robustness*

The notion of transition is essential to the concept of federalism, since the federal balance was described, in Section 2, as essentially contested. This implies an ongoing process of negotiation. It has been stated in the literature that 'the primary purpose of federal design' must be to keep these negotiation processes in check.[38] In that vein, the 'dangers federal bargaining poses' were defined as the possibility that it leads to disintegration, or transforms the system into a unitary state.[39] However, the federal balance is not an immobile equilibrium between the powers of the federal government and the federated entities that should be maintained overall,[40] and the stability of the federal structure is not an end in itself. Instead, to preserve the stability of the political system, checks on the process should not aim at keeping the federal balance as it is, but at robustness.

Robustness means that the political system has the ability to adapt to changing needs in a way that secures the system's stability[41] or, at least, its sustainability over the longer term. In other words, a robust system has the instruments to overcome, immediately or in the longer run, the contingencies that threaten it, and thereby secure the stability and sustainability of the system.

For this reason, the system needs instruments that facilitate peaceful transitions. Surely, transition can also come about in an informal way. That, however, offers fewer certainties. For example, in specific cases, a secession clause may serve this purpose, if it secures that the modalities of a secession are agreed upon by all parties. In Bossacoma Busquets' words: 'making State territorial borders unchangeable may entail more worrying objections and problems than constitutionalizing a qualified right to secede.'[42] Without such clause, secessionist movements may more easily turn to violence. Or, as the Spanish

38 Filippov, Ordeshook and Shvetsova (n 2) 33.

39 Filippov, Ordeshook and Shvetsova (n 2) 34.

40 Critical of the notion of federal balance in that sense: Preston King, *Federalism and Federation* (Croom Helm 1982) 56–68; Michael Burgess, *Comparative Federalism. Theory and Practice* (Routledge 2006) 45f.

41 Jenna Bednar, *The Robust Federation* (Cambridge University Press 2009) 13f.

42 Pau Bossacoma Busquets, *Morality and Legality of Secession* (Palgrave Macmillan 2020) 219.

case shows,[43] it may instigate secession processes outside the legal framework, in a way that leads the central government to react in a forceful way. This may cause instability in the long term, and create discontent that jeopardizes sustainability in the long term.

This raises the question which instruments are built in federal systems to enable changes and transitions. They are presented in the next sub-section.

### 4.3 *Hubs for Federal Transition*

The instruments that are built in federal systems to bring about institutional change are called 'institutional hubs for change'. They can be listed as follows:[44]

1. The *constitutional amendment procedure*.
2. *De-constitutionalization*. ie delegation to more flexible instruments such as ordinary legislation, super-majority laws, or bilateral or multilateral intergovernmental agreements. These agreements may concern the allocation of powers or the conditions under which a group may secede.
3. *Power allocation techniques*. For example, concurrent powers allow for shifts in power relations without formal constitutional amendments. They usually have centralising effects,[45] but these can be mitigated through the inclusion and design of subsidiarity clauses.[46]
4. *Political adjudicators of federalism conflicts*. In some systems they precede the judicial adjudication of conflicts. In others, such as Ethiopia,[47] they replace courts to resolve federalism disputes.
5. *Courts*. Judicial adjudicators of federalism conflicts tend to have a centralist impact, but in some systems they take a more balanced position.[48]

---

43 Benito Aláez Corral and Francisco J. Bastido Freijedo, 'Constitutionalizing secession in order to harmonize constitutionality and democracy in territorial decentralized states like Spain' in Alberto López-Basaguren and Leire Escajedo San-Epifanio (eds), *Claims for Secession and Federalism* (Springer 2019) 268.

44 In more detail: Popelier (n 16) 214.

45 Nico Steytler, 'The Currency of Concurrent Powers in Federal Systems' in Nico Steytler (ed), *Concurrent Powers in Federal Systems. Meaning, Making, Managing* (Brill/Nijhoff 2017) 3.

46 Popelier (n 16) 225. On subsidiarity and federal change: Jenna Bednar, 'Subsidiarity and Robustness: Building the Adaptive Efficiency of Federal Systems' (2014) 55 Federalism and Subsidiarity 231.

47 Gedion T. Hessebon and Abduletif Idris, 'The Supreme Court of Ethiopia: Federalism's Bystander' in Nicholas Aroney and John Kincaid (eds), *Courts in Federal Countries. Federalists or Unitarists?* (University of Toronto Press 2017) 184; Assefa Fiseha, 'Constitutional Adjudication in Ethiopia: Exploring the experience of the House of Federation' (2007) 1 Mizan Law Review 1.

48 Patricia Popelier, 'Federalism Disputes and the Behavior of Courts' (2017) 47 Publius 27, 41–44.

Much depends on extra-legal factors, but institutional-legal factors also play a role. For example, involving governments in the selection of judges and representation of Seconded National Experts in the bench seem to reduce centralist tendencies. This means that institutional design to some extent predetermines whether the court will take a centralist or balanced position.

6. *Global governance*. Powers can be transferred to international (or supranational) bodies in such a way that this affects the domestic power relations between central and subnational governments. For example, regional integration has a centralizing effect in mono-national federations but a decentralizing effect in multinational ones.[49] Also, treaties may establish international courts that in turn operate as judicial hubs for change.

All these instruments can instigate federal change. But they may also initiate a transition to a different type of federal system. The constitutional amendment procedure is the most examined tool for constitutional change, and scholars examining constitutional amendments are often interested in the rigidity of the procedure. More important for the purpose of this chapter, however, is which of these six 'hubs' is the most suitable one to bring about transition in a robust way. This is discussed in Section 5.

## 5 On Optimal Structures, and Robust Transitions

In the previous sections, it was argued that the search for the most adequate formal structure is not a search for the most longlasting structure, but for the one that best secures the stability and sustainability of the political system. In other words, the stability of the political system may necessitate a transition from one structure to another. To this end, types of federal systems that structure a political system were categorized in view of their federal balance, measured by degrees of institutional cohesion and institutional autonomy.

Building on these insights, this section presents propositions about which structure is the most adequate for which type of society, and how transitions should occur in order to best preserve the stability and sustainability of the political system. Importantly, they are based on hypotheses that still have to be tested in follow-up research. This means that the propositions present trains of

49 Paolo Dardanelli and others, 'Dynamic De/Centralization in Federations: Comparative Conclusio*ns*' (2019) 49 Publius 194, 205.

thought rather than truths. They are also based on informed intuitions about the sources of federal arrangements. This section explains what these intuitions are (5.1) before presenting the propositions (5.2).

### 5.1 *Sources of Federal Dynamics*

Sociologists have argued that institutions aim to reach the best fit with the underlying societal structure[50] and that federal arrangements are opted for mainly to accommodate diversity of any kind.[51]

The propositions below will take this view as an ideal. In reality, social structure and institutional design are not always perfectly aligned. The reason is that actors are needed to give shape to the institutional design, and to operate it in fact. Social as well as economic actors come into view but in the end political actors make the institutional arrangements.[52] Hence, politics come in between: political structure, bargains, culture and discourse.[53] The political landscape is assumed to reflect the social structure. But other factors also play a role in the political bargain: power relations and the level of trust between the political parties, pressure from social and economic actors, path dependency, and economic forces.[54]

In addition, institutional structure may impact on social structure and federal dynamics.[55] This is an expectation that guides the propositions below. Even Livingston admitted that the very fact that a political system adopts a federal structure may bring a feeling of distinctiveness to life, and create diversity where previously none existed.[56] To a certain extent, it is also agreed that federal institutions that institutionalize ethnic diversity may reinforce ethnic conflict[57] and thus decrease social cohesion. It is also an implication of the institutional conditions for stability mentioned in Section 1. The key question

50 Jan Erk, *Explaining Federalism* (Routledge 2010); Jan Erk and Edward Koning, 'New Structuralism and Institutional Change: Federalism between Centralization and Decentralization' (2020) 43 Comparative Political Studies 353, 355.

51 William S. Livingston, *Federalism and Constitutional Change* (Oxford University Press 1956); William S. Livingston, 'A Note on the Nature of Federalism' (1952) 67 Political Science Quarterly 81, 85.

52 For an overview of actors: Popelier (n 16) 205f.

53 Arthur Benz and Jörg Broschek, 'Federal Dynamics: Introduction' in Arthur Benz and Jörg Broschek (eds), *Federal Dynamics* (Oxford University Press 2014) 7.

54 For an overview: Popelier (n 16) 198–203.

55 See Richard Simeon, 'Constitutional Design and Change in Federal Systems: Issues and Questions' (2009) 39 Publius 241, 244.

56 Livingston (n 51) 8.

57 Philip G. Roeder, 'Ethnofederalism and the Mismanagement of Conflicting Nationalisms' in Jan Erk and Lawrence Anderson (eds), *The Paradox of Federalism* (Routledge 2010) 116.

is whether institutional engineering can change social dynamics, or merely accelerate or slow them down.

## 5.2 *Propositions*

*Proposition 1. Centralized or highly cohesive systems are the most adequate structures for political systems that meet the internal non-institutional conditions for stability.*

In Section 1, political symmetry, or the absence of diversity was marked as a critical (internal) condition for the stability of a political system. Political systems that fully meet these conditions show no or only minimal diversity and therefore have no reason to opt for federal arrangements, and the complexity that comes with it.

If there is no meaningful diversity at all, there is no reason to give substantial autonomy to territorial entities, or to build in institutional cohesion, since this implies the taking into account of groups with distinctive needs and preferences. At most, territorial entities can be delineated for the handling of local affairs, especially in vast political systems. Hence, turning to Table 1, a system with low cohesion and low autonomy seems the most adequate structure for an orderly handling of public affairs.

If there is some diversity – the conditions are met to some extent but not fully – a structure that combines high cohesion with low or at most medium autonomy seems more adequate.

This would explain the centralizing trends that have been noticed in traditional federal systems.[58] They may indicate that systems change to find the most optimal federal balance. At the same time, we consider the possibility that centralizing or integrating dynamics result from the very properties of such structure. The hypothesis would then read as follows: In systems with low diversity, a centralized or a cohesive structure impacts positively on social cohesion (ie minimizes even further possible feelings of distinctiveness between groups in society), which in turn triggers transition towards an even more centralized or a more cohesive structure.

*Proposition 2. The stability and sustainability of political systems is enhanced by federal structures that align institutional cohesion to social cohesion, with institutional cohesion being slightly higher than social cohesion.*

---

58 Erk and Koning (n 50) 353–378. For these centralizing trends, see Dardanelli and others (n 49) 211.

The more challenging question is: which structure is the most adequate one for political systems that do not meet the internal non-institutional conditions for stability – ie for multinational systems?

This question has been preoccupying political scholars in search for the optimal institutional design of divided societies. Two schools have been discerned. In brief, the accommodationist model promotes a system of group-based partisanship in political institutions, whereas the integrationist model endeavors to create a common political community and encourages political actors to rise above the interests of their own group.[59] In Table 1, the accommodationist model would be situated in the row of systems with medium cohesion: the relevant groups are represented in the central political institutions and decisions are made taking their needs and interests into account; but the system does not encourage them to go beyond the interests of their own group and promote a broader common interest. The integrationist model takes that extra step, which would bring it in the row of systems with high cohesion.

The proposition does not take side in this discussion. Both models have their merits and flaws. The accommodationist model is criticized for strengthening ethnic identity and thereby weakening social cohesion. The integrationist model is criticized for being too naïve. In divided societies, distrust between groups would cause the system to fail, especially in post-conflict systems where one group may have been oppressed by the other. In the end, we can expect that the degree of social cohesion determines which model is the most adequate one for a particular political system.

The scenario relevant for this paper is one where (all or some) ethnic groups are situated within a specific territory, inviting federal arrangements. The proposition suggests medium or high autonomy to allow these groups the development of policies according to their specific needs, preferences and identity. At the same time, by institutionalizing cohesion, efforts are made to keep the system together and prevent it from reinforcing regional identity. Thus, the proposition follows to a certain extent Gagnon's device for multinational federations as a combination of autonomy ('the encouragement of political autonomy for the member states') and cohesion ('the adoption of collaborative initiatives with a view to creating bonds between the peoples, the regions, and the orders

59 For a richer and more nuanced discussion: John McGarry, Brendan O'Leary and Richard Simeon, 'Integration or Accommodation? The Enduring Debate in Conflict Regulation' in Sujit Choudhry (ed), *Constitutional Design For Divided Societies* (Oxford University Press 2008); Lidia Bonifati, 'Comparative Constitutional Design for Divided Societies: A Model to Explain Constitutional Asymmetries' (PhD thesis, University of Bologna and University of Antwerp 2023) 20–33.

of government').[60] Our proposition, however, makes distinctions as to how much cohesion can be institutionalized.

As mentioned, the proposition is based on the idea that institutions ideally follow social structure. This means that the optimal degree of institutional cohesion depends on the degree of social cohesion already present. In turn, institutional cohesion is expected to impact on social cohesion. Low cohesion is expected to impact negatively on social cohesion on account of its emphasis on regional identity and the absence of a common public space. High cohesion creates a common public space and is therefore expected to impact positively on social cohesion. In both scenario's, the level of institutional cohesion affects the relationship between the political representatives of the ethnic groups, which in turn impact on social cohesion.

If this hypothesis is valid, the solution is a structure where the degree of institutional cohesion slightly exceeds the degree of social cohesion. This way social cohesion gradually increases, which in turn is expected to instigate a gradual integrationist dynamic. By contrast, if the degree of institutional cohesion is lower than the degree of social cohesion, this impacts negatively on the degree of social cohesion, thereby triggering disintegrating dynamics.

Importantly, by institutional cohesion we do not mean centralisation. It was noticed, for example, that in Nigeria multinational conflict was accommodated by a process of centralisation, whereas 'a culture of intergovernmental consultation and cooperation' – and thus more cohesion – has been proposed 'to solve the federation's problems more peacefully and expeditiously'.[61]

The proposition also implies that a differentiated structure is recommendable if social cohesion varies, meaning that a particular group displays a much weaker sense of belonging and national identity than the rest of the population. This is in particular the case if different groups push towards change into two directions – towards more centralisation and towards more decentralisation.[62] It is no surprise, then, that constitutional asymmetry is characteristic of multinational systems, as was noted in Ssection 1. Constitutional asymmetry seems to work in a more nuanced way: it was considered a threat to the stability of a political system, but may also contribute to its sustainability. Whether it works in one way or the other will depend on the social structure, and on how constitutional asymmetry is given shape.

60 Alain-G. Gagnon, 'Multinational federalism: challenges, shortcomings and promises' (2021) 31 Regional & Federal Studies 99, 108.

61 Majekodunmi (n 33) 107–118.

62 Anderson (n 19) 22 refers to Canada as an example.

*Proposition 3. To preserve stability, transition must be based on consensus, even if the preferred structure presents low or medium cohesion.*

To enhance the stability of a political system, the federal system must facilitate transitions. At the same time it must include safeguards to make sure that the transition process is aimed at finding the most optimal federal balance for this particular system at that moment, preferably in a way that causes as little disruption as possible from the normal handling of public affairs. The proposition states that this requires consensus, so that no party excluded from the negotiation feels the need to oppose the new federal balance in a way that jeopardizes the stability of the political system. This means that transformations towards more centralisation can also be a cause of instability.[63]

Benz already pointed out that institutional reform must rely on a process of joint decision-making.[64] The idea is that the federal balance relies on an agreement between all (relevant) participants. This procedure secures both cohesion, because it looks for consensus, and autonomy, because it provides veto powers. What prevails depends on the procedure. Individual vetoes are less cohesive because they can be used on the basis of self-interest, without consideration of the needs of others. Collective vetoes are more cohesive but they are less protective of each participant's autonomy. We will return to this when we discuss the joint decision trap.

First, distinction must be made between change and transition.

As pointed out in Section 4.2, change can be brought about in several ways, and built into the institutional design. Institutional hubs do not necessarily rely on joint decision-making. Much depends on how they are designed: constitutional amendments and super-majority laws depending on the procedure; multilateral intergovernmental agreements if all parties concerned are involved; political adjudicators of federalism conflicts depending on their composition; concurrent powers if the rule that is given priority relies on a process of joint decision-making.

This is not problematic for non-transformative changes that do not alter the federal balance. In that case, institutional hubs remain within the boundaries of the political agreement. That is different when it comes to transitions. The federal balance must rely on a consensus, so that no party excluded from the negotiation feels the need to oppose it in a way that jeopardizes the stability of the political system.

---

63 ibid 15–27.

64 Arthur Benz, 'Dimensions and dynamics of federal regimes' in Arthur Benz and Jörg Broschek (eds), *Federal Dynamics* (Oxford University Press 2014) 84.

Filippov, Ordeshook and Shvetsova see compliance with constitutional rules as a condition for a stability-enhancing transition.[65] Consensus, however, seems more important than compliance with constitutional rules. Imagine a governing political elite that uses a non-cohesive constitutional amendment procedure to strengthen its dominance in a more centralized structure. Such a constitutional but non-consensual transformation might instigate secessionist claims. The reverse scenario – a negotiated transformation that falls outside constitutional rules – is less threatening to the political system's stability. To this end, constitutional rules are stretched or simply bypassed. Or a process of deconstitutionalization occurs. Behnke and Benz refer to Canada as an example where it was impossible to implement the Charlottetown Accord through constitutional amendment, and instead it was realized through policy-specific intergovernmental agreements.[66]

The possibility exists, of course, that no consensus can be reached. Scharpf described the joint decision trap in situations where the various parties can veto proposals.[67] Then, much depends on the decision-making procedure and on the environment in which the process takes place.

Individual vetoes secure the autonomy of each participant and invite what Scharpf calls '"bargaining" by the appeal to the individual self-interest of all (necessary) participants and by resort to incentives'.[68] This is only medium cohesive because it gives few incentives to take the needs of others and the common interest into consideration. Parties are more likely to contest the outcome, especially if it is later felt that too many concessions were made to one party. By contrast, collective vetoes are more cohesive, but do not guarantee that a new federal balance relies on consensus by all relevant parties. At least, parties with distinctive interests and the means to endanger stability must be able to weigh on the decision.

Ideally, participants opt for a 'problem-solving' decision-making style, which implies an appeal to common values.[69] That style is more likely to be adopted if the negotiations take place within a highly cohesive environment. In such an environment, parties know each other, know each other's needs and interests,

65 Filippov, Ordeshook and Shvetsova (n 2) 13.

66 Nathalie Behnke and Arthur Benz, 'Federalism and constitutional change' in Xenophon Contiades and Alkmene Fotiadou (eds), *Handbook of Comparative Constitutional Change* (Routledge 2021) 176.

67 Fritz W. Scharpf, 'The Joint-Decision Trap. Lessons from German Federalism and European Integration' (1988) 66 Public Administration 239.

68 ibid 259.

69 ibid.

and share common values, which fosters trust between them. In less cohesive environments, joint decision-making will more easily lead to 'bargaining', or to 'confrontation' that implies recourse to power and coercion.[70]

If no consensus can be reached, exit options are needed. One option is constitutional asymmetry, for example through opt-outs or opt-ins. Another one is secession. As mentioned above, stability is better secured if the secession is consensual. In that vein, the Canadian Supreme Court even formulates a duty to negotiate.[71] Obviously, if secession leads to dissolution, a consensual secession does not secure the stability of the old political system – which no longer exists – but that of the newly established entities. The case of Czechoslovakia was already mentioned to illustrate this.[72]

## 6 Conclusion

The question central to this chapter was which structure is the most adequate for a given political system. It is not a question to which a conclusive and detailed answer that applies to all cases can be given. Nevertheless, some conclusions can be drawn as to the principles that govern the search for an adequate structure.

One conclusion concerns the notions of adequacy and stability. This paper held that a structure is adequate if – and for as long as – it enables a political system to orderly govern its public affairs. This refers to the short term (ie the stability of the political system) as well as the long term (its sustainability). The object of stability is the political system, not the federal structure. The question whether a type of federal system is stable in itself – refering to its longetivity – is misplaced. If it is no longer able to secure stability and sustainability, it should be replaced by another structure. Hence, the 'stickyness' of certain consociational structures that block necessary transition is contested rather than praised.[73]

This brings us to another conclusion: to secure stability of the political system and make it robust, an adequate federal structure must regulate the

70 ibid 260.

71 *Reference re: Secession of Quebec* [1998] 2 SCR 217. For a discussion see Bossacoma Busquets (n 42) 323–326.

72 Above, section 1.

73 Allison McCulloch, 'Introduction: Power-Sharing in Europe – From Adoptability to End-Ability' in Soeren Keil and Allison McCulloch (eds), *Power-Sharing in Europe* (Palgrave Macmillan 2021) 3.

transition process, and thus its own ending. To this end, the chapter proposes transition based on consensus. This, however, is not required for changes that maintain the overall balance. This way, optimalization of the institutional design, for example through courts, can avoid the danger of stalemate inherent to joint decision-making.

The third conclusion draws on this distinction between change and transition, and on the notion of sustainability. To be aware that a transition is taking place, and to assess whether subsequent transitions endanger the system's sustainability over time, an appropriate categorisation of federal systems is required. Therefore, the chapter presented a categorisation of types of federal systems based on the federal balance, ie the combination of a degree of overall cohesion and a degree of regional autonomy laid down in the institutional design. A structure is adequate if it aligns the federal balance to the specifities of the society for which it is designed. In this regard, the chapter made a distinction between societies with low diversity and societies with high diversity. It proposed that in the first case, centralized or highly cohesive systems are the most adequate structures, depending on how low diversity is. And that in the second case, the most adequate structure aligns institutional cohesion to social cohesion but in such a way that institutional cohesion is slightly higher than social cohesion.

## Bibliography

Aláez Corral B and Bastido Freijedo FJ, 'Constitutionalizing secession in order to harmonize constitutionality and democracy in territorial decentralized states like Spain' in López-Basaguren A and Escajedo San-Epifanio L (eds), *Claims for Secession and Federalism* (Springer 2019).

Anderson L, 'Both Too Much and Too Little: Sources of Federal Instability in Canada' (2014) 44 American Review of Canadian Studies 15.

Aubert JF, 'Essai sur le fédéralisme' (1963) 80 Revue Du Droit Public Et De La Science Politique 401.

Bauböck R, 'United in Misunderstanding? Asymmetry in Multinational Federations' (2002) ICE Working Paper Series 26.

Bednar J, *The Robust Federation* (Cambridge University Press 2009).

Bednar J, 'Subsidiarity and Robustness: Building the Adaptive Efficiency of Federal Systems' (2014) 55 Federalism and Subsidiarity 231.

Behnke N and Benz A, 'Federalism and constitutional change' in Contiades X and Fotiadou A (eds), *Handbook of Comparative Constitutional Change* (Routledge 2021).

Benz A, 'Dimensions and dynamics of federal regimes' in Benz A and Broschek J (eds), *Federal Dynamics* (Oxford University Press 2014).

Benz A and Broschek J, 'Federal Dynamics: Introduction' in Benz A and Broschek J (eds), *Federal Dynamics* (Oxford University Press 2014).

Bonifati L, 'Comparative Constitutional Design for Divided Societies: A Model to Explain Constitutional Asymmetries' (PhD thesis, University of Bologna and University of Antwerp 2023).

Bossacoma Busquets P, *Morality and Legality of Secession* (Palgrave Macmillan 2020).

Bossacoma Busquets P and Sanjaume-Calvet M, 'Asymmetry as a Device for Equal Recognition and Reasonable Accommodations of Majority and Minority Nations. A Country Study on Constitutional Asymmetry in Spain' in Popelier P and Sahadžić M (eds), *Constitutional Asymmetry in Multinational Federalism* (Palgrave Macmillan 2019).

Burgess M, *Comparative Federalism. Theory and Practice* (Routledge 2006).

Burgess M, *In Search of the Federal Spirit* (Oxford University Press 2012).

Dardanelli P and others, 'Dynamic De/Centralization in Federations: Comparative Conclusions' (2019) 49 Publius 194.

Dowding KM and Kimber R, 'The Meaning and Use of Political Stability' (1983) 11 European Journal of Political Research 229.

Duchacek ID, 'Dyadic Federations and Confederations' (1988) 18 Publius 5.

Elazar DJ, *Exploring Federalism* (University of Alabama Press 1987, Edn 1991).

Erk J, 'Austria: A Federation without Federalism' (2004) 34 Publius 1.

Erk J, *Explaining Federalism* (Routledge 2010).

Erk J and Koning E, 'New Structuralism and Institutional Change: Federalism between Centralization and Decentralization' (2020) 43 Comparative Political Studies 353.

Filippov M, Ordeshook PC and Shvetsova O, *Designing Federalism* (Cambridge University Press 2004).

Fiseha A, 'Constitutional Adjudication in Ethiopia: Exploring the experience of the House of Federation' (2007) 1 Mizan Law Review 1.

Gagnon AG, 'Multinational federalism: challenges, shortcomings and promises' (2021) 31 Regional & Federal Studies 99.

Gardner JA and Ninet AA, 'Sustainable decentralization: power, extraconstitutional influence and subnational symmetry in the United States and Spain' (2011) 59 The American Journal of Comparative Law 491.

Hessebon GT and Idris A, 'The Supreme Court of Ethiopia: Federalism's Bystander' in Aroney N and Kincaid J (eds), *Courts in Federal Countries. Federalists or Unitarists?* (University of Toronto Press 2017).

Hombrado A, 'Learning to catch the wave? Regional demands for constitutional change in contexts of asymmetrical arrangements' (2011) 21 Regional & Federal Studies 479.

Hug S, 'Federal Stability in Unequal Societies' (2005) 16 Constitutional Political Economy 113.

Illner M, 'Czechoslovakia. A peaceful disintegration' in Loughlin J, Kincaid J and Swenden W (eds), *Handbook of Regionalism and Federalism* (Routledge 2013).

King P, *Federalism and Federation* (Croom Helm 1982).

Kremyanskaya EA, 'Constitutional Asymmetry in Russia: Issues and Developments. A Country Study on Constitutional Asymmetry in the Russian Federation' in Popelier P and Sahadžić M (eds), *Constitutional Asymmetry in Multinational Federalism* (Palgrave Macmillan 2019).

Livingston WS, 'A Note on the Nature of Federalism' (1952) 67 Political Science Quarterly 81.

Livingston WS, *Federalism and Constitutional Change* (Oxford University Press 1956).

Majekondumni A, 'Federalism in Nigeria: the past, current peril and future hopes' (2015) 9 Journal of Policy and Development Studies 107.

Mastromarino A, 'Secessionist Claims in a Federal System: the Belgian Case' in Lopéz-Basaguren A and Escajedo San-Epifanio L (eds), *Claims for Secession and Federalism* (Springer 2019).

McCulloch A, 'Introduction: Power-Sharing in Europe – From Adoptability to End-Ability' in Keil S and McCulloch A (eds), *Power-Sharing in Europe* (Palgrave Macmillan 2021).

McGarry J and O'Leary B, 'Federation and managing nations' in Burgess M and Pinder J (eds), *Multinational Federalism* (Routledge 2007).

McGarry J, O'Leary B and Simeon R, 'Integration or Accommodation? The Enduring Debate in Conflict Regulation' in Choudhry S (ed), *Constitutional Design For Divided Societies* (Oxford University Press 2008).

N-VA, *Verandering voor vooruitgang* (2014) <https://www.n-va.be/sites/default/files/generated/files/dossier/definitieve_congresbrochure.pdf> accessed 15 March 2023.

Palermo F, 'Asymmetries in Constitutional Law – An Introduction' in Palermo F, Zwilling C and Kössler K (eds), *Asymmetries in Constitutional Law, Recent Developments in Federal and Regional Systems* (Europäische Akademie Bozen/Accademia Europea Bolzano 2009).

Palermo F and Kössler K, *Comparative Federalism: Constitutional Arrangements and Case Law* (Hart Publishing 2017).

Pinder J, 'Multinational Federations' in Burgess M and Pinder J (eds), *Multinational Federalism* (Routledge 2007).

Popelier P, 'Federalism Disputes and the Behavior of Courts' (2017) 47 Publius 27.

Popelier P, *Dynamic Federalism* (Routledge 2021).

Popelier P and Sahadžić M, 'Conclusion. A Country Studies-Based Deliberation on Constitutional Asymmetry in Multi-tiered Multinational Systems' in Popelier P and

Sahadžić M (eds), *Constitutional Asymmetry in Multinational Federalism* (Palgrave Macmillan 2019).

Popelier P and Sahadžić M, 'Linking Constitutional Asymmetry with Multinationalism' in Popelier P and Sahadžić M (eds), *Constitutional Asymmetry in Multinational Federalism* (Palgrave Macmillan 2019).

Roeder PG, 'Ethnofederalism and the Mismanagement of Conflicting Nationalisms' in Erk J and Anderson L (eds), *The Paradox of Federalism* (Routledge 2010).

Sahadžić M, *Asymmetry, Multinationalism and Constitutional Law* (Palgrave Macmillan 2019).

Scharpf FW, 'The Joint-Decision Trap. Lessons from German Federalism and European Integration' (1988) 66 Public Administration 239.

Simeon R, 'Constitutional Design and Change in Federal Systems: Issues and Questions' (2009) 39 Publius 241.

Stepan A, 'Federalism and Democracy: Beyond the U.S. Model' (1999) 10 Journal of Democracy 19.

Steytler N, 'The Currency of Concurrent Powers in Federal Systems' in Steytler N (ed), *Concurrent Powers in Federal Systems. Meaning, Making, Managing* (Brill/Nijhoff 2017).

Tarlton CD, 'Symmetry and Asymmetry as Elements of Federalism: A Theoretical Speculation' in Kincaid J (ed), *Federalism*, vol II (Sage Publications 2011).

Tronvoll K, 'The Anatomy of Ethiopian's Civil War' (2022) 121 Current History 163.

Watts RL, *Comparing Federal Systems* (McGill-Queen's University Press 2008).

CHAPTER 5

# Was the Iroquois (Haudenosaunee) Confederation a European Construction?

*John Kincaid and J. Wesley Leckrone*

## 1 Introduction

This chapter examines what has been commonly called the Iroquois Confederation in North America, which was founded about 1450 and lasted as a viable independent political arrangement until about 1789. The chapter does not address the debate as to whether the Iroquois Confederation influenced the framing of the US Constitution.[1] Instead, it examines the Iroquois Confederation in its own right, including the question of whether it was actually a confederation. It is possible that 'confederation' was the label applied to the Iroquois arrangement by Europeans seeking to understand it on their own terms rather than Iroquois terms. We take the characteristics of a confederation, as commonly known in European-American traditions to include (1) a definitive starting point and identifiable origin, (2) a written document setting forth the confederation agreement and terms, (3) sovereignty or autonomy retained by the member states, (4) constituent states having fixed boundaries, (5) only expressly delegated powers assigned to the confederation, (6) the confederation government being responsible for external relations, (7) no independent revenue sources assigned to the confederation, (8) the confederation lacking authority to enforce its rules against individuals, (9) individuals having member-state citizenship, (10) constituent governments selecting delegates to the Confederation Council, (11) each constituent member having one vote on confederation matters, (12) super-majority voting rules required for many confederation matters, (13) the Confederal Council meeting irregularly and (14) secession being permissible. Our hypothesis is that the Iroquois Confederation was a blend of kinship and consent similar to the so-called confederation of the tribes of ancient Israel whereby a 'family of tribes' became 'a nation by consenting to a common' law.[2] The Iroquois's agreement, while not a covenant

1 For example, see Bruce E. Johansen, *Forgotten Founders: Benjamin Franklin, the Iroquois, and the Rationale for the American Revolution* (Gambit 1982).

2 Daniel J. Elazar, *Covenant and Polity in Biblical Israel* (Transaction Publishers 1995) 12.

© JOHN KINCAID AND J. WESLEY LECKRONE, 2024 | DOI:10.1163/9789004528581_007

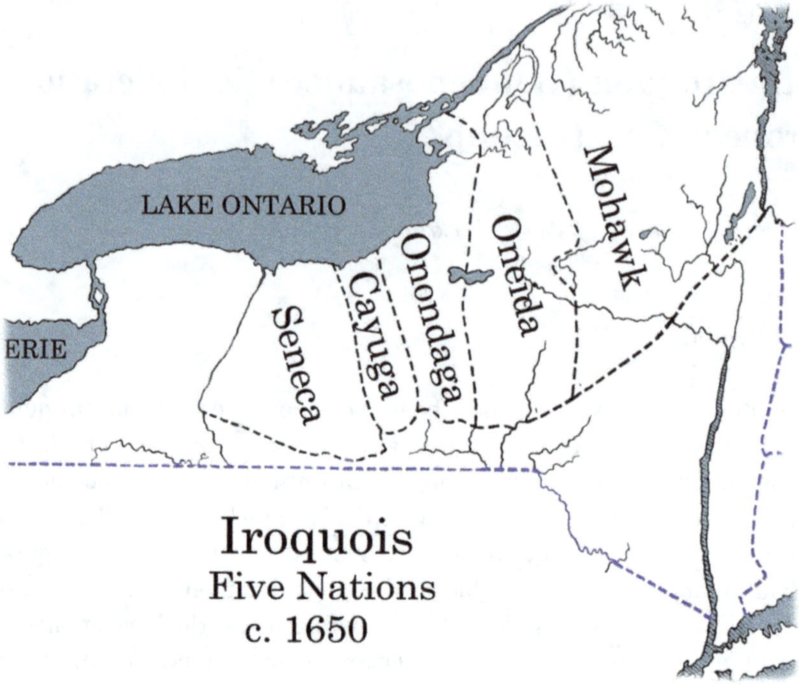


FIGURE 5.1 Map of the Five Nations of the Iroquois Confederation
SOURCE: R. A. NONENMACHER, PUBLIC DOMAIN, VIA WIKIMEDIA COMMONS <HTTPS://EN.M.WIKIPEDIA.ORG/WIKI/FILE:IROQUOIS_5_NATION_MAP_C1650.PNG> (ACCESSED 18 APRIL 2024).

with God, was a law based on the Great Peacemaker Deganawidah's vision from the Creator. Although the Iroquois union had unique characteristics endemic to North American native cultures, its characteristics seem to satisfy many criteria deemed to be characteristic of a confederation.

## 2 Background on Iroquois Confederation

Sometime between 1400–1600, five nations – the Cayugas, Mohawks, Oneidas, Onondagas and Seneca – joined together in a union designed to create eternal peace among the nations. They originally lived mostly in what is now New York, northern Pennsylvania, lower Ontario and Quebec. Their power and/or settlements at various times extended from north of Lake Ontario to the Carolinas in the south and from the Hudson River in the east to Michigan and Illinois in the west.

New York Governor DeWitt Clinton said the Iroquois sometimes called themselves the 'United people'.[3] Mostly, they called themselves 'the people of the Longhouse' or *Haudenosaunee* – meaning 'the entire house'. This was a kinship and spiritual union whose members sought to be of 'one heart, one mind, one law'. Longhouses were dwellings occupied by several families or a clan. The kinship connections of the longhouse came to represent the relationship between the five nations of the Iroquois, who collectively occupied a symbolic longhouse. The eastern nation, the Mohawks, were the Keepers of the Eastern Door facing the sunrise. The western nation, the Senecas, were the Keepers of the Western Door, facing the sunset. The Onondagas, the most geographically central nation, occupied the center. They were the union's 'firekeepers', and the Grand Council meetings were held at Onondaga. The other two communities were arrayed in the middle. The Iroquois called their arrangement a union of five fires, a term they later used to describe the United States as a union of thirteen fires.

The Mohawks, Onondagas and Senecas were considered to be the elders; the Oneidas and Cayugas were the younger brothers. At the Confederation Council, the nations were further divided into 'Two Sides' of the fire, with the Mohawks and Senecas on one side and the Oneidas and Cayugas on the other. The Onondagas retained the middle position as the Firekeepers.

## 3 Why Study the Iroquois?

The Five Nations (later Six Nations) or Iroquois are among the most fabled of North American indigenous communities. Their location in New York made them central to trading routes with the Dutch, English and French. They were formidable armed foes who were sought as allies, particularly in areas contested by the English and the French between 1610 to 1763. Their warrior culture made them central to trade and warfare with other indigenous nations in North America. One observer summed up the reasons for the mystique surrounding the Iroquois, arguing that they stood out because of 'the continued resilience, unity, and power they exhibited. Few other native peoples enjoyed the relative political, economic, and military self-sufficiency of this confederacy. Indeed,

3 William W. Campbell (ed), *The Life and Writings of De Witt Clinton* (Baker and Scribner 1849) 208.

few colonial governments of the time matched the League of the Iroquois in stability'.[4]

Confederations were not uncommon among North American indigenous nations. Around the period of European arrival in North America, the Dakota, Illinois, Miami, Three Fires and Wabanaki all had some form of confederal arrangement in addition to the Iroquois.[5] However, the Iroquois had the first 'known' constitution in North America. In fact, some claim that along with Iceland, the Isle of Man and Swiss cantons, the Iroquois polity is among the world's oldest continuously functioning democracies. As such, it is important to evaluate the structure of government created by this union.

The Iroquois have been studied widely for the democratic traits that have been ascribed to them. Some Europeans viewed them as the 'Romans of the New World'; Karl Marx and Friedrich Engels were interested in the values of equality and democracy they found in the Iroquois Constitution; and 19th-and 20th-century feminists admired the strong roles played by women in Iroquois society and governance, such as their role in appointing the chiefs who constituted the Grand Council.[6]

A few historians argue that the Iroquois Confederation influenced the United States' first form of government under the Articles of Confederation[7] as well as the later federal Constitution. This theory gained some credence around the time of the bicentennial of the US Constitution in 1987. In 1988, the US Congress went so far as to resolve that 'the confederation of the original Thirteen Colonies into one republic was explicitly modeled upon the Iroquois Confederacy as were many of the democratic principles which were incorporated into the [US] Constitution itself'. This highly contested theory is not addressed here. However, it shows the importance of the Iroquois to discussions of the structure of American government.

4 Daniel Murphree and Karim Tiro, 'Did the American Revolution cause a civil war within the Iroquois confederacy?' in Keith Krawczynski (ed), *History in Dispute*, vol 12 (Gale 2003) 174.

5 Anthony F. C. Wallace, 'Political Organization and Land Tenure Among the Northeastern Indians, 1600–1830' (1957) 13 Southwestern Journal of Anthropology 301, 305f.

6 William G. Spittal, *Iroquois Women: An Anthology* (Iroqrafts 1990); Jessica Nordell, 'Millions of Women Voted This Election: They Have the Iroquois to Thank' *The Washington Post* (Washington DC, 24 November 2016).

7 For example, see Samuel B. Payne, Jr., 'The Iroquois League, the Articles of Confederation, and the Constitution' (1996) 53 William and Mary Quarterly 605.

## 4 Research Question

William Starna argues that '[t]he appearance in the historical record of terms for the League, whether in Iroquoian languages or as glossed by Europeans, offers no clues whatever regarding its organization, structure, or operation'. He is only willing to claim that the Iroquois were an 'alliance (...) in pursuit of common political and economic goals'.[8] The goal of this research is to examine the structure and operation of the Iroquois Confederation and determine what sort of confederal arrangements were present.

### 4.1 *Europeans Name the Iroquois Polity*

In 1811, DeWitt Clinton, then New York City mayor, called the Iroquois 'the Romans of this Western World (...) who composed a federal Republic, and were denominated by the English, the Five Nations, the Six Nations, the Confederates; by the French, the Iroquois'. Clinton got these terms from Cadwallader Colden's *The History of the Five Indian Nations* (1727). Colden, who served several terms as colonial New York governor, wrote:

> The Five Nations (...) consist of so many Tribes or Nations joyn'd together by a League or Confederacy, like the United Provinces, without any Superiority of any one over the other. This Union has continued so long that the Christians know nothing of the Original of it (...). Each of the Nations are distinguished into 3 Tribes or Families, who distinguish themselves by three different sorts of Arms or Ensigns, viz. the Tortoise, the Bear & the Wolfe (...). Each Nation is an absolute Republick by its self, govern'd in all Publick Affairs of War and Peace by the Sachems or Old Men, whose Authority and Power is gain'd by and consists wholly in the Opinion the rest of the Nation have of their Wisdom and Integrity. They never execute their Resolutions by Compulsion or Force upon any of their People.[9]

Colden's influential *The History of the Five Indian Nations* was the first English-language book on the Iroquois. Its five editions (1727, 1747, 1750, 1755 and 1757) sold widely in the colonies, England and Europe. Benjamin Franklin was one of the book's admirers. It is no accident that Colden (1688–1776), in seeking to understand what he believed to be the Iroquois' government, described

8 William A. Starna, 'Respecting the Origins of the League of the Iroquois' (2008) 152 Proceedings of the American Philosophical Society 279, 291.

9 Cadwallader Colden, *The History of the Five Indian Nations* (William Bradford 1727) xv.

it in federal terms. His parents were Scottish; his father was a Presbyterian minister; and Colden studied for the ministry before switching to medicine before graduating from the University of Edinburgh in 1705. He was, therefore, steeped in the federal or covenant theology of Reformed Protestantism, rooted in Calvin's reformed theology, that pervaded Scotland, parts of England, the United Provinces of the Netherlands (1588–1795), parts of Switzerland and Huguenot France. The Scottish Covenanters (circa 1638–1688) had supported a Presbyterian Church of Scotland; the Acts of Union of 1707 secured Presbyterian Church government in Scotland; and the Presbyterian polity is federal.

### 4.2 *Colden's Flypaper Effect*

Colden's federal language stuck. The Iroquois eventually adopted Colden's language, although in the 18th century such language may have reflected the choices of English translators. For example, Onondaga chief Canasatego's famous speech at the 1744 Treaty Council at Lancaster, Pennsylvania, was translated as: 'Our wise Forefathers established Union and Amity between the Five Nations (…). We are a powerful Confederacy.'[10]

Contemporary scholars still use 'league', 'confederacy' and 'confederation' as well as, occasionally, 'nation' in referring to the Iroquois.

However:

(1) They do not use Colden's term 'republic' to describe the Iroquois;
(2) They use league, confederacy and confederation interchangeably; and
(3) They do not define these terms.

Colden appears to be the first person to use the term 'confederation' to describe the Iroquois government. His understanding of federal theology, Scottish covenantalism and the United Provinces of the Netherlands may well have led him to incorrectly identify the Iroquois as a confederation when it was perhaps a religious pact. He assumed that the Iroquois had a governmental structure, and he found it in the form of a confederation. This concept stuck and Europeans/ Americans used it to describe the Iroquois. However, Daniel Richter argues that, initially, it was a stateless society.

This is an important question because the Iroquois were considered to be formidable and well-organized people. Also knowing whether the Iroquois operated under a confederation is important because a strand of literature argues that the Iroquois had a strong influence on the US Articles of Confederation

10 Julian P. Boyd, *Indian Treaties Printed by Benjamin Franklin, 1736–1762* (Historical Society of Pennsylvania 1938) 78.

and Constitution. If the Iroquois arrangement was, in fact, not a confederation, then this is an important finding.

## 5 The Iroquois Confederation Constitution

A confederation is normally created by an agreement negotiated by human delegates from the constituent states. The Iroquois union was the product of the 'Good Message, the Power, and the Peace' brought to the five nations by a semi-divine man, Deganawidah, who was born of a virgin due to divine intervention. Together with a Mohawk chief, Hiawatha, he persuaded four of the nations to accept the message. They then humanized the chief of the Onondagas, who was a monster and great sorcerer and persuaded the Onondagas to join the union and be its firekeepers.[11]

There might have been an Iroquois equivalent of Athen's Solon, but the union was surely a product of human negotiation; however, the mythic semi-divine foundation signaled its spiritual core and helped legitimize the union in ways not characteristic of Western confederations.

The union's creation was similar to a Hobbesian covenant; it was established to end continual warfare among the five nations. Deganawidah warned that dissolution of the Great Peace would plunge the nations back into a war of all against all. However, unlike the Hobbesian covenant, the union did not establish a leviathan body-politic authorized to wield a sword to enforce the covenant. The union wielded no coercive authority; spirituality and kinship maintained the union instead. The union was to act as 'a single person' with 'a single mind'.

Colden and other Europeans believed the Great League/Confederacy of Peace and Power was the Iroquois government. The union had some federal characteristics, but it was a spiritual and kinship union limited to maintaining peace among the five nations. It operated by consensus; all decisions had to be unanimous. It was not a 'state' or 'government'.

The Iroquois union was neither a *Bundesstaat* nor *Staatenbund* because neither the union nor the constituent members were 'states'. However, it had the characteristic of a *Bundesstaat* in that it created a single people – the people of the longhouse – though not exactly a single *demos*.

---

11 Christopher Vecsey, 'The Story and Structure of the Iroquois Confederacy' (1986) 54 Journal of the American Academy of Religion 79; William N. Fenton, *The Great Law and the Longhouse: A Political History of the Iroquois Confederacy* (University of Oklahoma Press 1998).

It had the characteristic of a *Staatenbund* in that the constituent nations and clans retained plenary autonomy.

### 5.1 *Fundamental Purposes of the Iroquois Constitution*

The literature points to four primary explanations for the development of the League. First was the need for security against the outside threats from Europeans and other native nations. Second, the union was a military alliance to strengthen the Iroquois's role in trade with European traders and settlers. Third, it was a spiritual movement seeking to create 'social and political transformation'. Finally, the league or confederation developed out of informal ceremonies, particularly funeral rites, that were shared by the Iroquois nations. It is difficult to tease this out from a reading of the Constitution, partly because, as Starna states 'the question arises as to what came first: the ideology leading to confederation, the confederation to be subsequently justified by the ideology, or a complex mix of both processes'.[12]

The primary purpose of the confederation was to achieve peace between the warring nations that became the Iroquois. It was a means to end blood feuds and adopt peaceful funeral rites that brought the nations together instead of permanent infighting resulting from a tradition of retaliation at the death of a nation's member(s).[13] These ritual practices probably existed before the confederation was formed as native society became more complex and more elaborate networks of kin and clan were bound together in communities.[14] They then got codified in the Constitution (which follows Elazar's view of a covenant preceding a constitution). Overlapping clan membership also bound tribes together 'much as the weft strands bind the warp strands to the cloth'.[15]

However, as Birch[16] has noted, while a political apparatus is created to facilitate the objectives of a confederation, these structures are subject to change over time based on the development of the confederation. This seems to mirror the Iroquois's experience. Washburn claims there 'was often confusion on

12 Starna (n 8) 290.

13 Alan S. Mohl, 'The Rise and Fall of the Iroquois Confederacy: Its Influence on Early American History' (2007) 34 Journal of Psychohistory 347, 356.

14 William Englebrecht, 'New York Iroquois Political Development' in William W. Fitzhugh (ed), *Cultures in Contact: The European Impact on Native Cultural Institutions in Eastern North America, A.D. 1000–1800* (Smithsonian Institution Press 1985) 163.

15 Elisabeth Tooker, 'Northern Iroquoian Sociopolitical Organization' (1970) 72 American Anthropologist 90, 93.

16 Jennifer Birch, 'Premodern Confederacies: Balancing Strategic Collective Action and Local Autonomy' (2022) 4 Frontiers in Political Science 1 <https://www.frontiersin.org/articles/10.3389/fpos.2022.807239/full> accessed 30 March 2023.

the part of the Europeans in distinguishing between the Iroquois Great League of Peace as a cultural and ritual institution, and the Iroquois Confederacy as a political and diplomatic entity'.[17] Over time, it appears that there was a decision-making body that worked outside of the Great Council. This 'confederacy council' most likely developed over the course of the 1600s as a group of local leaders who deliberated on political issues. While there may have been overlap in the composition of these two bodies, the former retained stable structures and processes based on the Great Law of Peace, while the later was a continually evolving group that appeared to develop organically.[18] It would appear that the confederacy council served the purpose of creating what Crawford[19] calls the 'security regime' formed by the Constitution: a mechanism for collective relations with other nations and Europeans. In particular, this manifests itself in a policy of neutrality towards the French and English that helped hold the confederation together until the American Revolution of 1776.[20] Given the lack of written records, there is much about the Iroquois governance structure that remains impossible to verify.

## 6 Is This a Confederation?

This chapter's objective is to try to determine what form of governance structure was established by the Iroquois Constitution since the union may have been improperly termed a confederation by Europeans. The discussion begins with an examination of whether it would be more appropriate to evaluate the Iroquois as a league or a confederation. Having determined that the latter is a more appropriate term, the Iroquois union is then examined in light of 14 elements of a confederation that have been gleaned from the literature.

---

17 Wilcomb E. Washburn, 'Foreward' in Daniel K. Richter and James H. Merrell (eds), *Beyond the Covenant Chain: The Iroquois and Their Neighbors in Indian North America, 1600–1800* (Pennsylvania State University Press 2003) xx.

18 Daniel K. Richter, 'Ordeals of the Longhouse: The Five Nations in Early American History' in Daniel K. Richter and James H. Merrell (eds), *Beyond the Covenant Chain: The Iroquois and Their Neighbors in Indian North America, 1600–1800* (Pennsylvania State University Press 2003).

19 Neta C. Crawford, 'A Security Regime Among Democracies: Cooperation Among Iroquois Nations' (1994) 48 International Organization 345.

20 Richard Haan, 'The Problem of Iroquois Neutrality: Suggestions for Revision' (1980) 27 Ethnohistory 317.

### 6.1 *The Iroquois Should Be Evaluated as a Potential Confederation, Not League*

The concepts of 'league' and 'confederation' are closely related and have had fuzzy, not fixed, universally accepted definitions. In fact, they are often conflated in discussions of federal arrangements.[21] For example, Freeman's study of the history of federalism interchangeably uses the terms league and confederation to discuss the Greek governments of Aetolia and Achaia.[22] Art III of the US Articles of Confederation states that the 'states hereby severally enter into a firm league of friendship with each other'. In his pre-Constitutional Convention notes and *The Federalist*, James Madison explored confederacies and leagues as though they were synonymous.[23]

Elazar seems to argue that leagues are proto-confederations.[24] He defines them as 'linkages of politically independent polities for specific purposes, which function through a common secretariat rather than a government and from which members may unilaterally withdraw'.[25] They 'serve to link entirely discrete polities in some lasting way'.[26] Leagues and confederations share federal qualities. For example, one of the four political ends federalism seeks to achieve is 'to institute workable political arrangements'. This is the least rigorous of the four ends, and 'confederations and leagues in their federal dimension are designed for these limited ends'.[27] However, Elazar[28] implies that a confederation, while having elements of a league, is something more than a pact of convenience between sovereign entities.

For analyzing the Iroquois, we define 'league' to mean an alliance of nations, states or city-states, such as the League of Nations, created to achieve one or more common objectives, but having little or no internal governmental capacity. Leagues typically are formed to address the external problems of

---

21 Daniel J. Elazar, *Exploring Federalism* (University of Alabama Press 1987) 8 is careful to note that leagues are not technically 'species' of federalism 'generally speaking'.

22 Edward A. Freeman, *The History of Federal Government in Greece and Italy* (2nd edn, Macmillan 1893) 252.

23 Alexander Hamilton, John Jay and James Madison, *The Federalist: The Gideon Edition* (Liberty Fund 2001); James Madison, 'Notes on Ancient and Modern Confederacies, [April–June?] 1786' (*Founders Online, National Archives*) <https://founders.archives.gov/documents/Madison/01-09-02-0001> accessed 30 March 2023.

24 Elazar (n 21) 120f.

25 ibid 8.

26 ibid 58.

27 ibid 104.

28 Daniel J. Elazar, 'Confederation and Federal Liberty' (1982) 12 Publius 1.

members.[29] Other types of leagues, such as the *Lega Nord* (a federation of political parties), the American League of Women Voters (a civil-society association) and sports leagues are not relevant to an examination of the Iroquois.

Confederation is defined to mean a voluntary political association or union of sovereign, independent city-states or nation-states established to manage matters of common concern to the member states, such as defense and trade. The verb 'confederate' has traditionally meant to form an alliance that carries out the will of a coalition of interests, none of which surrender sovereignty to the confederation even while delegating certain express powers to the union. A confederation is ordinarily bound together by a treaty or agreement and normally attends to the corporate interests of the member states.

We argue that the Iroquois union was more like a confederation than a league because it was more than an alliance and had little to do with external relations. The independence of each constituent nation to engage in foreign relations makes the Iroquois arrangement different from a typical confederation, league or alliance. The union was not established for commercial or trading purposes, and scholars differ on whether it was founded for any defensive purpose. Its primary purpose was to create a perpetual peace among its five members, thus creating a fundamental shift in the lifestyles of the members of the Iroquois confederation. Based on kinship and consent, the Constitution creates a system of rituals, such as Condolence Ceremonies, that were designed to express grief without violence. The Iroquois Constitution embodied a set of ideals and codified a formal structure of social, political and cultural interactions that would achieve 'the good life' for both the individual nations of the Iroquois and the union as a whole. It also outlines the qualities of good leaders who personify the values of a good citizen in the confederation.

## 6.2 *Confederations Have Definitive Starting Points and Identifiable Origins*

Like some ancient Greek leagues and confederations, there is no agreed-upon date for the Iroquois union's formation. Most creation estimates lie between 1400 and 1600, although some date the union's formation as 31 August 1142. It is generally agreed that the union existed before Europeans arrived in the area circa 1603. According to Fenton, a leading authority on the topic, 'Iroquois

29 Donald S. Lutz, 'The Iroquois Confederation Constitution: An Analysis' (1998) 28 Publius 99, 102.

nationalists claim (…) their confederacy is 600 years old'.[30] This would make the confederacy approximately 649 years old in 2024.

The origin story of the Iroquois union is mythological, which is not the case of other confederations with the possible exception of ancient Israel. The supernatural-like figure of Deganawiah brought the idea of peace to the five nations and persuaded recalcitrant parties to join in the Great Peace. The Constitution was created when the origin myth was merged with the distribution of powers among the Iroquois and the rituals of peace that emerged from a council of members of the five nations. Starna claims that 'it is generally understood that that outcome of deliberations at this assembly was the creation of the bylaws of the League or, as it also came to be called, the Iroquois Confederacy'.[31] Lutz[32] states that the Iroquois moved beyond myth and the traditional kinship society when the words of the Constitution were agreed upon. He claims that the Constitution, by allowing individuals or groups outside the five main nations to join the Great Binding Law and be protected by the mythological Tree of Great Peace, moved the union from myth to a political pact because others could enter the confederation. Additionally, Section 16 allowed for 'addition or change of this law', therefore providing a way to amend the product of the founding myth. Thus, while there is no definitive date of its origin and the union grew out of myth, it had a starting point at the time in which the five nations agreed to the language of the Constitution.

### 6.3 *There Is a Written Document Setting Forth the Confederation Agreement and Terms*

The Iroquois had no written constitution. Rather, as was traditional in Native American culture, the details of the agreement were passed down orally. While treaties and alliances were often memorialized in elaborate wampum belts, there is no identifiable wampum related to the Great Binding Law. Exact terms are not codified because an oral tradition can never precisely capture wording. Under the agreement, the laws of the Great Peace could be recited at the request of members of the union, there was the ability to amend the Constitution, and every five years the Iroquois nations were required to reconsent to the Great Binding Law or face the dissolution of the union. What scholars consider to be the 'written constitution' may have been a vestige of a

30 William N. Fenton, 'The Lore of the Longhouse: Myth, Ritual and Red Power' (1975) 48 Anthropological Quarterly 131, 139.

31 Starna (n 8) 288.

32 Lutz (n 29) 102.

19th-century interpretation of the Iroquois as seen through the eyes of anthropologists and missionaries and thus not an accurate portrayal of what existed in reality.[33]

### 6.4 *'Sovereignty' or Autonomy Is Retained by the Member States*

State sovereignty is a western construct and probably not a concept held by the Iroquois. A more appropriate concept would be to say that the Iroquois member states retained self-governing autonomy within the union. The nations surrendered little power in joining the union because its purpose was unity, focused on not making war on each other. All other decision-making was retained by the nations.

Several provisions of the Constitution reflect the member states' autonomy. First, the constituent nations retained self-rule under Section 97 of the Constitution: 'The five Council Fires shall continue to burn as before and they are not quenched. The Lords of each nation in future shall settle their nation's affairs at this council fire governed always by the laws and rules of the council of the Confederacy and by the Great Peace.' Second, the Constitution's most explicit mention of constituent self-rule involves religious practices. Section 99 states that 'the rites and festivals of each nation shall remain undisturbed and shall continue as before because they were given by the people of old times as useful and necessary for the good of men'.

### 6.5 *Constituent States Have Fixed Boundaries*

The Iroquois did not have fixed concepts of private, individual land-ownership, but each nation occupied a roughly defined territory. The boundaries of the nations were semi-fluid, expanding and contracting over time. The addition of the Tuscarora to the Iroquois union in 1722 contracted the territory of the Onondaga and Oneida, as the new nation was carved out of the two existing nations.

### 6.6 *Only Expressly Delegated Powers Are Assigned to the Confederation*

The competences of the Iroquois union are not clearly defined in the Constitution beyond the conduct of condolence rituals. There are really no powers delegated to the Council, whose primary purpose is to make peace. The only real power delegated to the union is using the Council as a forum for deliberation on issues to maintain peace among the five nations.

33 Richter (n 18).

## 6.7 *Confederation Responsible for External Relations*

The union's unanimity rule did not permit it to make the kinds of diplomatic and military decisions normally made by leagues. The Iroquois realized that expecting the union to do more would risk fracturing the Great Peace. The Great Peace of the union did not prohibit the constituent nations from engaging in external relations, including war and trade. Sometimes the nations competed for favorable trade with other nations and Europeans. The only area where the Grand Council deliberated on external relations was the absorption of new nations into the confederation. This was also subject to a unanimous vote of the original five nations.

The Iroquois's diplomatic and military power was separate from this union. It consisted of diplomatic initiatives and war-making conducted by chiefs of single nations and coalitions of chiefs from two or more nations. By maintaining peace among the five nations, the Great Peace enabled the Iroquois to project considerable power, but those projections were highly fluid and not organized constitutionally or systematically. Richter estimates that 538 different headmen 'participated in four hundred separate diplomatic encounters with the Dutch, French, and English during a seventy-year period beginning in 1663'.[34]

## 6.8 *No Independent Revenue Sources Are Assigned to the Confederation*

It does not appear that there was any direct taxation of individuals. Rather, all sources of revenue were gathered by the individual nations and given to the confederation. The Onondagas maintained a central treasury for the confederation that stored wampum (the primary currency) and commodities such as animal pelts and corn meal for use as 'currency' in trading.[35] According to Stites, 'in order to meet necessary expenses, the Confederacy also possessed a treasury of its own, filled by tributes exacted from dependent people, and by gifts from the Iroquois tribes themselves'.[36] Thus, part of the Iroquois's funding came from tributes paid by vassal nations, which served as an independent source of revenue for the union. Confederation funds were used for the cost of provisions during meetings and to host ambassadors from outside the union.

---

34 Daniel K. Richter, *The Ordeal of the Longhouse* (University of North Carolina Press 1992) 6.

35 James Cicarelli, 'Economic Thought Among American Aboriginals Prior to 1492' (2012) 71 American Journal of Economics and Sociology 77, 116.

36 Sara Henry Stites, *Economics of the Iroquois* (New Era Printing Company 1905) 69.

## 6.9 *The Confederation Has No Authority to Enforce Its Rules against Individuals*

The confederation does not appear to have had the authority to enforce any rules or legislation against individuals. The purpose of the Grand Council was to resolve disputes among the nations. Any policies that they unanimously agreed to were implemented through the constituent units. By way of example, Section 20 of the Constitution prohibits an Iroquois Sachem from committing murder. However, it is up to the leaders of an individual nation to determine guilt and to remove the Sachem from his post by exiling him from the confederation. Thus, the Iroquois could prohibit the activity of murder, but could not directly hold the individual Sachem accountable for his actions without consent from his nation.

## 6.10 *Member-State Citizenship*

The Iroquois did not adhere to a western concept of citizenship. However, they understood belonging and duties based on kinship. There were two primary identifying groups for each person: their clan and then their nation. However, unlike most confederations, the Iroquois union created a single people who thereby retained multiple identities as members of a family, clan, nation and the Great Binding Law. Section 59 of the Constitution mandates a wampum belt be constructed from equal contributions of each of the five nations to serve as 'a token that the men have combined themselves into one head, one body and one thought'.

Individuals or groups could be adopted and given membership in a nation through consent of the nation. At this point, adoptees had the full rights and privileges of their new nation and were fully integrated into the society. Once adopted, the Constitution required that 'no one of our nation ever mention the original name or nation of their birth'. Individuals also had the right to 'abandon their birth nation' and move outside of confederation territory.

## 6.11 *Constituent Governments Select Delegates to the Confederation Council*

Normally, constituent units of western confederacies select delegates to represent their government to the Confederation Council. Among the Iroquois, each Sachem on the Council was chosen by women in his clan based on clan lineage. Each clan owned the name of a founding chief of the Great Peace. When the founding chief died, the newly appointed chief was given the name of the founding chief. The name was owned by the clan. This is a different form of representation than that found in western democracies. However, while the Sachems were chosen from the elites, their people had 'the right to correct their erring [Sachems]'. Section 59 outlines the process by which the Sachem can be removed through a process involving representatives from both individual nations and the confederation.

## 6.12 *Each Constituent Member of the Confederation Has One Vote on Confederation Matters*

Technically, like most confederations, each nation had one vote. This was despite the fact that each nation had different numbers of Sachems on the 50-member Council (eg, Mohawks had 9, Onondagas had 14). Given the need for unanimity, each nation also had a veto power.

However, there was an asymmetric power relationship between the nations, with some having the power to initiate and others the final say or power to veto. The Mohawks were the first among equals within the Iroquois union. They began deliberation on any issue, and according to Section 6 of the Constitution, it was 'against the Great Binding Law to pass measures in the Confederate Council after the Mohawk Lords have protested against them'. Therefore, the Mohawks had an absolute veto.

The Onondaga appear to have had a qualified veto. Questions were addressed by each nation in the following order: Mohawk and Seneca, then Oneida and Cayuga. The Mohawk then relayed the two decisions to the Onondaga, 'who shall render a decision as they see fit in the case of a disagreement by the two bodies or confirm the decisions of the two bodies if they are identical' (Section 10). However, if the Two Sides deliberate and agree, the Onondaga are 'compelled to confirm their joint decision' (Section 11).

The Iroquois were evangelistic about the benefits of the Great Peace and sought to bring new nations into the agreement. However, new nations were not accorded the right to vote, a privilege that extended only to the original five members of the Iroquois union. The Tuscarora became the sixth nation of the union in 1722, but were given no vote on the union Council.

## 6.13 *Super-Majority Voting Rules Are Required for Many Confederation Matters*

Unlike most confederations, everything was done by consensus under a rule of unanimity, subject to provisions discussed above. There were no provisions for simple-majority or qualified-majority voting on different matters. Given the narrow scope of the confederation and its emphasis on internal peace, unanimity was perhaps an essential rule.

### 6.14 *Confederal Council Meets Irregularly*

Section 55 of the Constitution states: 'Every five years the Five Nations Confederate Lords and the people shall assemble together and shall ask one another if their minds are still in the same spirit of unity for the Great Binding Law and if any of the Five Nations shall not pledge continuance and steadfastness to the pledge of unity then the Great Binding Law shall dissolve.'

This was the only regularly scheduled meeting of the Council. Otherwise, the Council met to mourn the dead, but then only in the autumn or winter. There is some debate concerning meeting times, as some observers contend the Grand Council met at least once a year.

### 6.15 *Secession Permissible*

Every five years, the nations met to re-consent to the Great Binding Law. If one nation did not 'pledge continuance', then the Iroquois union would dissolve (Section 55). In principle, then, any nation could secede from the union. Individual villages could and did secede. Whole nations, or portions of them, could be driven out of the union if they violated the Great Binding Law or sought to destroy the union (Section 92).

## 7 Reasons for Decline of Iroquois Confederation

European colonization of North America led to the gradual downfall of the Iroquois Confederation by the end of the 18th century. The Iroquois became increasingly reliant on trade with Europeans and pursued a policy of neutrality when dealing with them to avoid disruption of trade and trade routes. The ability of the Iroquois to remain neutral towards European powers slowly eroded over the 1700s.[37] The American Revolution forced the Iroquois to take sides between the British and the colonists, thus ending their neutrality.[38] Most Oneidas and some of the Tuscarora allied with the colonists; most members of the other nations worked with the British. The split led to the Council Fire being extinguished by the Onondagas in 1777.[39] All nations of the Iroquois faced

37 Sam Bleiweis, 'The Downfall of the Iroquois' (2013) 5 Emory Endeavors in History 84.

38 Barbara Graymont, *The Iroquois in the American Revolution* (Syracuse University Press 1972); Jon Parmenter, 'After the Mourning Wars: The Iroquois as Allies in Colonial North American Campaigns, 1676–1760' (2007) 64 William and Mary Quarterly 39.

39 Karim Tiro, 'A Civil War? Rethinking Iroquois Participation in the American Revolution' (2000) 4 Explorations in Early American Culture 148.

destructive raids on their villages during the war, sometimes led by members of their confederation. This led to displacement and dwindling populations.[40]

The 1783 Treaty of Paris, ending the American Revolution, included no language concerning the status of Native Americans. Most of the Iroquois land was inside the boundaries of the new United States. Over time, much of the Iroquois land was absorbed through military action and treaty.[41] The Oneidas and Tuscarora were allowed to keep land due to their allegiance to the colonists during the war.[42] However, even that land was encroached upon by land speculators and settlers. Some Iroquois relocated to what would become Canada. Left without their traditional lands, the Iroquois Confederation fractured,[43] proving the wisdom of Thomas Franck, who stated that 'the sharing of such things as culture, language and standard of living, while helpful to the cause of federalism, is not an ultimate guarantee against failure'.[44]

## 8 Conclusion

This chapter has questioned whether the governing structure of the Iroquois union was mischaracterized as a confederation by Europeans. To explore this possibility, the Iroquois Constitution was examined from the perspective of 14 commonly accepted characteristics of confederations. Overall, Iroquois governance appears to have operated within the guise of some characteristics of a confederation. The Iroquois union was federal in a broad sense. It met two key criteria of federalism: (1) unity with diversity and (2) shared rule and self-rule. Otherwise, it was very different from common western notions of a confederation. First and foremost, it was a spiritual union with supernatural roots centered on maintaining internal peace through regular condolence rituals for deceased members of the five nations. Second, the union was framed in kinship terms. The union's founders were called grandparents. Their successors

40 Murphree and Tiro (n 4).

41 David J. Lehman, 'The End of the Iroquois Mystique: The Oneida Land Cession Treaties of the 1780s' (1990) 47 William and Mary Quarterly 523; Barbara Graymont, 'New York State Indian Policy After the Revolution' (1997) 78 New York History 438.

42 Ester V. Hill, 'The Iroquois Indians and Their Lands Since 1783' (1930) 11 Quarterly Journal of the New York State Historical Association 335; Mohl (n 13) 358.

43 Alan Taylor, 'The Divided Ground: Upper Canada, New York, and the Iroquois Six Nations, 1783–1815' (2002) 22 Journal of the Early Republic 55.

44 Thomas M. Franck, 'Why Federations Fail' in Thomas M. Franck (ed), *Why Federations Fail: An Inquiry into the Requisites for Successful Federalism* (New York University Press 1968) 171.

were called grandchildren. The Iroquois union was a blend of kinship and consent,[45] which, while not a covenant with God, was a law based on the Great Peacemaker Deganawidah's vision from the Creator.

The overarching purpose of the union was to prevent a Hobbesian war of all against all among the tribes and clans of the longhouse. However, unlike Hobbes's sword-wielding leviathan, the union's narrow and singular focus on internal peace did not require establishment of a sword-wielding governmental structure. Such a structure would have been required if the Iroquois had sought to broaden the policy scope of their union. Broadening the union's policy scope might have fractured the union. Instead, by maintaining internal peace, allowing the constituent nations plenary self-government and framing the union in spiritual kinship terms, the Iroquois peoples and their cultures were able to survive into today even though their constituent nations were politically, economically and often socially, decimated by the European settlers by 1789.

## Bibliography


Birch J, 'Premodern Confederacies: Balancing Strategic Collective Action and Local Autonomy' (2022) 4 Frontiers in Political Science 1 <https://www.frontiersin.org/articles/10.3389/fpos.2022.807239/full> accessed 30 March 2023.

Bleiweis S, 'The Downfall of the Iroquois' (2013) 5 Emory Endeavors in History 84.

Boyd JP, *Indian Treaties Printed by Benjamin Franklin, 1736–1762* (Historical Society of Pennsylvania 1938).

Campbell WW (ed), *The Life and Writings of De Witt Clinton* (Baker and Scribner 1849).

Cicarelli J, 'Economic Thought Among American Aboriginals Prior to 1492' (2012) 71 American Journal of Economics and Sociology 77.

Colden C, *The History of the Five Indian Nations* (William Bradford 1727).

Crawford NC, 'A Security Regime Among Democracies: Cooperation Among Iroquois Nations' (1994) 48 International Organization 345.

Elazar DJ, 'Confederation and Federal Liberty' (1982) 12 Publius 1.

Elazar DJ, *Exploring Federalism* (University of Alabama Press 1987).

Elazar DJ, *Covenant and Polity in Biblical Israel* (Transaction Publishers 1995).

Englebrecht W, 'New York Iroquois Political Development' in Fitzhugh WW (ed), *Cultures in Contact: The European Impact on Native Cultural Institutions in Eastern North America, A.D. 1000–1800* (Smithsonian Institution Press 1985).


45 Elazar (n 2).

Fenton WN, 'The Lore of the Longhouse: Myth, Ritual and Red Power' (1975) 48 Anthropological Quarterly 131.

Fenton WN, *The Great Law and the Longhouse: A Political History of the Iroquois Confederacy* (University of Oklahoma Press 1998).

Franck TM, 'Why Federations Fail' in Franck TM (ed), *Why Federations Fail: An Inquiry into the Requisites for Successful Federalism* (New York University Press 1968).

Freeman EA, *The History of Federal Government in Greece and Italy* (2nd edn, Macmillan 1893).

Graymont B, *The Iroquois in the American Revolution* (Syracuse University Press 1972).

Graymont B, 'New York State Indian Policy After the Revolution' (1997) 78 New York History 438.

Haan R, 'The Problem of Iroquois Neutrality: Suggestions for Revision' (1980) 27 Ethnohistory 317.

Hamilton A, Jay J and Madison J, *The Federalist: The Gideon Edition* (Liberty Fund 2001).

Hill EV, 'The Iroquois Indians and Their Lands Since 1783' (1930) 11 Quarterly Journal of the New York State Historical Association 335.

Johansen BE, *Forgotten Founders: Benjamin Franklin, the Iroquois, and the Rationale for the American Revolution* (Gambit 1982).

Lehman JD, 'The End of the Iroquois Mystique: The Oneida Land Cession Treaties of the 1780s' (1990) 47 William and Mary Quarterly 523.

Lutz DS, 'The Iroquois Confederation Constitution: An Analysis' (1998) 28 Publius 99.

Madison J, 'Notes on Ancient and Modern Confederacies, [April–June?] 1786' (*Founders Online, National Archives*) <https://founders.archives.gov/documents/Madison/01-09-02-0001> accessed 30 March 2023.

Mohl AS, 'The Rise and Fall of the Iroquois Confederacy: Its Influence on Early American History' (2007) 34 Journal of Psychohistory 347.

Murphree D and Tiro K, 'Did the American Revolution cause a civil war within the Iroquois confederacy?' in Krawczynski K (ed), *History in Dispute*, vol 12 (Gale 2003).

Nordell J, 'Millions of Women Voted This Election: They Have the Iroquois to Thank' *The Washington Post* (Washington DC, 24 November 2016).

Parmenter J, 'After the Mourning Wars: The Iroquois as Allies in Colonial North American Campaigns, 1676–1760' (2007) 64 William and Mary Quarterly 39.

Payne, SB Jr, 'The Iroquois League, the Articles of Confederation, and the Constitution' (1996) 53 William and Mary Quarterly 605.

Richter DK, *The Ordeal of the Longhouse* (University of North Carolina Press 1992).

Richter DK, 'Ordeals of the Longhouse: The Five Nations in Early American History' in Richter DK and Merrell JH (eds), *Beyond the Covenant Chain: The Iroquois and Their Neighbors in Indian North America, 1600–1800* (Pennsylvania State University Press 2003).

Spittal WG, *Iroquois Women: An Anthology* (Iroqrafts 1990).

Starna WA, 'Respecting the Origins of the League of the Iroquois' (2008) 152 Proceedings of the American Philosophical Society 279.

Stites SH, *Economics of the Iroquois* (New Era Printing Company 1905).

Taylor A, 'The Divided Ground: Upper Canada, New York, and the Iroquois Six Nations, 1783–1815' (2002) 22 Journal of the Early Republic 55.

Tiro K, 'A Civil War? Rethinking Iroquois Participation in the American Revolution' (2000) 4 Explorations in Early American Culture 148.

Tooker E, 'Northern Iroquoian Sociopolitical Organization' (1970) 72 American Anthropologist 90.

Vecsey C, 'The Story and Structure of the Iroquois Confederacy' (1986) 54 Journal of the American Academy of Religion 79.

Wallace AFC, 'Political Organization and Land Tenure Among the Northeastern Indians, 1600–1830' (1957) 13 Southwestern Journal of Anthropology 301.

Washburn WE, 'Foreward' in Richter DK and Merrell JH (eds), *Beyond the Covenant Chain: The Iroquois and Their Neighbors in Indian North America, 1600–1800* (Pennsylvania State University Press 2003).

# PART 3

## *The Making and Ending of Federalism – Theory and Case Studies*

CHAPTER 6

# The Constitutional Eschatology of Federalism

*Anna Gamper*

## 1 Introduction

The *making* of federalism has been among the great topics of federal theory, and is still perhaps its greatest. Also the miracle about the idea of federalism has been traditionally linked to the foundation process of a federal system:[1] in particular, is a federal system made through a federal contract, and what does 'federal contract' mean – is it rather a kind of political idea that becomes constitutionalized or a constitutional idea that needs to be transformed into a federal political culture?[2] Both practically and theoretically, the federal contract has received much attention from the earliest beginning of federal states. This is not surprising, since the term 'federalism', deriving from the Latin word for covenant or agreement (*foedus*), became connoted with the prototypes of (con-)federal systems that emerged in the 18th century.[3] It was the idea of a constitutional compact, previous to the enactment of or identical with an 'original' federal constitution, that was understood as the big bang of a federal system.[4] While, until the end of the First World War, federal states were usually founded in accordance with this idea, the way of 'making' federal systems changed over the last century.[5] This flexibilisation of the practice how federal systems are made has apparently had impact on the theory of federalism, challenging traditional definitions and attempting to draw new maps in which all kinds of multi-tiered[6] or

1 See, summarizingly, Francesco Palermo and Karl Kössler, *Comparative Federalism. Constitutional Arrangements and Case Law* (Hart 2017) 38ff.

2 The idea of a federal contract has recently been revisited by Stephen Tierney, *The Federal Contract* (Oxford University Press 2022).

3 Critically on that connotation ibid 7ff (in particular 9ff). Even though US federalism, when compared to the former confederation, appears as the result of a centralizing process, neither the term 'federalism' nor the chosen title of the 'Federalist Papers' can be deprived of its etymological origin and connotation of compact.

4 Palermo and Kössler (n 1) 38ff; Anna Gamper, 'Entstehung und Constitutional Engineering des Bundesstaats' in Peter Bußjäger (ed), *3. November 1918 – Die Länder und der neue Staat* (new academic press 2019) 20ff and 27ff.

5 Palermo and Kössler (n 1) 38ff.

6 See, eg, Patricia Popelier, *Dynamic Federalism* (Routledge 2021) 70.

© ANNA GAMPER, 2024 | DOI:10.1163/9789004528581_008

plurinational[7] systems can be found and weighted so as to fit into a radical deconstruction of 'classical' federalism that thus remains hardly recognizable. But while it is not controversial today that federalism may be either grounded on a 'historically first'[8] federal constitution or be the result of a constitutional transformation process, the answers to the question what should then be the main constitutional factors for recognizing federalism as a distinct form of the state are somewhat opaque.[9]

Even more opaque is the question of *unmaking* federal constitutions which, unlike popular topics such as 'changes' or 'dynamics' of federalism,[10] has been much more neglected by federal theory.[11] Federal constitutions cannot only be unmade by disruptive processes leading to the enactment of a new 'historically first' constitution that itself could be either federal or not, but also by amendments to a constitution that, even though it is formally continued, loses its former federal character. Federal constitutions could choose to entrench federalism as an unamendable constitutional value or let the abolition of federalism depend on the consent of all federal components or a majority of them; they could also provide sundry other amendment procedures and either distinguish or not distinguish amendments regarding federalism from other constitutional amendments.

This paper focuses on the constitutional ways of abolishing – not just: changing – federalism in formal constitutional terms or, to put it theologically, on the constitutional eschatology[12] of federalism. In classifying the possibilities of constitutional entrenchment of federalism, differences between the constitutions of younger and older, coming-together and keeping-together, symmetric

---

7 See, eg, Tierney (n 2) 227ff.

8 Hans Kelsen, *Reine Rechtslehre* (2nd edn, Verlag Österreich 1960) 47 and 203; Clemens Jabloner, 'Verfassungsrechtliche Grundordnung und historisch erste Verfassung' in Thomas Olechowski and Klaus Zeleny (eds), *Methodenreinheit und Erkenntnisvielfalt* (Manz 2013).

9 Palermo and Kössler (n 1) 39ff.

10 See, eg, from a more general perspective, Arthur Benz and Felix Knüpling (eds), *Changing Federal Constitutions* (Budrich 2012); Ronald L. Watts, *Comparing Federal Systems* (3rd edn, McGill-Queen's University Press 2008) 179ff; Popelier (n 6) 193ff; Tierney (n 2) 253ff; Peter Bußjäger, *Föderale Systeme* (Jan Sramek Verlag 2017) 75ff; John Kincaid and G. Alan Tarr (eds), *Constitutional Origins, Structure, and Change in Federal Countries* (McGill-Queen's University Press 2005).

11 Theoretical chapters on the 'end' of federalism are largely missing even in leading handbooks of federalism such as Watts (n 10) or Palermo and Kössler (n 1). See, however, Bußjäger (n 10) 49ff and Emilian Kavalski and Magdalena Zolkos (eds), *Defunct Federalisms* (Ashgate 2008).

12 The term alludes to the 'last things', ie the end of federalism and thus clearly goes beyond a mere 'pathology' of federations treated, eg, by Watts (n 10) 179ff.

and asymmetric federations shall be analysed with regard to the question how the component units partake in federal constitutional amendments that target their abolition as parts of a federal compound. The paper finally discusses whether definitions of federalism should be more concerned with the eschatology of federalism and whether the fading concept of *foedus* should play its final role in the constitutional unmaking of federalism.

## 2 The Constitutional Entrenchment of Federalism

### 2.1 *The Making and Unmaking of Federalism: A Constitutional Perspective*

What could be the reasons for the neglect with which both federal theory and comparative research on federalism have treated the constitutional unmaking of federalism? A simple reason may be that scholars of federalism dislike treating the end of something that is their object of study. Rather, however, federal constitutions have hitherto been quite successful so that there is little empirical evidence on their abolition. Excluding sham federal constitutions relating to illiberal and undemocratic regimes, instable post-colonial constitutions and similar cases,[13] there are hardly any cases where effective federal constitutions were unmade, unless they were replaced by new, but still federal constitutions.[14] In contrast, there are many recent cases where unitary constitutions were unmade and thus transformed into or replaced by a federal constitution.[15] This seems to tell rather a success story of federalism.

Ultimately, however, very much depends on the question what it means to 'abolish' federalism in constitutional terms. If some constitutional ingredients were considered requisites for a federal system, the abolition of these ingredients would *e contrario* entail the constitutional unmaking of federalism. From theoretical perspective, however, there is much controversy on what these ingredients exactly are.[16] While some tend to regard these ingredients not as strong pillars but rather as fluctuating variables that may to large extent be replaced by each other,[17]

13 See the case-studies in Kavalski and Zolkos (n 11); Bußjäger (n 10) 49ff.

14 Bußjäger (n 10) 58f.

15 See, with examples on the development Palermo and Kössler (n 1) 34ff; Watts (n 10) 29ff; Daniel J. Elazar (ed), *Federal Systems of the World: A Handbook of federal, confederal and Autonomy Arrangements* (2nd edn, Longman Group 1994).

16 See, most recently, the surveys on the literature given by Popelier (n 6) 9ff; Palermo and Kössler (n 1) 13ff.

17 Popelier (n 6).

some[18] make their essentiality dependent on mindsets such as a 'federal culture' or a 'federal spirit'. Other authors increase the degree of abstraction of these ingredients, which, however, leaves the constitutional design of a federal system very much open.[19]

What 'federalism' means in terms of a concrete federal constitution and if and how it can be abolished, can, moreover, be answered only by the interpretation of that constitution and not by either practical or theoretical assessments. When, eg, the Austrian Constitutional Court construes federalism as a constitutional principle that essentially depends on elements such as a distribution of powers and the existence of a federal second chamber,[20] an 'abolition' of federalism would, in constitutional terms, already happen if, eg, the federal second chamber was abolished, even though the distribution of powers or other elements were maintained. Whether such an interpretation would be challenged or shared by theoreticians, is irrelevant to its inherent constitutional authority.

When both eternity clauses and constitutional amendment procedures will be analysed in the following,[21] attention will therefore have to be drawn to the fact that the respective protection shields may neither extend to federalism 'as such' nor any element related to federalism, but rather to particular elements; whether the abolition of such elements entails the downfall of federalism 'as such' will again depend on the respective constitutional design of federalism which derives from the individual interpretation of a constitution but cannot be defined by a universalist theory.

---

18 Erika Arban, Giuseppe Martinico and Francesco Palermo, 'Introduction: Why is the trajectory of Italian regionalism comparatively important and what does it have to offer?' in Erika Arban, Giuseppe Martinico and Francesco Palermo (eds), *Federalism and Constitutional Law – The Italian Contribution to Comparative Regionalism* (Routledge 2021) 2; Michael Burgess, *In Search of the Federal Spirit* (Oxford University Press 2012); Félix Mathieu and Alain-G. Gagnon, '(Still) in Search of the Federal Spirit' in Tracy B. Fenwick and Andrew C. Banfield (eds), *Beyond Autonomy: practical and theoretical challenges to 21st century federalism* (Brill/Nijhoff 2021).

19 Palermo and Kössler (n 1) 64ff accordingly entitle their respective chapter 'living without definitions'. A 'dynamic and flexible relationship between authority and democratic legitimacy', stressed by Tierney (n 2) 297 as the constitutional idea of federalism, could be achieved by a unitary or moderately decentralized constitution, too.

20 VfSlg 2455/1952.

21 Some of these instruments are, although with a different focus, discussed by Tierney (n 2) 258ff; Popelier (n 6) 214ff; Markus Kaltenborn, 'Constitutional Amendment Rules in Federal and Unitary States' in Arthur Benz and Felix Knüpling (eds), *Changing Federal Constitutions* (Budrich 2012); Palermo and Kössler (n 1) 178ff.

Technically, federal constitutions can be unmade as well as all other constitutions, in various ways: first, a constitution could itself include a sunset clause according to which the federal constitution as a whole – or at least the relevant provisions relating to federalism – enters out of force at a given date or under certain conditions. Second, a federal constitution could be unmade disruptively, ie through a revolutionary process which – even though illegally – discontinues the prevailing constitutional regime, after which a new 'historically first constitution', with or without federal character, might be enacted. Third, a federal constitution could be unmade just with regard to its federal character by a constitutional amendment, while the constitution as such continues to be in force.

## 2.2 *Eternity Clauses on Federalism*

The most rigid instrument a constitution can use in order to protect itself from being amended is an eternity or unamendability clause. No constitution across the globe, however, prohibits every kind of constitutional amendment, even though about a third of all constitutions explicitly provide an eternity clause.[22]

Only few federal constitutions, however, entrench federalism or certain aspects related to federalism as an unamendable principle:[23] eg, Art 60 para 4 subpara I Constitution of Brazil generally prohibits the abolition of the 'federalist form of the State'. Art 79 para 3 German Basic Law declares the division of the federation into the *Länder* and their participation on principle in the legislative process but also the principles entrenched in, *inter alia*, Art 20 – among them the principle of Germany being a 'federal state' – as unamendable. Still,

22 Richard Albert, 'Introduction: The State of the Art in Constitutional Amendment' in Richard Albert, Xenophon Contiades and Alkmene Fotiadou (eds), *The Foundations and Traditions of Constitutional Amendment* (Hart 2017) 7f; Anna Gamper, 'Änderung und Schranken der Verfassung' in Peter Bußjäger, Anna Gamper and Arno Kahl (eds), *100 Jahre Bundes-Verfassungsgesetz* (Verlag Österreich 2020) 52f and 70ff; Peter Häberle, 'Verfassungsrechtliche Ewigkeitsklauseln als verfassungsstaatliche Identitätsgarantien' in Yvo Hangartner and Stefan Trechsel (eds), *Völkerrecht im Dienste des Menschen: Festschrift für Hans Haug* (Haupt 1986); Yaniv Roznai, 'Unconstitutional Constitutional Amendments – The Migration and Success of a Constitutional Idea' (2013) 61 AJCL 657; Yaniv Roznai, 'Amendment Power, Constituent Power, and Popular Sovereignty: Linking Unamendability and Amendment Procedures' in Richard Albert, Xenophon Contiades and Alkmene Fotiadou (eds), *The Foundations and Traditions of Constitutional Amendment* (Hart 2017); Silvia Suteu, *Eternity Clauses in Democratic Constitutionalism* (Oxford University Press 2021).

23 See also, with examples, Palermo and Kössler (n 1) 40ff. The inverse case is constituted by Art 37 para 5 Constitution of Indonesia according to which provisions relating to the form of the unitary state of the Republic of Indonesia may not be amended.

since the division of a 'federation' into *Länder* has to be maintained and since Art 79 para 3 const cit refers to the principles mentioned in Art 20 const cit which explicitly states that Germany is a 'federal state', the abolition of federalism *per se* – which would naturally include the amendment of these elements – is prohibited, too. Another example of an aspect-related unamendability clause is Art 132 para 1 in conjunction with Art 3 para 3 Constitution of Somalia which declares the fundamental principles of power sharing in a federal system unamendable.[24]

A different case is constituted by those constitutions that expressly prohibit infringements of the national territory. Normally, neither federal nor unitary constitutions admit unilateral secessions, although there are some very few exceptions to this rule.[25] The entrenchment of an unamendability clause on territorial integrity takes one step further: even though eternity clauses that entrench territorial integrity are rather usual for unitary constitutions,[26] such clauses could be used for safeguarding federalism, too, inasmuch as the constitution could not be amended with a view to allowing a component unit to leave the federal compound. Among federal constitutions, Art 115 Constitution of Comoros entrenches such a rule according to which no procedure of constitutional revision may be initiated or pursued when it infringes the unity of the territory and the inviolability of the internationally recognized frontiers. Likewise, Art 274 para 1 Constitution of Nepal declares territorial integrity unamendable. The perspective from which federalism is protected under such a clause does not, however, relate to the protection of the component territories from the possible establishment of a unitary state with a unitary territory.

---

24 A couple of constitutions of non-federal, but still decentralized countries declare the autonomy of local power (Art 285 para 1 subpara e Constitution of Cape Verde), the principle of autonomy of the decentralized territorial collectivities (Art 163 Constitution of Madagascar) or the autonomy of regional and local power (Art 154 para g Constitution of São Tomé and Príncipe) unamendable.

25 Art 39 para 1 and 4 Constitution of Ethiopia, Sec 338ff Constitution of Papua New Guinea, Sec 113 and 115 in conjunction with Schedule 3 Constitution of St Kitts and Nevis, Art 89 and 93 para 7 Constitution of Uzbekistan; see already Anna Gamper, 'Regionalismus und Sezession – verfassungsrechtliche Herausforderungen und Antworten im europäischen Vergleich' in Walter Obwexer and others (eds), *Integration oder Desintegration? Herausforderungen für die Regionen in Europa* (Nomos 2018) 62ff and Anthony Beauséjour, 'Indivisibility and Secession Clauses in Current Constitutions and the Prevalence of Secessionist Movements – Empirical Paper Series on Secession and Constitutionalism, Part 1' (2019) 13 ICL Journal 147.

26 See, eg, Art 236 para b Constitution of Angola, Art 285 para 1 subpara a Constitution of Cape Verde, Art 248 Constitution of El Salvador, Art 91 para 2 Constitution of Kazakhstan.

Rather, such clauses protect federalism only to the extent that a secession is prohibited – which would disrupt the federal system inasmuch as it would lose the seceding unit. An eternity clause relating to territorial integrity thus protects a federal state only from further fragmentation, while it does not protect it from the contrary development, namely from amalgamation into a unitary state.

Moreover, the unamendability of federalism or some of its features may not just result from an explicit eternity clause. Following a landmark decision of the Indian Supreme Court[27] which was rooted in French and German constitutional theory,[28] an increasing number of apex courts[29] across the globe apply the 'basic structure doctrine' according to which certain fundamental constitutional principles must not be amended even though an explicit eternity clause is missing.[30] In India, also federalism is considered to be part of the implicit 'basic structure'.[31] Still, an implicit 'basic structure' is a highly diffuse yardstick which ultimately leaves it open to judges to determine whether federalism as such or certain elements pertaining to federalism will be considered unamendable or not.

A similar case is constituted by the Italian Constitution, which, apart from an explicit eternity clause protecting the republican form of state entrenched in Art 139 const cit, entrenches a number of principles which, according to the interpretation of the Italian Constitutional Court,[32] are considered to be related to the constitutional understanding of 'republic' and, thus, implicitly

27 The leading case was *Kesavananda Bharati v State of Kerala*, AIR 1973 SC 1461.

28 Monika Polzin, 'The basic-structure doctrine and its German and French origins: a tale of migration, integration, invention and forgetting' (2021) 5 Indian Law Review 45; Thomas Fleiner and Cheryl Saunders, 'Constitutions embedded in different legal systems' in Mark Tushnet, Thomas Fleiner and Cheryl Saunders (eds), *Routledge Handbook of Constitutional Law* (Routledge 2013) 24.

29 The most recent example is the 'Building Bridges Initiative' case law in Kenya, in which the application of the basic structure doctrine had been affirmed by lower courts, but was ultimately refused by the Kenyan Supreme Court (see Silvia Suteu, 'The BBI Judgment: Of Basic Structure Doctrines and Participatory Constitution-Making' [*Blog of the International Journal of Constitutional Law*, 2022] <http://www.iconnectblog.com/2022/09/the-bbi-judgment-of-basic-structure-doctrines-and-participatory-constitution-making> accessed 30.11.2022).

30 ibid; Roznai (n 22) 657; Anna Gamper, 'Constitutional transplants oder autochthones Verfassungsrecht?' in Peter Bußjäger and Anna Gamper (eds), *100 Jahre Liechtensteinische Verfassung* (Verlag Österreich/Schulthess 2022) 32.

31 Wen-Chen Chang and others (eds), *Constitutionalism in Asia* (Hart 2014) 290.

32 See, eg, sent 1146/1988.

unamendable: one of these is Art 5 const cit which obliges the Republic to, *inter alia*, recognize and promote local autonomies and to adapt the principles and methods of its legislation to the requirements of autonomy and decentralisation. While this clause protects regionalism to some extent, it at the same time puts an obstacle to a full-fledged federal system.[33]

Eternity clauses may, moreover, not just refer to the *abolition* of federalism or certain elements pertaining to federalism, but to any or a specific kind of its *transformation*: the aforementioned Brazilian provision, eg, relates to the '*abolition*' of the federalist form of the State, whereas, according to the aforementioned German and Somalian provisions, the '*amendment*' of federalism or certain features of federalism is prohibited. Whilst, in the first case, constitutional amendments relating to federalism are admitted, as long as this does not amount to an abolition, the latter category of clauses prohibits even the amendment of federalism or certain features of federalism. Even though it is not excluded that these different techniques of formulating an eternity clause will to some part be overshadowed by a kind of interpretation that, eg, understands the term 'amend' as inclusive of the term 'abolish' or 'significantly amend', the distinction between the prohibition to amend federalism and the prohibition to abolish federalism is obvious. An 'amendment' of federalism might, moreover, even include the improvement of the federal system and is not necessarily targeted at weakening or reducing federalism.

However, the very unamendability of federalism or its features might accelerate disruptive processes that overturn the federal constitution. Paradoxically, the rigidity of a constitution may thus have a self-destroying effect, because reforms cannot be properly made under a rigid constitution so that, following a revolutionary overturn, a 'historically first' new constitution might be adopted by a constituent assembly or through a referendum.

It is, therefore, highly questionable whether an eternity clause is really useful for the purpose of protecting federalism. And why should a federal constitution not even be amended in order to accommodate federalism in a better way? More precisely, why should a federal constitution not be amended if even the component units want it to be amended? In turn, however, how can they protect federalism from being amended or even abolished?

33 On the differences, see Arban, Martinico and Palermo (n 18).

## 3 Constitutional Amendments Related to Federalism

### 3.1 *General Remarks*

The political attitudes taken towards constitutional amendments related to federalism may differ widely between the federal and the component governments. While a federal government might – although not necessarily – favour centralisation, the component units will rather oppose a constitutional reform that reduces or abolishes federalism; this neither excludes possible trade-offs between them nor even diverging views among the component units, though.

The question, therefore, is whether a federal constitution should rather take the view that it ought to protect federalism as much as possible which means that the most rigid amendment procedure – let alone an eternity clause – should apply if federalism was amended; or, whether the amendment procedure should substantially focus on the participation of the component units while other guarantees of constitutional rigidity could be neglected. In other words: the protection of federalism does perhaps not necessarily require a rigid constitution. Rather, it needs a constitution that allows the component units to take part in the choice in what direction federalism should be amended. The need for participation of the component units in the amendment procedure might contribute to the rigidity of the respective constitution, but it is not the only kind and not necessarily the most rigid of procedural hurdles: a constitutional amendment procedure, eg, could do well without rigid elements such as parliamentary supermajorities, referendums or the re-election of a parliament, while it could still allow the component units a say in constitutional amendments that affect federalism. It depends on the actual political circumstances, whether a constitutional amendment can in practice be achieved more easily through the one or the other hurdle.

From comparative perspective, written constitutions differ very much with regard to the constitutional amendment procedures they provide.[34] While some constitutions establish only one uniform amendment procedure that

34 See, for a survey, Michael Hein, 'Do constitutional entrenchment clauses matter? Constitutional review of constitutional amendments in Europe' (2020) 18 ICON 78; Ewald Wiederin, 'Über Inkorporationsgebote und andere Strategien zur Sicherung der Einheit der Verfassung. Rechtsvergleichende Beobachtungen und Vorschläge de constitutione ferenda' (2004) 56 ZöR 175, 193ff; Anna Gamper, 'Hierarchiefragen der Verfassungsänderung' in Clemens Jabloner and others (eds), *Scharfsinn im Recht: Liber Amicorum Michael Thaler zum 70. Geburtstag* (Jan Sramek Verlag 2019) 165ff; Albert (n 22) 8ff; Yaniv Roznai, 'Rigid (Entrenched)/Flexible Constitutions' in Rüdiger Wolfrum, Frauke Lachenmann and Rainer Grote (eds), *Max Planck Encyclopaedia of Comparative Constitutional Law* (Oxford University Press 2018) para 14ff; Richard Albert, Xenophon Contiades and Alkmene

applies to every type of constitutional amendment, other constitutions vary as to different types of constitutional amendment and respective procedures. In the latter case, two or even more different amendment procedures apply, depending on which kind of amendment is made – just an amendment of 'ordinary' constitutional law or regarding certain enumerated provisions, principles or values or with regard to whether the constitution is revised 'partially' or 'totally'.[35]

Typical amendment hurdles include a qualified quorum and/or majority in the parliament (which is regularly provided as a minimum hurdle by all written constitutions), an absolute veto power of the second chamber (where such a chamber exists), the dissolution and re-election of a parliament, the need for a repeated parliamentary decision, a nationwide referendum, the consent of the component units and sometimes even a combination of these elements.[36]

Federal constitutions do not necessarily refer to all of these elements when it comes to constitutional amendments, but it is usual for them to give the component units some say in federal constitutional amendments. In order to verify this in detail, however, federal constitutions shall be examined with regard to three aspects in the following: first, whether federal constitutions on the whole tend to be rigid or flexible constitutions;[37] second, whether federal constitutions tend to establish specific amendment procedures with regard to amendments relating to federalism or perhaps even several types of amendment relating to federalism; third, whether federal constitutions require the component units' direct and/or indirect, unanimous or majoritarian approval for all or specific types of constitutional amendments, and whether federal constitutions involve the component units only through veto powers or also other participatory instruments, eg the right of initiative, in the amendment procedure.

The 17 constitutions selected for this comparison are those of Argentina, Australia, Austria, Belgium, Bosnia and Herzegovina, Brazil, Canada, Germany, India, Italy, Mexico, Nepal, Russia, South Africa, Spain, Switzerland and the US. This range does not, of course, consider all federal constitutions that would be

---

Fotiadou (eds), *The Foundations and Traditions of Constitutional Amendment* (Hart 2017); Gamper (n 22) 52ff.

35 See, eg, the distinction in Art 44 para 3 Austrian Federal Constitutional Act, Art 195 and 196 Constitution of Costa Rica, Art 191 and 193 Constitution of Nicaragua, Art 32 para 1 Constitution of Peru, Sec 168 para 1 Constitution of Spain, Sec 75 lit b Constitution of Sri Lanka, Art 138 and 139 Swiss Federal Constitution.

36 Gamper (n 22) 54f with further references.

37 See the classical distinction by James Bryce, *Studies in History and Jurisprudence*, vol 1 (Oxford University Press 1901) 145 and Roznai (n 34).

worth considering in this context, but seeks to give a representative sample of most 'mature' federal systems, as well as some newer federal or 'quasi-federal' systems[38] that have drawn more attention in recent scholarship on federalism.

### 3.2 *Rigid or Flexible Federal Constitutions*

The vast majority of the selected federal constitutions ranges between a moderately and highly rigid character. Some of them, as shown before, even include explicit eternity clauses or have been interpreted in line with the 'basic structure doctrine'.[39] Hardly any of these constitutions make federal constitutional amendments depend on just the minimum requirement of a qualified quorum and/or majority in the federal parliament or one of its chambers, but they usually provide one or even more further hurdles, at least with regard to some types of constitutional amendment. None of these constitutions, moreover, has an 'unwritten' character in the sense that ordinary laws could formally not be distinguished from constitutional laws.

### 3.3 *Uniform or Specific Constitutional Amendment Procedures*

The majority of the selected constitutions provides more than just one uniform constitutional amendment procedure, but differentiates between a basic procedure required for ordinary constitutional amendments and one or more other, more specific amendment procedures. Not all of these specific procedures are targeted at issues of federalism, though. While the constitutions of Argentina, Belgium, Bosnia and Herzegovina, Brazil, Germany, Italy, Mexico, Spain and Switzerland do not distinguish between different types of constitutional amendments and corresponding procedures as to whether federalism is concerned – even though some of them distinguish between different types of constitutional amendments in accordance with other distinction criteria[40] – the constitutions of Australia,[41] Austria,[42] Canada,[43] India,[44] Nepal,[45] Russia,[46] South Africa[47] and the US[48] distinguish between two or even more

38 On that term Watts (n 10) 25 and Palermo and Kössler (n 1) 45.

39 See above 147.

40 The constitutions of Spain and Switzerland, eg, distinguish between a 'partial' and 'total' revision of the constitution.

41 Sec 128 Constitution of Australia.

42 Art 2 para 3, Art 35 para 4, Art 44 para 1, 2 and 3 Austrian Federal Constitutional Act.

43 Sec 38–47 Constitution Act 1982.

44 Art 368 para 2 Constitution of India.

45 Art 274 Constitution of Nepal.

46 Art 135–137 Constitution of Russia.

47 Sec 74 para 1, 2, 3 and 8 Constitution of South Africa.

48 Art v US Constitution.

types of constitutional amendment, at least one of which specifically relates to federalism.

However, these specific amendment procedures do not refer to 'federalism' in general, but to specific issues related to federalism: typically, they refer to changes regarding the representation of the component units in the federal second chamber, their powers and/or territorial boundaries.[49] Some of them even establish more than one amendment procedure that is specifically federalism-related: according to the Austrian Federal Constitution, eg, an ordinary constitutional amendment procedure requires just a qualified quorum and majority in the first chamber of the Federal Parliament, but four specific procedures, all of them relating to federalism, provide additional hurdles: firstly, if the territory of a component *Land* is abolished or if the rights of the *Länder* to take part in certain boundary changes are restricted, the approval of the *Länder* – each through the enactment of a *Land* constitutional law – will be needed additionally to the required federal constitutional amendment.[50] Secondly, a federal constitutional amendment that alters Art 34 or 35 of the Federal Constitutional Act – which regulate the basic organisation of the federal second chamber – additionally depends on a qualified[51] approval of the federal second chamber.[52] If, thirdly, the *Länder* are to lose a competence, the respective constitutional amendment will need the qualified approval of the federal second chamber as well.[53] Fourthly, if the federal constitution is submitted to a 'total revision' – which means the serious alteration or abolition of at least one of the leading constitutional principles –, a nation-wide referendum will be needed.[54] Since federalism belongs to the leading principles of the Austrian Federal Constitution, the abolition of federalism would constitute a 'total revision',[55] but also require the other procedures.

## 3.4 *The Participation of the Component Units*

### 3.4.1 Indirect Participation

Irrespective of whether federal constitutions provide more than one constitutional amendment procedure and, in that case, even one or more specific

49 Palermo and Kössler (n 1) 178ff.

50 Art 2 para 3 Austrian Federal Constitutional Act.

51 A majority of the delegates of at least four out of nine *Länder* need to approve, in addition to the ordinary requirements according to which a third of all members must be present and the simple majority approve.

52 Art 35 para 4 Austrian Federal Constitutional Act.

53 Art 44 para 2 Austrian Federal Constitutional Act.

54 Art 44 para 3 Austrian Federal Constitutional Act.

55 See the Austrian Constitutional Court's landmark case VfSlg 2455/1952.

procedures related to federalism, a crucial question is if and how the component units are involved in constitutional amendment procedures – both in uniform amendment procedures and in those that are specifically related to issues of federalism.

As the comparison between the selected federal constitutions shows, this is done in a very different manner.[56] Some of them do not directly involve the component units at all: such cases are, eg, constituted by Argentina, Belgium, Bosnia and Herzegovina and Germany. In these countries, the respective federal constitution does not provide any direct participatory rights of the component units, in particular not with regard to initiating or vetoing a proposed constitutional amendment. Still, the respective second chambers – as well as those of the selected countries in which the component units directly participate in amendment procedures – are regularly involved in the amendment procedure.

The position of the federal second chambers within the respective constitutional amendment procedures differs with regard to the type of participatory right: participatory rights include the right of initiative, absolute or relative veto rights, the right to partake in a mediation procedure, the right to submit a bill to a constitutional court and the right to convoke a referendum on the respective amendment.[57] In perfectly bicameral systems, the federal second chamber has an equally strong position as the respective first chamber, even though a constitution may deny some of the aforementioned participatory rights to both chambers. With regard to imperfectly bicameral systems, the federal second chamber may not possess all of these rights for all kinds of constitutional amendment procedures, even though the first chamber may: however, the right of initiative is, eg, granted to the federal second chambers with regard to all types of constitutional amendments in Australia,[58] Austria,[59] Belgium,[60] Brazil,[61] Canada,[62] Germany,[63] India,[64] Italy,[65] Nepal,[66] Russia,[67]

56 See some examples in Palermo and Kössler (n 1) 183ff.

57 See, on these categories already Anna Gamper, 'Legislative Functions of Second Chambers in Federal Systems' (2018) 10 Perspectives on Federalism E – 117, E – 120f.

58 Art 128 para 2 Constitution of Australia.

59 Art 41 para 1 Austrian Federal Constitutional Act.

60 Art 77 para 1 Constitution of Belgium.

61 Art 60 Constitution of Brazil.

62 Sec 46 para 1 Constitution Act 1982.

63 Art 76 para 1 German Basic Law.

64 Art 368 para 2 Constitution of India.

65 Art 138 para 1 Constitution of Italy.

66 Art 274 para 2 Constitution of Nepal.

67 Art 134 Constitution of Russia.

Spain,[68] Switzerland[69] and the US,[70] while this right is more limited in case of the South African National Council of Provinces.[71]

Both chambers are equally strong with regard to veto powers in most of the selected federal countries (even with imperfectly bicameral federal parliaments) when federal constitutional amendments are concerned.[72] Exceptions can, however, be found in Austria,[73] Canada,[74] South Africa[75] or Spain,[76] where the federal second chamber can, at least with regard to some federal constitutional amendments, be overruled.[77]

In Austria, moreover, a third of the members of the federal second chamber may convoke a referendum on any kind of constitutional amendment (unless in case of a 'total revision' for which a referendum is already provided)[78] as well as challenge[79] the amendment before the Constitutional Court if one of the aforementioned specific amendment hurdles was not kept. A referendum may also be convoked by one tenth of the members of the Spanish[80] Senate, which, as well as the German *Bundesrat*,[81] is also entitled to possibly partake in

68 Sec 87 para 1 and 166 Constitution of Spain.

69 While a partial revision of the Swiss Federal Constitution may be, *inter alia*, initiated by the Federal Assembly as a whole (Art 194 para 1 const cit), a total revision may be also initiated by each of the two chambers (Art 193 para 1 const cit). Similarly, Art 30 Constitution of Argentina and Art 135 Constitution of Mexico respectively entitle the Congress as a whole to initiate a constitutional amendment.

70 Art v US Constitution.

71 Sec 74 para 1 subpara b, para 2 subpara b and para 3 subpara b Constitution of South Africa.

72 See, with examples Palermo and Kössler (n 1) 183ff.

73 The consent of the Federal Council is only required for constitutional amendments under Art 35 para 4 and Art 44 para 2 Austrian Federal Constitutional Act.

74 Sec 47 para 1 Constitution Act 1982.

75 Sec 74 Constitution of South Africa.

76 Sec 167 para 2 Constitution of Spain.

77 In some cases, the Federal Parliament as a whole, in which one of the chambers may be numerically privileged, decides (eg, Art 30 Constitution of Argentina which, however, further requires a convention, Art x para 1 Constitution of Bosnia and Herzegovina and Art 135 Constitution of Mexico), while in other cases a dissent between both chambers is finally left to the decision of either the component units (Sec 128 Constitution of Australia) or the federal people in a referendum (Art 193 para 2 Swiss Federal Constitution).

78 Art 44 para 3 Austrian Federal Constitutional Act.

79 Art 140 para 1 subpara 2 Austrian Federal Constitutional Act.

80 Sec 167 para 3 Constitution of Spain; in case of a total revision of the Constitution a referendum is absolutely required by Sec 168 para 3 const cit.

81 Art 77 para 2 German Basic Law.

a joint mediation committee,[82] or by one fifth of the members of the Italian[83] Senate respectively.

Apart from the problem that these second chambers often lack a 'federal culture',[84] their members may not always exclusively represent the territorial units, but also other entities.[85] In all cases, moreover, no unanimous votes are required so that the representatives of a single component unit in the federal second chamber could be overruled by the other members.[86]

### 3.4.2 Direct Participation

Among the selected constitutions, a majority of them – those of Australia, Austria, Brazil, Canada, India, Mexico, Nepal, Russia, South Africa, Switzerland and the US – entitles the component units – apart from indirect particaption – to directly participate in federal constitutional amendment procedures.[87] Again, direct participatory rights do not just include (absolute or relative) veto powers, but also rights such as legislative initiative, the power to convoke a referendum or to request a pre-legislative scrutiny from the constitutional court.[88] Federal constitutions do not only, however, differ with regard to the respective participatory right, but also as to whether the component units may participate in all constitutional amendments or just in a few exceptional cases.

While the Australian,[89] the Canadian,[90] the Mexican,[91] the Swiss[92] and the US[93] constitutions entrench absolute veto powers of the component units within the ordinary constitutional amendment procedure, the constitutions of India,[94] Russia[95] as well as, in exceptional cases,

82 Sec 167 para 1 Constitution of Spain.

83 Art 138 para 2 Constitution of Italy.

84 Arban, Martinico and Palermo (n 18) 2.

85 At least in exceptional cases, they include honorary members or non-territorial entities, including minorities. See also Palermo and Kössler (n 1) 185.

86 See already Anna Gamper, 'Suum Cuique tribuere – Acommon Narrative of Federalism and Equality?' in Eva Maria Belser and others (eds), *The Principle of Equality in Diverse States* (Brill/Nijhoff 2021) 24.

87 See some examples in Palermo and Kössler (n 1) 179ff.

88 See also ibid 179.

89 Sec 128 Constitution of Australia.

90 Sec 38 para 1, 2, 3, Sec 41 and 43 Constitution Act 1982 provide these rights in a highly differentiated manner, while Sec 44 enumerates some exceptional matters for which constitutional amendments may be made by the Federal Parliament exclusively.

91 Art 135 Constitution of Mexico.

92 Art 140 para 1 subpara a Swiss Federal Constitution.

93 Art v US Constitution.

94 Art 368 para 2 Constitution of India.

95 Art 136 Constitution of Russia.

Austria,[96] Nepal[97] and South Africa[98] provide such veto powers of the component units only with regard to certain types of constitutional amendment.

In most of the selected cases, the approval of the component units is given by their parliaments and not by their executives;[99] only in very rare cases,[100] the peoples of the component units must approve the amendment in a referendum.

Unanimity between the component units is rarely – and never in the regular amendment procedures – a requirement. One important exception is Sec 41 of the Canadian Constitution Act 1982 which, being embedded in Part V regulating the amendment provisions, requires the consent of the legislative assembly of each province when an amendment to the Constitution is made referring to, *inter alia*, the Lieutenant Governor of a province, or the right of a province to a number of members in the House of Commons not less than the number of Senators by which the province is entitled to be represented when Part V came into force, or, subject to section 43, the use of the English or the French language, or the composition of the Supreme Court of Canada, or when an amendment[101] to Part V is made. While such amendments – which refer to key issues of Canadian federalism or at least to issues of particular constitutional interest – are thus not absolutely excluded, every single province is entitled to veto them; as a result, the federal constitutional amendment cannot be enacted.[102] Also a few other constitutions provide similar rights, which mostly refer to changes in the representation of the component units in the second chamber or the alteration of territorial boundaries: in the US, every State that is deprived of its equal suffrage in the US Senate is entitled to an absolute veto.[103] In Australia, likewise, alterations regarding the proportionate representation of any State in either chamber, or the minimum number of representatives of a State in the House of Representatives, or that

96 Art 2 para 3 Austrian Federal Constitutional Act.

97 Art 274 para 4 Constitution of Nepal.

98 Sec 74 para 8 Constitution of South Africa.

99 See, with examples, Palermo and Kössler (n 1) 179ff.

100 Sec 128 Constitution of Australia and Art 140 para 1 subpara a and Art 142 para 3 Swiss Federal Constitution; see Palermo and Kössler (n 1) 182f.

101 While some federal constitutions, unlike the Canadian provision, do not expressly entrench the amendment provision, such an entrenchment may implicitly be assumed from a systematic und purposive interpretation of the amendment provision; see, generally, Richard Albert, 'Amending constitutional amendment rules' (2015) 13 ICON 655.

102 In contrast, an amendment under Art 38 para 3 const cit that is vetoed by a single province does not have effect in that province, but in all other provinces that did not veto it.

103 Art V US Constitution.

increases, diminishes, or otherwise alters the limits of the State, or in any manner affects the provisions of the Constitution in relation thereto, needs the approval of that State.[104] Sec 74 para 8 South African Constitution provides that an amendment to the South African Constitution referring to a matter that affects the National Council of Provinces, or alters provincial boundaries, powers, functions or institutions or amends a provision that deals specifically with a provincial matter and that concerns only one or more specific province or provinces needs to be approved by that province or provinces. Similarly, Sec 43 of the Canadian Constitution Act 1982 provides that a federal constitutional amendment in relation to any provision that applies to one or more, but not all, provinces, including any alteration to boundaries between provinces, and any amendment to any provision that relates to the use of the English or the French language within a province requires the approval of the legislative assembly of each province to which the amendment applies. *Vice versa*, a constitutional amendment that derogates from the legislative powers, the proprietary rights or privileges of the legislature or government of a Canadian province shall not have effect in a province the legislative assembly of which has expressed its dissent.[105] Amendments to the Constitution of Nepal that are related to the alteration in the borders of any Province or matters related to their competences, too, need the approval of the Provincial Assembly.[106] The Austrian Federal Constitution vests the Austrian *Länder* that are threatened to lose their territories or their participatory rights regarding boundary changes by a federal constitutional law with the right of consent (to be given through a *Land* constitutional law).[107]

In these latter cases, however, the respective requirement is not necessarily unanimity: if the respective constitutional amendment is just targeted at one specific state or states, the approval just needs to be given by that state or these states as an individual vote which is not the same requirement as a unanimous vote, ie an approval by all, ie each and every component unit. The need for a unanimous vote in these latter category of individual veto powers may result from the fact that all of them are affected by a federal constitutional amendment, but if this is not the case, unanimity is no requirement.

Moreover, the said constitutions differ very much as to how the respective approval of the component units needs to be given in these specific

104 Sec 128 Constitution of Australia.

105 Sec 38 para 3 Constitution Act 1982.

106 Art 274 para 4 Constitution of Nepal.

107 Art 2 para 3 Austrian Federal Constitutional Act.

amendment procedures: while, eg, the US Constitution[108] just mentions the consent of a 'state', without specifying the respective body at state level, the Canadian Constitution Act 1982[109] empowers the legislative assembly of each province; the Australian Constitution,[110] in turn, makes the respective amendment dependent on the majority of the electors voting in the concerned states, while in Austria[111] a constitutional law passed by each concerned *Land* is necessary.

In contrast to direct veto powers, the right to directly[112] initiate a federal constitutional amendment is granted to the component units only in rather few cases and, even there, sometimes only with regard to specific types of constitutional amendment. A general right of initiative for a federal constitutional amendment is given to more than one half of the State Legislatures of the federal entities, each of them expressing itself by a simple majority of its members by Art 60 subpara III of the Brazilian Constitution. Likewise, Sec 48 para 1 of the Canadian Constitution Act 1982 empowers the legislative assembly of each province to initiate a federal constitutional amendment. Art V US Constitution obliges the Congress, on the application of the legislatures of two thirds of the several States, to call a convention for proposing amendments to the Federal Constitution. Art 134 Constitution of Russia vests the legislative (representative) bodies of the constituent entities of the Russian Federation with the right of initiative.

Apart from rights of initiative, the Italian Constitution entitles five regional councils to request a referendum on constitutional amendments,[113] while the South African Constitution requests that at least 30 days before a constitutional amendment is introduced, the person or committee intending to introduce the Bill must submit particulars of the proposed amendment to the provincial legislatures for their views and submit any written comments received by them to the first chamber and, in case of certain amendments, also to the second chamber of the Federal Parliament.[114]

108 Art V US Constitution.

109 With regard to different kinds of constitutional amendment, Sec 41 and 43 Constitution Act 1982.

110 Sec 128 Constitution of Australia.

111 Art 2 para 3 Austrian Federal Constitutional Act.

112 An indirect right of initiative is given to the assemblies of the self-governing communities by Sec 166 and Sec 87 para 2 Constitution of Spain.

113 Art 138 para 2 Constitution of Italy.

114 Sec 74 para 5 and 6 South African Constitution.

### 3.5 *Comparative Observations*

Where a federal constitution allows to amend and even abolish the federal system, the comparative analysis shows that some constitutions provide a uniform amendment procedure, while some distinguish between different types of constitutional amendments which may be related to federalism or not.

By comparison, it appears that older and full-fledged federal constitutions, particularly those of North American origin and/or with common-law tradition, vest the component units with stronger direct rights, which, in particular cases, include even unanimity votes or at least individual veto powers. Younger federal systems, particularly those of European origin, but also some South American federal systems, vest the component units with fewer or weaker direct rights or even no direct rights at all, although their amendment procedures may be rigid due to other hurdles.[115]

In contrast, the second chamber of the federal parliament is regularly involved in the constitutional amendment procedures at federal level in the selected countries, but cannot always be considered an 'authentic' or effective representative institution of the component units. Where the component units are directly involved, moreover, this does usually not replace the role played by the second chambers in these systems.

## 4 The Eschatology of Federalism and the Meaning of *foedus*

A first conclusion from this short comparison is that the overall rigidity of a federal constitution may but need not particularly relate to federalism – neither in the sense that particularly rigid amendment procedures necessarily relate to issues of federalism nor that particularly federal elements play a role in a rigid amendment procedure. Even where other hurdles of an amendment procedure, such as nationwide referendums, parliamentary supermajorities, the dissolution or re-election of parliaments etc, prove a serious obstacle to the abolition of a federal system, they are no tools that could be exercised by the component units themselves.

Where, however, constitutions grant both direct and indirect participatory rights of the component units, federalism will be better protected from the

115 The German Basic Law is an interesting example here: while it strongly protects elements of federalism through both an eternity clause and the requirement that all constitutional amendments not falling under that clause need a qualified approval of the *Bundesrat* which efficiently represents the interests of the *Länder*, the *Länder* themselves are still neither entitled to approve of changes in federalism directly nor unanimously.

perspective of the component units. Older and full-fledged federal constitutions usually seem to give the component units a better position for shaping the constitutional design – including the abolition – of federalism, not only with regard to veto powers but also legislative proposals that could trigger institutional innovation. On the whole, however, their powers are more reactive than pro-active: while the component units could thus successfully veto the abolition of the federal system or even other, less significant changes or perhaps even all kinds of constitutional amendments, they could neither positively enforce their own desired amendments nor – in most cases – initiate them directly.

A second conclusion is that, when the abolition of a federal system is concerned, the idea of *foedus* seems to be rather neglected by federal constitutions: it is remarkable that those federal constitutions based on 'original' federal constitutions (that rely on a constitutional compact or are at any rate 'historically first' federal constitutions) vest the component units with more direct rights either in all constitutional amendment procedures or at least in those where they are particularly affected. It could thus seem that the old idea of a *foedus* that underlies the 'making' of federalism is to some extent revived when it comes to the possible 'unmaking' of federalism. 'Derived' federal constitutions, in turn, do not provide such rights, even though it is not excluded that they protect federalism through other hurdles; neither the genesis nor the eschatology of these federal systems are, however, concerned with a *foedus* composed by different partners. Still, while the idea of *foedus* is based on the voluntary consent and, thus, unanimity of all partners, unanimity is not the general rule even in those cases where a federal constitution entitles the component units to directly partake in federal constitutional amendment procedures.

If we accept that, in constitutional terms, federal systems may emerge just from an amendment to a hitherto unitary constitution, would it at least be required for the qualification as a 'derived' federal constitution that it made the abolition of federalism depend on rigid hurdles? But would, in that case, any kind of constitutional rigidity suffice or would the respective rigid procedures have to involve the component units directly and in a decisive, even unanimous manner?

As said before,[116] the existence of an original *foedus* is considered more or less irrelevant according to most modern federal theories. Even when we accept this notion of irrelevance, however, for what reasons should we then

116 See above 141f.

continue to speak of 'federalism' at all? As long as we use terms in accordance with a rational understanding of the underlying linguistic semantics, 'federalism' suggests a particular contractual quality for which neither 'decentralisation' nor 'regionalism', neither 'multi-tierism' nor the 'demotic composition of the polity'[117] or 'internal pluralism'[118] are exact synonyms. And whatever terms we use, we would still be able to perceive that the genesis, design and protection mechanisms of some so-called federal constitutions are different from those of others; and why group distinctive types of constitutions under an undistinctive umbrella that is pronounced to be federalism? In other words, should we replace previous classifications by shifting the focus to a large vocabulary of constitutional terms vaguely circling around the ideas of 'pluralism' or 'multi-levelism' at the expense of a more minute and undazzled perception of differences? Admittedly, the critical stance taken here neither resolves the difficulties around definitions of federalism nor supports a return to the idea that the *foedus* can only be achieved through an original constitutional compact between independent states – but it also avoids the opposite extreme, namely to call this original type of federalism 'distorting'[119] for the sake of a deconstructive and inclusive application of 'federalism' to all kinds of pluridemotic systems.

A possible option for a both meaningful and distinctive understanding of federalism could be to set the focus more on the end than on the beginning of federalism, ie not to let federalism necessarily depend on an original *foedus*, but rather on the protection given to the *foederati* by the constitution so that the (original or derived) federal system could not be abolished without the consent of those that compose the federal system.

Following such a definition, the 'federal hurdle' would, however, less depend on the *directness* of participation of the component units but on the *relevance* of their participation. Granted that the component units – and just them – were democratically represented in a federal second chamber, participatory rights of that chamber could not *per se* be considered less federalistic than direct participatory rights of the respective executive, parliament or people of the component units: if, eg, the abolition of federalism required the unanimous consent of all members of a federal second chamber (or at least that of all delegations of all component units as represented in the federal second chamber), this would, in terms of federalism, be equal to a requirement asking for the unanimous direct consent of all component units. The empirical

117 Tierney (n 2) 296.
118 ibid.
119 ibid 293.

evidence shows, however, that decisions in federal second chambers usually do not need to be made unanimously, but just require (simple or qualified) majorities of members, delegations or both of them. Decisions – including a possible abolition of federalism – could thus be made against the will of a minority such as a represented single component unit, which would be aggravated in asymmetrically composed second chambers.

However, if each and every component unit has the – direct or indirect – right to successfully veto a federal constitutional amendment that seeks to abolish the federal system, the *foedus* will remain intact as long as there is at least one partner that wants to maintain it. If all component units – quite apart from other actors in the constitutional amendment procedure whose approval will be required, such as the first chamber of a bicameral federal parliament – agree to abolish it, however, this will end the federal system. It will in that case be an *agreement* that ends the federal system even though it was not originally based on an agreement. One partner could thus effectively prevent federalism from being abolished, even when all other partners wished for an abolition; but neither could one partner enforce its wish to abolish federalism unless all other partners agreed. This idea inversely mirrors the stance taken by the Canadian Supreme Court[120] with regard to a secession of Quebec: not to allow one unit to leave the federal compound unless this is negotiated with all the other partners, including both the other component units and the federation.

Where, however, an amendable federal constitution does not make the abolition of federalism dependent on the consent of each individual *foederatus* but is grounded on an original *foedus*, it could be argued that each of the components that unanimously enforced the original federal constitution including its provisions on constitutional amendments also agreed to accept a possible amendment on an abolition of federalism even against the individual will of each of them, if the agreed amendment provisions were kept.

In my opinion, one important aspect of 'shared rule' as one of the two much acclaimed essential elements of federalism[121] has so far been underrated, and that is 'shared rule' with regard to the specific question of abolishing a federal

120 *Reference re: Secession of Quebec* [1998] 2 SCR 217, in particular 86, 94, 151.

121 Palermo and Kössler (n 1) 18 and 39; Watts (n 10) 8; Stephen Tierney, 'Federalism and the Plurinational Challenge' in Amnon Lev (ed), *The Federal Idea* (Hart 2017) 229f; Jean-François Gaudreault-DesBiens, 'Towards a Deontic-Axiomatic Theory of Federal Adjucation' in Amnon Lev (ed), *The Federal Idea* (Hart 2017) 88; Daniel J. Elazar, *Exploring Federalism* (University of Alabama Press 1987) 84; Sean Mueller, 'Self-Rule and Shared Rule' (*50 Shades of Federalism*, 2017) <http://50shadesoffederalism.com/theory/self-rule-shared-rule/> accessed 1 December 2022.

system. 'Shared rule' should therefore not be reduced to a snapshot of the institutional architecture of a living federal constitution, but needs to take care of the component units also regarding the future, in particular the possible end of federalism – and, thus, their own end as *foederati*. To leave it to any kind of actor but the component units – each of them, ideally – to decide on the eschatology of federalism, however, is not what a meaningful use of the term 'federalism' would suggest.

## Acknowledgments

The author's sincere thanks go to Jakob Linser for his editorial help with the footnotes.

## Bibliography

Albert R, 'Amending constitutional amendment rules' (2015) 13 ICON 655.

Albert R, 'Introduction: The State of the Art in Constitutional Amendment' in Albert R, Contiades X and Fotiadou A (eds), *The Foundations and Traditions of Constitutional Amendment* (Hart 2017).

Albert R, Contiades X and Fotiadou A (eds), *The Foundations and Traditions of Constitutional Amendment* (Hart 2017).

Arban E, Martinico G and Palermo F, 'Introduction: Why is the trajectory of Italian regionalism comparatively important and what does it have to offer?' in Arban E, Martinico G and Palermo F (eds), *Federalism and Constitutional Law – The Italian Contribution to Comparative Regionalism* (Routledge 2021).

Beauséjour A, 'Indivisibility and Secession Clauses in Current Constitutions and the Prevalence of Secessionist Movements – Empirical Paper Series on Secession and Constitutionalism, Part 1 of 2' (2019) 13 ICL Journal 147.

Benz A and Knüpling F (eds), *Changing Federal Constitutions* (Budrich 2012).

Bryce J, *Studies in History and Jurisprudence*, vol 1 (Oxford University Press 1901).

Burgess M, *In Search of the Federal Spirit* (Oxford University Press 2012).

Bußjäger P, *Föderale Systeme* (Jan Sramek Verlag 2017).

Chang WC and others (eds), *Constitutionalism in Asia* (Hart 2014).

Elazar DJ, *Exploring Federalism* (University of Alabama Press 1987).

Elazar DJ (ed), *Federal Systems of the World: A Handbook of federal, confederal and Autonomy Arrangements* (2nd edn, Longman Group 1994).

Fleiner T and Saunders C, 'Constitutions embedded in different legal systems' in Tushnet M, Fleiner T and Saunders C (eds), *Routledge Handbook of Constitutional Law* (Routledge 2013).

Gamper A, 'Legislative Functions of Second Chambers in Federal Systems' (2018) 10 Perspectives on Federalism E – 117.

Gamper A, 'Regionalismus und Sezession – verfassungsrechtliche Herausforderungen und Antworten im europäischen Vergleich' in Obwexer W and others (eds), *Integration oder Desintegration? Herausforderungen für die Regionen in Europa* (Nomos 2018).

Gamper A, 'Entstehung und Constitutional Engineering des Bundesstaats' in Bußjäger P (ed), *3. November 1918 – Die Länder und der neue Staat* (new academic press 2019).

Gamper A, 'Hierarchiefragen der Verfassungsänderung' in Jabloner C and others (eds), *Scharfsinn im Recht: Liber Amicorum Michael Thaler zum 70. Geburtstag* (Jan Sramek Verlag 2019).

Gamper A, 'Änderung und Schranken der Verfassung' in Bußjäger P, Gamper A and Kahl A (eds), *100 Jahre Bundes-Verfassungsgesetz* (Verlag Österreich 2020).

Gamper A, 'Suum Cuique Tribuere – A Common Narrative of Federalism and Equality?' in Belser EM and others (eds), *The Principle of Equality in Diverse States* (Brill/Nijhoff 2021).

Gamper A, 'Constitutional transplants oder autochthones Verfassungsrecht?' in Bußjäger P and Gamper A (eds), *100 Jahre Liechtensteinische Verfassung* (Verlag Österreich/Schulthess 2022).

Gaudreault-DesBiens JF, 'Towards a Deontic-Axiomatic Theory of Federal Adjucation' in Lev A (ed), *The Federal Idea* (Hart 2017).

Häberle P, 'Verfassungsrechtliche Ewigkeitsklauseln als verfassungsstaatliche Identitätsgarantien' in Hangartner Y and Trechsel S (eds), *Völkerrecht im Dienste des Menschen: Festschrift für Hans Haug* (Haupt 1986).

Hein M, 'Do constitutional entrenchment clauses matter? Constitutional review of constitutional amendments in Europe' (2020) 18 ICON 78.

Jabloner C, 'Verfassungsrechtliche Grundordnung und historisch erste Verfassung' in Olechowski T and Zeleny K (eds), *Methodenreinheit und Erkenntnisvielfalt* (Manz 2013).

Kaltenborn M, 'Constitutional Amendment Rules in Federal and Unitary States' in Benz A and Knüpling F (eds), *Changing Federal Constitutions* (Budrich 2012).

Kavalski E and Zolkos M (eds), *Defunct Federalisms* (Ashgate 2008).

Kelsen H, *Reine Rechtslehre* (2nd edn, Verlag Österreich 1960).

Kincaid J and Tarr GA (eds), *Constitutional Origins, Structure, and Change in Federal Countries* (McGill-Queen's University Press 2005).

Mathieu F and Gagnon AG, '(Still) in Search of the Federal Spirit' in Fenwick TB and Banfield AC (eds), *Beyond Autonomy: practical and theoretical challenges to 21st century federalism* (Brill/Nijhoff 2021).

Mueller S, 'Self-Rule and Shared Rule' (*50 Shades of Federalism*, 2017) <http://50shadesoffederalism.com/theory/self-rule-shared-rule/> accessed 1 December 2022.

Palermo F and Kössler K, *Comparative Federalism. Constitutional Arrangements and Case Law* (Hart 2017).

Polzin M, 'The basic-structure doctrine and its German and French origins: a tale of migration, integration, invention and forgetting' (2021) 5 Indian Law Review 45.

Popelier P, *Dynamic Federalism* (Routledge 2021).

Roznai Y, 'Unconstitutional Constitutional Amendments – The Migration and Success of a Constitutional Idea' (2013) 61 AJCL 657.

Roznai Y, 'Amendment Power, Constituent Power, and Popular Sovereignty: Linking Unamendability and Amendment Procedures' in Albert R, Contiades X and Fotiadou A (eds), *The Foundations and Traditions of Constitutional Amendment* (Hart 2017).

Roznai Y, 'Rigid (Entrenched)/Flexible Constitutions' in Wolfrum R, Lachenmann F and Grote R (eds), *Max Planck Encyclopaedia of Comparative Constitutional Law* (Oxford University Press 2018).

Suteu S, *Eternity Clauses in Democratic Constitutionalism* (Oxford University Press 2021).

Suteu S, 'The BBI Judgment: Of Basic Structure Doctrines and Participatory Constitution-Making' (*Blog of the International Journal of Constitutional Law*, 2022) <http://www.iconnectblog.com/2022/09/the-bbi-judgment-of-basic-structure-doctrines-and-participatory-constitution-making> accessed 30 November 2022.

Tierney S, 'Federalism and the Plurinational Challenge' in Lev A (ed), *The Federal Idea* (Hart 2017).

Tierney S, *The Federal Contract* (Oxford University Press 2022).

Watts RL, *Comparing Federal Systems* (3rd edn, McGill-Queen's University Press 2008).

Wiederin E, 'Über Inkorporationsgebote und andere Strategien zur Sicherung der Einheit der Verfassung. Rechtsvergleichende Beobachtungen und Vorschläge de constitutione ferenda' (2004) 56 ZöR 175.

CHAPTER 7

# Municipalities and Public Policies in the Brazilian Federation

*Gilberto M.A. Rodrigues, Klaus Frey and Vanessa Elias de Oliveira*

## 1 Introduction

In the large majority of federations, municipalities are 'creatures' of the states, subordinate to them, although in many cases with broad administrative autonomy. In Brazil, the model of federalism adopted by the 1988 Constitution resulted in a unique federalism, in which municipalities are autonomous entities, with administrative, political and financial autonomy. This means that they can administer local services, but also create municipal laws, collect and manage local taxes, and also establish municipal taxes, oriented towards the administration of municipal public services. Thus, the federation is composed of the Union, the 26 states, the Federal District and the 5,570 municipalities. Through a cooperative model of federalism, the federated entities must cooperate among themselves to produce public policies.

If, on the one hand, this model allows policies aimed at the demands and needs of each territory of the extensive country, it demands, on the other hand, efficient federal coordination instruments in order to overcome regional inequalities. This has been the main challenge of the Brazilian federation, as we will argue throughout this chapter.

To present the role of municipalities in Brazilian cooperative federalism, especially their performance in public policies as well as the problems and challenges faced, the text will be divided into five parts. First, we will present the Federal Constitution and how it deals with municipalities and their role in the federation. Then, we will deal with the challenges imposed on intergovernmental relations, considering the intense decentralization and demand for coordination present in Brazilian federalism. Thirdly, we will deal with multilevel governance and how it takes place in a specific public policy, characterised by an intrinsic need for federative cooperation, namely the water management policy – which cannot be linked to administrative territorial divisions, but rather to the design of hydrographic basins, thus challenging tight federative arrangements. Fourth, we will analyse another public policy, health policy, which has also faced the need for federative cooperation worldwide,

© GILBERTO M.A. RODRIGUES ET AL., 2024 | DOI:10.1163/9789004528581_009

but which in Brazil has been impacted by the extreme right-wing and anti-scientific government of Jair Bolsonaro, with impacts for intergovernmental relations and for the very configuration of federalism in Brazil. We will conclude with some reflections on Brazilian federalism, the place and role of municipalities in it and how the institutional design adopted in Brazil helps us thinking about federalism and intergovernmental relations in other contexts.

## 2 Municipalities in the Federal Constitution: Actors and Legal Subjects

Municipalities in Brazil have a peculiar political and legal trajectory. Since the colonial period (1500–1822), they have developed degrees of autonomy that will mark their position in the country's political-legal system in contemporary times.[1] After the mid-twentieth century, municipalist movements took shape around associations of municipalities, both at the state and national level.

Although the Brazilian federation, born with the Constitution of 1891, favoured a dual system (Union and federated states), which prevailed over the decades and was maintained in successive constitutions,[2] something new happened during the constituent process that ended the previous authoritarian period (1964–1985) and resulted in the Federal Constitution of 1988: municipalities started to be recognised as federated entities.[3]

In effect, in the Title on Fundamental Principles, Art 1 of the 1988 Federal Constitution reads: 'The Federative Republic of Brazil, formed by the permanent union of the states, the municipalities, and the Federal District, is a democratic State ruled by the law.'[4] The interpretation that this article elevates municipalities to the position of federative entities is defended by part of the specialists and literature of Political Science and Law, and is not exempt of polemics, however, there are decisions of the Supreme Federal Court (STF) that

1 Celina Souza, 'Federal Republic of Brazil' in John Kincaid and G. Alan Tarr (eds), *Constitutional Origins, Structure, and Change in Federal Countries* (McGill-Queen's University Press 2005).

2 ibid.

3 Gilberto M.A. Rodrigues, 'Les villes sont-elles des unités constituantes dans le fédéralisme brésilien?' in Félix Mathieu, Dave Guénette and Alain-G. Gagnon (eds), *Cinquante Déclinaisons de Féderalisme Théorie, Enjeux et Études de Cas* (Presses de l'Université du Québec 2020).

4 Federal Supreme Court, *Constitution of the Federative Republic of Brazil* (STF, Secretaria de Altos Estudos, Pesquisas e Gestão da Informação 2022) <https://www.stf.jus.br/arquivo/cms/legislacaoConstituicao/anexo/BrazilFederalConstitution_125_comcapa_versao_digital_PAGINAS_SIMPLESEC125.pdf> accessed 16 May 2023.

have been marking the degrees of autonomy that municipalities have in the Brazilian federation throughout decades. More recently, during the COVID-19 pandemic, the STF took decisions that favoured municipal autonomy over that of the Union.[5]

In fact, the wording of Art 1 of the Federal Constitution should be read systematically with other constitutional provisions, especially those dealing with the powers of each entity of the federation, and the interpretations made by state and federal courts and, ultimately, by the Supreme Court.

In this sense, the Federal Constitution reserves a considerable share of competences to the municipalities – both common and exclusive. The fact that municipalities share common competencies on equal terms with the Union and the states is an important fact and reveals their federative autonomy.

Art 23 of the Federal Constitution states that '[t]he Union, states, Federal District and municipalities have the collective power'. What this article then presents is an extensive list of core areas of government and public governance which include, among others: health, protection of historical heritage, protection of the environment, access to culture and education, housing and combating poverty. As can be seen, all these areas depend on public policies for their realisation.

In addition, Art 30 of the Federal Constitution grants municipalities exclusive competence to legislate on matters of local interest and to regulate state and federal legislation. As autonomous entities, with an Executive Power (Mayor's Office) and a Legislative Power (City Council), elected by direct, secret and universal vote, municipalities have the legal and political attributes to exercise their powers and implement the public policies derived therefrom.[6]

Furthermore, it should be noted that municipal autonomy is also manifested in international relations, based on increasingly common experiences of decentralised cooperation and paradiplomacy in the fields under their common or exclusive competences.[7]

---

5 Vanessa Elias de Oliveira and Lígia Mori Madeira, 'Judicialização da política no enfrentamento à COVID-19: um novo padrão decisório do STF?' (2021) 13 (35) Revista Brasileira de Ciência Política 1 <https://www.scielo.br/j/rbcpol/a/zVR7JRsKnppq8TBw9VLMPXx/?format=pdf> accessed 16 May 2023; Gilberto M.A. Rodrigues and others, 'Brazil and the fight against COVID-19: Strengthening State and Municipal Powers' in Nico Steytler (ed), *Comparative Federalism and COVID-19: Combating the Pandemic* (Routledge 2021).

6 Gilberto M.A. Rodrigues, 'Concurrent Power and Local Interest in Brazil's Federalism' in Nico Steytler (ed), *Concurrent Powers in Federal Systems: Meaning, Making, Managing* (Brill/ Nijhoff 2017).

7 Gilberto M.A. Rodrigues, *Paradiplomacia: cidades e estados na cena global* (Desatino 2021).

## 3 Intergovernmental Relations: The Permanent Challenge

Although the Federal Constitution has provided municipalities with autonomy and a relevant role in the achievement of constitutional objectives, among them the formulation and implementation of public policies, the same Constitution did not include general mechanisms for intergovernmental relations for coordinated and cooperative actions among the Union, states, and municipalities. This absence of an express legal provision has been filled by political initiatives and mechanisms, whose design has varied from government to government, but which in the view of specialists and literature constitutes an important gap in the Brazilian system, resulting in difficulties for concerted and effective actions in the areas of common competence already mentioned.

With the exception of the Unified Health System (SUS), which was foreseen by the Federal Constitution of 1988 as a mechanism for cooperation among all federated entities for public health policy, and has become an effective and internationally recognised system over decades, the other areas lack stable cooperative mechanisms that are independent of circumstantial political moods for their effective operation.

Despite this, infra-constitutional federal laws that regulate the action of municipalities, within the scope of Urban Law, such as the City Statute (2001) and the Metropolis Statute (2015), try to establish and regulate both mechanisms of citizen participation at the local level, as well as mechanisms of intergovernmental relations within metropolitan regions, which constitute territories in which most public policies depend on articulation and collective governance.

The experience and practice of intermunicipal federation has revealed some examples of successful intergovernmental relations, even if they are subject to recurrent budgetary problems. The case of the ABC region in the state of São Paulo, with its Consortium of municipalities, is one such example.

While it is true that the Brazilian federation recognises municipalities as political actors and subjects of law that are politically and legally autonomous, therefore as constituent parts of the federation, and their common and exclusive competencies directly aimed at carrying out public policies, it is also true that the Brazilian federation does not yet have permanent and effective mechanisms for intergovernmental relations between the Union, states, and municipalities to ensure federative governance in relation to public policies in many areas and on a continuous basis.

Notwithstanding the lack of constitutional regularisation of intergovernmental relations in the Brazilian federation, the 1988 Constitution aimed to establish a balance in federative relations with administrative, political and financial decentralisation, intenting to foster cooperative practices for the expansion of social policies.[8] The challenge facing the New Republic – and that posed for any federation – was to reconcile municipal autonomy (diversity) with the promotion of greater territorial equity through federal authority (Unity),[9] in other words, to seek 'unity in diversity'[10] as a precondition for the implementation of public policies in a country with 5,570 municipalities and high socioeconomic and territorial heterogeneity.

However, in view of the perverse effects of decentralisation observed during the post-constitutional democratic transition process, which manifested themselves in phenomena such as clientelism, patrimonialism, corruption, patronage, fiscal war, fiscal irresponsibility and inefficiency in municipal management,[11] the government of Fernando Henrique Cardoso in the mid-1990s began a conflictive process of recentralisation of power at the national level. The Cardoso government, concerned in making viable an effective fiscal adjustment policy, demonstrated its governing capacity by imposing the Law of Fiscal Responsibility and, above all, by means of a Provisional Measure, the Program of Incentives to Reduction of the State Public Sector in Banking Activity (PROES), liquidating or privatizing most of the state banks; but also advanced in the regulation and financing of public policies as in the case of the creation of the Fund for Maintenance and Development of Basic Education and the Appreciation of the Teaching Profession (FUNDEF) and the law that established the SUS.[12]

---

8 Fernando Luiz Abrucio and Cristina Toth Sydow, 'Federalismo e Governança Multinível em Regiões Metropolitanas: o caso brasileiro' in José Mario Brasiliense Carneiro and Klaus Frey (eds), *Governança multinível e desenvolvimento regional sustentável. Experiências do Brasil e da Alemanha* (Oficina Municipal 2018).

9 Ronald L. Watts, 'Origins of Cooperative and Competitive Federalism' in Scott L. Greer (ed), *Territory, Democracy and Justice: Regionalism and Federalism in Western Democracies* (Palgrave Macmillan 2006); Fernando Luiz Abrucio, 'Reforma do Estado no federalismo brasileiro: a situação das administrações públicas estaduais' (2005) 39 Revista Brasileira de Administração Pública 401; Celina Souza, 'Coordenação, uniformidade e autonomia na formulação de políticas públicas: experiências federativas no cenário internacional e nacional' (2019) 35 (suppl 2) Cadernos de Saúde Pública 1 <https://www.scielo.br/j/csp/a/45DWPg6xBf99zWHR57q4hcK/?lang=pt> accessed 16 May 2023.

10 Abrucio (n 9).

11 Marcus André Melo, 'Crise Federativa, Guerra Fiscal e "Hobbesianismo Municipal" efeitos perversos da descentralização?' (1996) 10 (3) São Paulo em Perspectiva 11.

12 Marta Arretche, 'Um federalismo centralizado' (*DADOS – Revista de Ciências Sociais*, 25 March 2020) <dados.iesp.uerj.br/um-federalismo-centralizado/> accessed 16 May 2023.

This protagonism of the federal government in public policies was sustained into the new millennium, with the Workers' Party (PT) governments modifying, consolidating and expanding the actions of the Union in public policies, especially social policies, aimed at reducing the extreme social and territorial inequalities that characterise the country, putting into practice, according to Souza, 'the constitutional commandments regarding social policies and the principles that govern them – decentralisation, participation and universalisation'.[13]

Therefore, this continuous strengthening of the function and capacity of coordination at the federal level, supported by the instrument of financial induction, significantly contributed to the improvement of public policy indicators,[14] at least until the economic-financial crisis that shook the worldwide economy from the year – 2008 – constraining the possibilities of social policies.

This process occurs based on the distinction between those who regulate and deliberate on programme and policy guidelines (national government) and those who execute them (subnational governments), but this does not eliminate the possibilities of decision-making autonomy of municipalities and states. In this way, both levels of government are considered strong, but in different senses; suggesting, therefore, the existence of sufficient space for local innovation in the production of public policies by the latter.[15]

Since the 1988 'Citizen's Constitution', several constitutional amendments, ordinary laws regulating public policies and formal and informal governance arrangements have contributed to an increasingly complex federation, marked

(1) by public policies decided at the centre, approved by Congress and imposed on the subnational instances;
(2) by binding tax resources from the three spheres of government to policies such as basic education and health;
(3) by limitations on the capacity of the subnational spheres to legislate on their own policies; and
(4) by the coordination of the federal sphere in the management of federal conflicts.[16]

---

13 Souza (n 9) 7.

14 Marta Arretche, *Democracia, federalismo e centralização no Brasil* (Editora Fiocruz 2012).

15 Klaus Frey and others, 'Política ambiental local na federação brasileira: Um desafio para a autonomia local' in Klaus Frey and Lúcio Nagib Bittencourt (eds), *Poder local, políticas públicas e relações federativas: o caso do ABC paulista* (Editora CRV 2022).

16 Celina Souza and Flavio Fontanelli, 'Antídotos institucionais do federalismo brasileiro: a COVID-19 mudou a dinâmica federativa?' in Leonardo Avritzer, Fábio Kerche and Marjorie Marona (eds), *Governo Bolsonaro: retrocesso democrático e degradação política* (Autêntica Editora 2021) 137.

Souza and Fontanelli conclude optimistically that 'the design of Brazilian federalism contemplates institutional instruments capable of managing the tensions and dilemmas of federation'.[17] However, these studies, when analysing the functionality of federalism in terms of the effectiveness of public policies, usually adopt the perspective of the Union level and the federal government's capacity to manage federal conflicts, but do not necessarily take the perspective of local power adequately into account.

The promotion of the municipality as a federative entity would certainly contradict the expectations of the constituents if its role was restricted to the implementation of centrally conceived and elaborated public policies. Having assured competencies to create its own Organic Law (Art 29), to legislate on matters of local interest (Art 30, item I), and administrative, political, and financial autonomy in the Federal Constitution of 1988, one should expect that the federative arrangement provides municipalities with political and financial conditions that allow them, besides implementing federal public policies, to adapt such policies to specific local conditions, as well as to produce their own local policies in line with the popular demands that manifest themselves in the political processes of local democracy.

Therefore, recent research[18] attempted to investigate the degree of autonomy of municipalities in different public policies, including the formulation of policies adapted to the specificities of their socioeconomic and territorial conditions. But before delving deeper into this discussion, we will see below how new institutional arrangements of intermediation of interests and conflicts have emerged that favour on one side a greater vertical cooperation between the Union, the states and the municipalities, and on the other, the intermunicipal cooperation, conceived in this work as new practices of multilevel and polycentric governance.

## 4 New Governance Practices in Brazilian Federalism – Collaborative Networks and Innovations

The concept of governance describes a phenomenon that has gained prominence in political science and public administration as a 'shift from government

17 ibid 139.

18 Klaus Frey and Lúcio Nagib Bittencourt (eds), *Poder local, políticas públicas e relações federativas: o caso do ABC paulista* (Editora CRV 2022).

to governance',[19] associated with an increasing involvement of civil society and citizens in the processes of policy-making and networking, involving the private sector, the voluntary or third sector, and growing intersectoral cooperation within the public sector.[20] The increase in networking and partnership practices derives from the public sector's recognition of its own limitations, as becomes clear from Stoker's definition of governance as 'a concern with governing, achieving collective action in the realm of public affairs, in conditions where it is not possible to rest on recourse to the authority of the state'.[21]

However, network governance depends on a continuous process of dialogue and negotiation. When dialogue comes to a standstill, trust between members tends to decrease and, as a consequence, the network tends to disintegrate.[22] Openness to dialogue depends, on the one hand, on actors, on leadership capable of instigating dialogue and keeping it going; on the other, on institutional structures that support interactive processes and collaboration. Since the 1988 Constitution, several institutional arrangements have been created with the potential to support negotiated collaborative processes aimed at overcoming the impasses related to institutional compartmentalisation and to competitive intergovernmental relations that have often marked Brazilian federalism. In the following, we will briefly address the experiences gained, firstly, with the River Basin Committees as part of integrated water resources management, drawing on the concept of multilevel and polycentric governance, and secondly, with intermunicipal cooperation through public consortia, focusing on the case of the Greater ABC Intermunicipal Consortium in the São Paulo metropolitan region.

### 4.1 *Polycentric and Multilevel Governance in Water Resources Management*

The concept of polycentric governance, on the one hand, has gained prominence in the research of Nobel Laureate in Economics Elinor Ostrom, studying practices of self-government of local communities in the management of common-pool resources. According to Ostrom and her collaborators,

---

19 R. A. W. Rhodes, 'Understanding Governance: Ten Years On' (2007) 28 Organization Studies 1243; Jon Pierre and B. Guy Peters, *Governance, Politics and the State* (2nd edn, Red Globe Press 2020) 94.

20 Gerry Stoker, 'Urban political science and the challenge of urban governance' in Jon Pierre (ed), *Debating governance: Authority, Steering, and Democracy* (Oxford University Press 2000).

21 ibid 93.

22 ibid 104.

polycentric governance, that is, collective action at multiple scales and levels, supported by multiple decision-making centres, favours collective action problem solving.[23] The imperfections that always exist in governance processes could be counterbalanced or minimized by 'back-up institutions' at the various levels of governance.[24]

The concept of Multilevel Governance, on the other hand, has its origins in political and administrative sciences and is conceived as a possible response to deficits in the implementation of public policies. The approach analyses the transformations of organisational structures and how institutions adapt their interactive practices to better coordinate political and administrative actions among different governmental levels.[25] The objective is to understand better how government structures deal with the existing interdependencies between different levels of government and which policy coordination mechanisms governments mobilise to this end.

Nevertheless, the two approaches share the emphasis on the potential of institutional arrangements to strengthen governability and both consider informal institutional rules and practices fundamental for governance regimes dealing with complex issues as in the case of water resources policy in crisis situations.[26]

Frey and others[27] analysed emerging practices of polycentric and multilevel water governance, adopting the conceptual perspective of Elinor and Vincent Ostrom, which emphasises the need of adopting an interdisciplinary and intersectoral perspective, and valuing the political in governance as crucial aspect for understanding the potential and limits of polycentric governance for sustainability.[28] The main authors' interest was to understand the behaviour of a polycentric governance structure, that is to say, its resilience in the context of

23 Elinor Ostrom, 'A Long Polycentric Journey' (2010) 13 Annual Review of Political Science 1; Krister P. Andersson and Elinor Ostrom, 'Analyzing decentralized resource regimes from a polycentric perspective' (2008) 41 Policy Sciences 71.

24 Andersson and Ostrom (n 23).

25 Arthur Benz, 'Multilevel governance' in Arthur Benz and others (eds), *Handbuch Governance: Theoretische Grundlagen und empirische Anwendungsfelder* (Verlag für Sozialwissenschaften 2007).

26 Klaus Frey and others, 'Polycentric Water Governance in the Urban Global South' in Walter Leal Filho, Ulisses Miranda Azeiteiro and Andréia Faraoni Freitas Setti (eds), *Sustainability in Natural Resources Management and Land Planning* (Springer International Publishing 2021).

27 ibid.

28 It is important to recognise that for the Ostroms', polycentric governance already includes the multilevel dimension, so that in the following, in the Ostromian manner, we will exclusively use the more complex term of polycentric governance.

crisis and uncertainty, particularly during the water crises in the years 2014 and 2015 that affected the São Paulo Macrometropolis (SPMM), a region consisting of 174 municipalities.

The Brazilian Integrated Water Resources Management System was established in 1997 by the Federal Water Policy, making the river basin the basic unit for planning and management of water resources, having been considered as a privileged space for participation, articulation, and conflict resolution by the literature.[29] The municipalities are responsible for providing services of basic sanitation to its citizens, for wastewater treatment, water management and drainage, and together with the provincial and the federal state, for the monitoring and supervision of the management of water resources in its territory.[30] And in order to adequately fulfil their tasks, municipalities are participating, together with representatives from the local and regional civil society, in the regional water governance at the scale of the watersheds, mainly in the water basin committees, backed by the regulatory and operational agencies.

However, in the case of the SPMM, the water supply system is not controlled by the hydrographic basin committees, but by the Basic Sanitation Company of the State of São Paulo (SABESP), which is a mixed capital company responsible for water and sanitation services in the majority of the municipalities in the SPMM, and thus used to be a strong, decisive player in the regional water and sanitation governance regime. This has become evident during the water crisis.

Despite the existence of the formal structure of participatory and decentralized water management in basin committees, other political and technical policy makers, formal and informal in nature, have become crucial in the water crisis. The São Paulo State Government became the final decision-making authority while social control mechanisms have de facto been suspended. As a consequence, priority in water supply has been given to the economic interests of the powerful private sector to the detriment of the poorest and most vulnerable communities living in the urban periphery, who suffered from periodic water rationing during the crisis,[31] which calls into question the ability of local

29 Rodrigo Constante Martins, 'Boundaries between inequality and difference in water governance [Fronteiras entre desigualdade e diferença na governança das águas]' (2015) 18 Ambiente & Sociedade 211 <https://www.scielo.br/j/asoc/a/Tr5sX63b7Bskms9L6QprksR/?lang=en> accessed 16 May 2023.

30 Marussia Whately and Estela Maria S. C. Neves, *O município e a governança da água. Subsídios para a agenda municipal de cuidado com a água* (2017) <https://sinapse.gife.org.br/download/o-municipio-e-a-governanca-da-agua-subsidios-para-a-agenda-municipal-de-cuidado-com-a-agua> accessed 22 April 2024.

31 Ana Paula Fracalanza and Thais Magalhães Freire, 'Crise da água na Região Metropolitana de São Paulo: a injustiça ambiental e a privatização de um bem comum' (2015) 19 GEOUSP

governments to take responsibility for the water supply of all citizens under the condition of outsourcing the provision of the service to SABESP.

In accordance with the theory of polycentric governance, the existence of different administrative units and multiple autonomous decision-making centres, taking action and decisions in a relatively coordinated way, has to be considered favourable for constructive political dispute processes and for the governance of common-pool resources.[32] However, in the case of water governance in the SPMM, we observed that irrespective of the polycentric structure of the water governance arrangements, the water crisis proved to be the trigger for the aggravation of conflicts between the river basin committee, civil society, local governments, the São Paulo State Government, and the basic sanitation company, revealing the asymmetric power relations that characterise the governance arrangements, and the predominance of the latter two agents once the situation became acute.[33]

Ostrom's assumption that polycentric arrangements forgo a predominant central authority, seems accurate for the general day-to-day water governance before the crisis, when the different decision-making actors and arenas still enjoyed relative autonomy within their area of competence.[34] The 'critical juncture'[35] of the water crisis led to the creation of a governmental crisis committee excluding civil society and local governments from crisis management, which as a consequence was marked by lack of transparency, the suspension of democratic practices, and thus developed towards an authoritarian and technocratic practice of monocentric governance.[36]

To what extent the critical juncture of the water crisis constituted the starting point for a new path-dependent process able to override the polycentric governance arrangement of the Brazilian federal and state legislation concerning the water resource policy, continuously weakening the inclusive participatory forums of deliberation in favour of the state government and market forces, still has to be analysed in the future. However, the election of a

---

Espaço e Tempo 464 <https://www.revistas.usp.br/geousp/article/view/103064/112861> accessed 16 May 2023.

32 Ostrom (n 23).

33 Frey and others (n 26).

34 Elinor Ostrom, *Understanding institutional diversity* (Princeton University Press 2005).

35 Giovanni Capoccia and R. Daniel Kelemen, 'The Study of Critical Junctures: Theory, Narrative, and Counterfactuals in Historical Institutionalism' (2007) 59 World Politics 341.

36 Pedro Roberto Jacobi, Nicolas Luis Bujak and Alexandre do Nascimento Souza, 'Pénurie hydrique et crise de gouvernance dans la Région métropolitaine de São Paulo' (2018) 13 Brésil(s). Sciences humaines et sociales <http://journals.openedition.org/bresils/2506> accessed 16 May 2023.

right-wing government in the state of São Paulo defending the privatisation of SABESP seems indicative of a more far-reaching institutional change of water governance in the state of São Paulo, at the expense of civil society participation and municipal autonomy.[37]

### 4.2 *Intermunicipal Cooperation – The Experience of the Greater* ABC *Intermunicipal Consortium*

As mentioned before, the lack of cooperation used to be identified as a main obstacle to effective policy-making in Brazilian federalism. Although the top-down approach of federal coordination has proven to be quite effective in social policy in times of relative economic and political stability, this pattern of policy-making has not withstood the rise of right-wing populism in recent years (see next section). Moreover, the comprehensive municipal autonomy, to the extent that it fostered a kind of 'municipal autarchism'[38] and triggered competitive relations amongst municipalities,[39] represents an additional impediment to put the constitutionally envisaged cooperative federalism into practice.

In view of these limitations, local governments started already in the 1990s to join forces in favour of institutional collective action.[40] Especially in metropolitan regions, intermunicipal cooperation was increasingly seen as vital to overcome the governance vacuum left by the new Constitution.[41] One of the most important experiences took place in the so-called Greater ABC, a region consisting of seven municipalities with about 2.7 million inhabitants, a subregion of the São Paulo metropolitan area and known as its industrial heart. Due to the industrial decline suffered by this region, these municipalities started to establish a regional governance regime from 1990 onwards, supported

37 Elected in 2022 with the support of the then President Jair Bolsonaro, São Paulo governor Tarcisio de Freitas took office in January 2023.

38 Celso Daniel, 'Autonomia municipal e as relações com os estados e a União' in Wilhelm Hofmeister and José M. C. Brasiliense (eds), *Federalismo na Alemanha e no Brasil* (Fundação Konrad Adenauer 2001).

39 Melo (n 11); Eduardo José Grin, 'Federalismo, governança e cooperação intermunicipal no Brasil: um balanço da literatura' in José Mario Brasiliense Carneiro and Eder dos Santos Brito (eds), *Consórcios Intermunicipais e Políticas Públicas Regionais* (Oficina Municipal 2019).

40 Richard C. Feiock, 'Metropolitan Governance and Institutional Collective Action' (2009) 44 Urban Affairs Review 356; Richard C. Feiock, 'The Institutional Collective Action Framework' (2013) 41 Policy Studies Journal 397.

41 Celina Souza, 'Regiões metropolitanas: reforma do regime político e vazio de governança' in Eli Diniz (ed), *Globalização, Estado e Desenvolvimento: dilemas do Brasil no novo milênio* (FGV 2007).

by an institutional structure consisting of a Regional Chamber, a Regional Development Agency and, finally, the Greater ABC intermunicipal Consortium to strengthen their administrative, financial, political, and planning capacities for joint action to better address the issues affecting the region as a whole.[42]

The Consortium's joint approach favours fundraising from state and federal resources, enables intermunicipal coordination of policies, explores intercommunity synergies and forms joint partnerships with the state government or with the region's universities, as in the case of the intensive cooperation in the field of risk management or, more recently, regarding the management of the COVID-19 pandemic, as explained in the following section.

The Greater ABC Consortium was founded in 1990 as an association under private law and served as a reference model for the Federal Law of Public Consortia adopted in 2005. In 2010, its legal form was adapted to the requirements of this law by transforming it into a public consortium, thus becoming part of the indirect administration of the Consortium municipalities, with legitimacy to plan and implement regional public policies. The creation of the regional governance regime coincided with the phase of political democratisation in which several municipalities of the region were experimenting with new practices of citizen participation. Under the leadership of the Mayor of Santo André, Celso Daniel, the Regional Chamber of the Greater ABC was established as an informal forum of regional political dialogue between the seven municipalities, the state government and organised civil society, where opportunities for regional development and policy were discussed and joint agreements were reached to overcome the socio-economic crises of the Greater ABC.[43]

---

42 Jeroen Klink, 'Recent Perspectives on Metropolitan Organization, Functions, and Governance' in Eduardo Rojas, Juan R. Cuadrado-Roura and José Miguel Fernández Güell (eds), *Governing the Metropolis: Principles and Cases* (Inter-American Development Bank 2008); Klaus Frey, 'Abordagens de governança em áreas metropolitanas da América Latina: avanços e entraves' (2012) 4 urbe. Revista Brasileira de Gestão Urbana 87 <https://www.redalyc.org/pdf/1931/193123768007.pdf> accessed 16 May 2023; Frey and Bittencourt (n 18); Bessy Thuranira and Klaus Frey, 'Planning and Governance for Resilient Metropolises in Brazil and Germany – Arrangements for Institutional Collective Action' (2023) 15 urbe. Revista Brasileira de Gestão Urbana <https://www.scielo.br/j/urbe/a/kDFwVPf83MxKSTkxCy94YZc/?format=pdf&lang=en> accessed 16 May 2023.

43 Luis Paolo Bresciani, 'Tradição e transição: o caso do Consórcio Intermunicipal do Grande ABC' (2011) 12 Cadernos Adenauer 161; Luis Paulo Bresciani, 'Políticas públicas no Grande ABC: os desafios da integração regional na encruzilhada do novo ciclo' in Klaus Frey and Lúcio Nagib Bittencourt (eds), *Poder local, políticas públicas e relações federativas: o caso do abc paulista* (Editora CRV 2022).

This bottom-up approach, in which civil society played an essential role in the mobilisation process, was crucial to the success of this experience of intermunicipal cooperation, as well as the previously existing regional identity related to the industrialisation process and the strong labour movement, which had a pivotal role in the resistance against the military regime and the democratisation process. Apart from that, the institutionalisation of the cooperation through the establishment of the Consortium and the development agency, the provision of appropriate staff for both agencies and agreements on their funding guaranteed the sustainability of the experience.

However, in these more than 30 years of intermunicipal cooperation, there have also been crises to overcome. Changes in party political conditions in the different cities of the region and, relatedly, in regional political leadership, as well as the general socio-economic context, had different impacts on the effectiveness of collective political action. Significantly, the political upheaval that accompanied the impeachment of Dilma Rousseff in 2016 also changed the political landscape in the ABC region to a great extent, leading to a strong shift to the right by the governments that took office in 2017.[44]

As a result, the regional pact was disrupted, and the regional coordination function of the Consortium was severely weakened.[45] The governance system went into crisis and three of the seven municipalities took initial measures to leave the Consortium. Possibly because of the significant transaction costs associated with the exit option – to return to Feiock's analytical scheme – the Consortium did not ultimately collapse, and the governments came together again in the face of the pandemic as this renewed crisis reminded them of the importance of effective institutional collective action (see next section).

Frey's and Bittencourt's research on public policy in the municipalities of the ABC region analysed the similarities and differences in terms of politics and polity in the different policies, notably in the areas of public health, education, social welfare, culture, and environment; and how the Consortium contributed to shape these different policies.[46] The authors found significant differences in the degree of local autonomy and state capacity in the seven municipalities. The larger cities, such as Santo André and São Bernardo, which

44 Klaus Frey, 'Governança metropolitana e democracia na América Latina: algumas sugestões para a ampliação da agenda de pesquisa' in Marco Aurélio Costa, Lizandro Lui and Sara Tavares Rebello (eds), *Governança Metropolitana na América Latina: um panorama das experiências contemporâneas sob uma mirada comparativa* (IPEA 2021); Bresciani (n 43); Frey and Bittencourt (n 18).

45 Bresciani (n 43).

46 Frey and Bittencourt (n 18).

have extensive economic and industrial structures and thus significant tax revenues, were able to adapt policies formulated at the national level to their specific local needs and develop adequate policies in line with local requirements, while smaller cities such as Rio Grande da Serra or Ribeirão Pires lack qualified staff and adequate technical and financial capacity to develop appropriate policies. However, these smaller municipalities benefited from measures of regional integration on the part of the intermunicipal Consortium in projects such as the shelter house 'Casa Abriga', which helps victims of domestic violence and serves women from the entire region, or the mutual aid agreement for local disasters, in which local governments committed to providing mutual technical assistance with their civil defence equipment and staff. Therefore, it can be said that intermunicipal cooperation has contributed to building trust and regional solidarity over time, strengthening regional and municipal capacities for the benefit of the local population, and this despite the discontinuities and alternations of power observed since the establishment of the Greater ABC Intermunicipal Consortium.

In the next section, we will look at the role of municipalities and public consortia during the COVID-19 pandemic and how they opposed the denialist and grossly negligent policies of the federal government.

## 5 Federalism in the Context of the COVID-19 Pandemic and Right-Wing Populism – The New Protagonism of Subnational Governments

Health policy in Brazil relies heavily on multilevel governance, mainly due to the model of cooperative federalism adopted in the country. According to the Federal Constitution of 1988 and the laws governing the SUS, which is Brazil's public system, health policy should be universal and integral, with shared management among the three levels of government. This means that states, municipalities and the federal government must act jointly to guarantee citizens the right to health, with the responsibility of each level of government defined according to the amount of the services provided, in a complex federative system of the SUS.[47]

The difficulty imposed by this model of cooperation for the implementation of health policy is the result of the model of federalism adopted in Brazil.

47 Marcia C. Castro and others, 'Brazil's unified health system: the first 30 years and prospects for the future' (2019) 394 Lancet 345.

As presented earlier, municipalities are autonomous entities in the federation, being able to decide on local public policies. This autonomy facilitates the adoption of public policies aimed at local demands and needs, on the one hand, but hinders intergovernmental cooperation in health, on the other.

The absence of mechanisms inducing intergovernmental cooperation makes regionalisation of the SUS very difficult to achieve. As happens worldwide, not all municipalities or regions are able to offer all services and medical specialties. Regionalisation serves to guarantee access of citizens to all types of health care, enabling the transit of patients according to health demands. However, given the autonomy of the federated entities and the absence of efficient mechanisms for resource transfers between municipalities and/or states, inequalities in access to services are enormous, according to the capacities of the different regions of the country. Health inequalities are therefore strongly affected by the model of federalism adopted, which in turn hinders intergovernmental cooperation in the SUS.

During the Bolsonaro government (2019–2022) and especially during the health crisis arising from COVID-19, this problem was further aggravated. This is because the absence of efficient mechanisms for federative coordination was exacerbated by the absence of guidance from the federal government on how states and municipalities should act in the management of the pandemic. Added to this, the federal government's anti-scientific posture caused states and municipalities to seek judicial authorisation from the Supreme Court to adopt restrictive measures and mandatory vaccination, which was rejected by the Bolsonaro government.[48]

The Brazilian Ministry of Health acted slowly. Since the beginning of 2020, the threat of COVID-19 was already clear, but the Ministry only act when the WHO declared the pandemic situation and, what is more, very slowly in some central issues to confront the disease, such as the expansion of the number of beds and in the demand for equipment and inputs.[49] But the worst was the confrontation between President Bolsonaro and his own health minister, Luiz Henrique Mandetta. While the minister encouraged states and municipalities to adopt measures of social distancing and restrictions on economic activities, the president stressed the bad economic effect of such measures. This led to

48 Rodrigues and others (n 5); Vanessa Elias de Oliveira and Michelle Fernandez, 'Política de Saúde no Governo Bolsonaro: desmonte e negacionismo' in Leonardo Avritzer, Fábio Kerche and Marjorie Marona (eds), *Governo Bolsonaro: retrocesso democrático e degradação política* (Autêntica 2021).

49 Oliveira and Fernandez (n 48).

a conflict between members of government, which then spilled over to the Supreme Court.

This situation led to the exoneration of Minister Mandetta. With his departure, the situation worsened. The president appointed as minister the doctor Nelson Teich, who was said to be aligned with the president. However, as a specialist in health management he also disagreed with the president's anti-scientific stance, which insisted on the use of chloroquine as a treatment for COVID-19. His tenure lasted less than a month.

The two 'failed' experiments – in the eyes of the president – with ministers with a more technical profile led to the politicisation of the Ministry of Health.[50] After the second minister had left during the pandemic, the general of the armed forces Eduardo Pazuello took over. As soon as he took over, Pazuello launched a protocol for the treatment of COVID-19, authorising the use of chloroquine in health services, even without studies proving its effectiveness. It was also during Pazuello's administration that we had the attempts to suspend the counting of cases, which were later revoked, with a change in the counting methodology.

The anti-scientific attitude of the federal government, which questioned the restrictive measures adopted by states and municipalities, generated a federative conflict never seen before in the country. This situation was called 'Bolsonarist federalism',[51] a logic according to which there should be an autocratic concentration of power in the hands of the Union, with very little room for dialogue and federative negotiations on issues involving federal programmes. Thus, intergovernmental confrontation becomes a daily element of federal relations, making the cooperation expected by the model of federalism adopted in the 1988 Constitution, and, above all, essential for the management of the COVID-19 pandemic, unfeasible.

The confrontation between the president and the measures adopted by states and municipalities for the management of the pandemic flowed into the judiciary. The STF proved to be a court capable of standing up to the president's authoritarian practices; the court clearly opposed the president's measures on issues concerning the fight against the pandemic.[52]

---

50 ibid.

51 Fernando Luiz Abrucio and others, 'Combating COVID-19 under Bolsonaro's federalism: a case of intergovernmental incoordination' (2020) 54 Revista de Administração Pública 663<https://www.scielo.br/j/rap/a/bpdbc9zSGCKZK55L3ChjVqJ/?format=pdf&lang=en> accessed 16 May 2023.

52 Rodrigues and others (n 5); Vanessa Elias de Oliveira and Gilberto M.A. Rodrigues, 'Federal Responses to Corona Pandemic: Brazil' (2021) 22 Jahrbuch des Föderalismus 161; Oliveira and Madeira (n 5).

States and municipalities thus preserved their autonomy for the management of the pandemic. However, it should be noted that this had already been the position adopted by the Court in federal conflicts involving the SUS, which is in line with what the Constitution and the provisions of the SUS say: health management is shared between the three levels of government. The novelty, in the case of the Bolsonaro government, was the absence of the role of the coordinator of health cooperation, which had been the keynote of the federal government since the re-democratisation.

The conflicts between the federal government and subnational governments during the pandemic, added to the absence of a coordinating role by the federal government, greatly aggravated regional disparities in health. Municipalities and regions with low local state capacities had higher rates of Covid deaths than more developed regions with a more complex and consolidated network of public health services (IDS-COVID-19).

The IDS-COVID-19 Index contains national data on social disparities in health associated with COVID-19. It is comprised of three elements: (a) a socioeconomic indicator (income, education and housing conditions); (b) a sociodemographic indicator (household density, percentage of elderly in poverty and percentage of black, brown and indigenous people); and (c) the difficulty of access to health services (rate of ICU beds and respirators, per 100,000 inhabitants, considering the distance between the municipalities of the health macro-region and the population of each municipality). This composite index was measured in four distinct moments of the pandemic and presents the evolution of social inequality in health in the course of the pandemic. The quintiles vary from a situation of very low social inequality in health (quintile 1) to a situation of very high social inequality in health (quintile 5).

The data demonstrate the huge regional inequalities in Brazil, with the North and Northeast regions as the most unequal in terms of health inequalities. According to one of the project coordinators, 'Brazil entered the pandemic period already with a wide inequality among regions. In the first measure, with data from February 2020, before the pandemic, 98% of municipalities in the North region were in clusters 4 and 5, the two worst groups classified by IDS-COVID-19. In the Southeast region, it was 35% of municipalities and in the South, only 7%'.[53] The enormous inequalities in health had drastic effects on the pandemic. The Northern region suffered from a lack of public services

53 In <https://cidacs.bahia.fiocruz.br/idscovid19/indice-de-desigualdades-sociais-para-covid-19-ids-covid-19-e-lancado-e-mostra-um-brasil-mais-desigual/> accessed 27 December 2022.

and basic items for Covid treatment, such as respirators and drugs, with high mortality rates.[54]

Health inequalities, which existed before the pandemic, were not addressed by the federal government during the pandemic. The conflict between the federal government and subnational governments placed the latter in an even more serious situation during the health crisis. In response, some states and municipalities sought regional solutions to the problem, thus overcoming the absence of national federative coordination. In the ABC region of São Paulo, the ABC Intermunicipal Consortium, presented in the previous section, established guidelines for the region, monitored cases and sought joint solutions – including demanding federal government actions for the region.

In the Northeast region of the country, the Northeast Consortium, which had been created in 2019 to promote regional integration, established a Scientific Committee to support the fight against the new COVID-19 pandemic, with the objective of advising the region's governors in taking measures related to the pandemic. In this way, it took actions in the coordination of state actions, seeking synergies and partnerships for the best use of regional state capacities. The purchase of equipment and supplies during the pandemic is an example of what regional cooperation made possible, generating gains for states and municipalities and overcoming the inaction of the federal government in this area. Although it was not created to face the pandemic, the Northeast Consortium proved to be an important instrument of regional federative coordination.

These two examples (of the ABC Paulista and the Northeast Consortium) demonstrate that forms of regional cooperation have been created to overcome the problems of coordination of the Brazilian federation, which worsened throughout the Bolsonaro government, whose authoritarian attitude did not seek dialogue, but the imposition of its visions on public policies for states and municipalities. The absence of top-down dialogue and cooperation strengthened bottom-up initiatives. Successful federal solutions with the participation of the federal government, such as those verified in the German[55] and Canadian[56] cases, were not the standard response to the health crisis given by Brazilian federalism.

---

54 Lewis F. Buss and others, 'Three-quarters attack rate of SARS-CoV-2 in the Brazilian Amazon during a largely unmitigated epidemic' (2021) 371 Science 288.

55 Scott L. Greer and others, 'Alignment and authority: Federalism, social policy, and COVID-19 response' (2023) 127 Health Policy 12.

56 Johanne Poirier and Jessica Michelin, 'Facing the coronavirus pandemic in the Canadian federation: Reinforced dualism and muted cooperation?' in Nico Steytler (ed), *Comparative federalism and COVID-19 Combating the Pandemic* (Routledge 2021).

## 6 Final Remarks

The Brazilian federation has a peculiar institutional arrangement. The more than five thousand municipalities are autonomous entities with administrative, fiscal, and political power to legislate. This autonomy enables them to conduct public policies focused on the needs of each municipality in the country. To do so, they rely on the transfer of federal and state resources, in addition to their own, locally collected resources. This model is based on a highly cooperative federalism, in which states, municipalities and the federal government share responsibility for a large part of public policies.

However, for it to work it also depends on coordination instruments, which were not introduced by the Constitution. Many of them emerged later, through infra-constitutional legislation related to the distinct areas of public policies. They derive from policies, not from polity. This means that federative cooperation depends more on the institutional advances achieved by the distinct policy areas, their actors and advocacy coalitions, than on the permanent and consolidated constitutional guarantees.

Consequently, federative coordination is fragile and highly dependent on the actions of the federal government to promote it throughout the national territory. When the federal government exercises its coordinating power, it is able to reduce regional inequalities.[57] In areas where it is not ensured through public policy designs and incentives for cooperation, or at times when the federal government exempts itself from exercising its coordinating role, as was the case in the Bolsonaro government, it is up to states and municipalities to find their own forms and instruments of intergovernmental cooperation. This becomes, therefore, cyclical, imposing enormous costs on municipalities, especially the smaller ones and those with lower state capacity. Inequalities are exacerbated and the federation becomes more heterogeneous.

The cooperative model of federalism is already known to be challenging, despite the possible gains in terms of public policies. In the Brazilian case, this challenge is even greater, considering the broad municipal autonomy, particularly in cases of crises such as the COVID-19 pandemic or the water crisis in the metropolitan region, where federal conflicts tend to worsen.

The federative coordination, in constant transformation, is far from ideal. This does not mean that decentralisation itself should be reconsidered, but that it is still necessary to build institutional instruments of cooperation that

57 Arretche (n 14).

can guarantee it beyond the will of the different governments, in addition to promoting the institutional resilience needed to face crises and uncertainties.

## Bibliography


Abrucio FL, 'Reforma do Estado no federalismo brasileiro: a situação das administrações públicas estaduais' (2005) 39 Revista Brasileira de Administração Pública 401.

Abrucio FL and others, 'Combating COVID-19 under Bolsonaro's federalism: a case of intergovernmental incoordination' (2020) 54 Revista de Administração Pública 663 <https://www.scielo.br/j/rap/a/bpdbc9zSGCKZK55L3ChjVqJ/?format=pdf&lang=en> accessed 16 May 2023.

Abrucio FL and Sydow CT, 'Federalismo e Governança Multinível em Regiões Metropolitanas: o caso brasileiro' in Carneiro JMB and Frey K (eds), *Governança multinível e desenvolvimento regional sustentável. Experiências do Brasil e da Alemanha* (Oficina Municipal 2018).

Andersson KP and Ostrom E, 'Analyzing decentralized resource regimes from a polycentric perspective' (2008) 41 Policy Sciences 71.

Arretche M, *Democracia, federalismo e centralização no Brasil* (Editora Fiocruz 2012).

Arretche M, 'Um federalismo centralizado' (*DADOS – Revista de Ciências Sociais*, 25 March 2020) <dados.iesp.uerj.br/um-federalismo-centralizado/> accessed 16 May 2023.

Benz A, 'Multilevel governance' in Benz A and others (eds), *Handbuch Governance: Theoretische Grundlagen und empirische Anwendungsfelder* (Verlag für Sozialwissenschaften 2007).

Bresciani LP, 'Tradição e transição: o caso do Consórcio Intermunicipal do Grande ABC' (2011) 12 Cadernos Adenauer 161.

Bresciani LP, 'Políticas públicas no Grande ABC: os desafios da integração regional na encruzilhada do novo ciclo' in Frey K and Bittencourt LN (eds), *Poder local, políticas públicas e relações federativas: o caso do abc paulista* (Editora CRV 2022).

Buss LF and others, 'Three-quarters attack rate of SARS-CoV-2 in the Brazilian Amazon during a largely unmitigated epidemic' (2021) 371 Science 288.

Capoccia G and Kelemen RD, 'The Study of Critical Junctures: Theory, Narrative, and Counterfactuals in Historical Institutionalism' (2007) 59 World Politics 341.

Castro MC and others, 'Brazil's unified health system: the first 30 years and prospects for the future' (2019) 394 Lancet 345.

Daniel C, 'Autonomia municipal e as relações com os estados e a União' in Hofmeister W and Brasiliense JMC (eds), *Federalismo na Alemanha e no Brasil* (Fundação Konrad Adenauer 2001).

Federal Supreme Court, *Constitution of the Federative Republic of Brazil* (STF, Secretaria de Altos Estudos, Pesquisas e Gestão da Informação 2022) <https://www.stf.jus.br/arquivo/cms/legislacaoConstituicao/anexo/BrazilFederalConstitution_125_comcapa_versao_digital_PAGINAS_SIMPLESEC125.pdf> accessed 16 May 2023.

Feiock RC, 'Metropolitan Governance and Institutional Collective Action' (2009) 44 Urban Affairs Review 356.

Feiock RC, 'The Institutional Collective Action Framework' (2013) 41 Policy Studies Journal 397.

Fracalanza AP and Freire TM, 'Crise da água na Região Metropolitana de São Paulo: a injustiça ambiental e a privatização de um bem comum' (2015) 19 GEOUSP Espaço e Tempo 464 <https://www.revistas.usp.br/geousp/article/view/103064/112861> accessed 16 May 2023.

Frey K, 'Abordagens de governança em áreas metropolitanas da América Latina: avanços e entraves' (2012) 4 urbe. Revista Brasileira de Gestão Urbana 87 <https://www.redalyc.org/pdf/1931/193123768007.pdf> accessed 16 May 2023.

Frey K, 'Governança metropolitana e democracia na América Latina: algumas sugestões para a ampliação da agenda de pesquisa' in Costa MA, Lui L and Rebello ST (eds), *Governança Metropolitana na América Latina: um panorama das experiências contemporâneas sob uma mirada comparativa* (IPEA 2021).

Frey K and Bittencourt LN (eds), *Poder local, políticas públicas e relações federativas: o caso do ABC paulista* (Editora CRV 2022).

Frey K and others, 'Polycentric Water Governance in the Urban Global South' in Leal Filho W, Azeiteiro UM and Setti AFF (eds), *Sustainability in Natural Resources Management and Land Planning* (Springer International Publishing 2021).

Frey K and others, 'Política ambiental local na federação brasileira: Um desafio para a autonomia local' in Frey K and Bittencourt LN (eds), *Poder local, políticas públicas e relações federativas: o caso do ABC paulista* (Editora CRV 2022).

Greer SL and others, 'Alignment and authority: Federalism, social policy, and COVID-19 response' (2023) 127 Health Policy 12.

Grin EJ, 'Federalismo, governança e cooperação intermunicipal no Brasil: um balanço da literatura' in Carneiro JMB and Brito EdS (eds), *Consórcios Intermunicipais e Políticas Públicas Regionais* (Oficina Municipal 2019).

Jacobi PR, Bujak NL and Souza AdN, 'Pénurie hydrique et crise de gouvernance dans la Région métropolitaine de São Paulo' (2018) 13 Brésil(s). Sciences humaines et sociales <http://journals.openedition.org/bresils/2506> accessed 16 May 2023.

Klink J, 'Recent Perspectives on Metropolitan Organization, Functions, and Governance' in Rojas E, Cuadrado-Roura JR and Güell JMF (eds), *Governing the Metropolis: Principles and Cases* (Inter-American Development Bank 2008).

Martins RC, 'Boundaries between inequality and difference in water governance. [Fronteiras entre desigualdade e diferença na governança das águas]' (2015) 18

Ambiente & Sociedade 211 <https://www.scielo.br/j/asoc/a/Tr5sX63b7Bskms9L6QprksR/?lang=en> accessed 16 May 2023.

Melo MA, 'Crise Federativa, Guerra Fiscal e "Hobbesianismo Municipal" efeitos perversos da descentralização?' (1996) 10 (3) São Paulo em Perspectiva 11.

Oliveira VE, 'Autonomia Dependente: o federalismo brasileiro e as políticas municipais de saúde no ABC paulista' in Frey K and Bittencourt LN (eds), *Poder local, políticas públicas e relações federativas: O caso do ABC paulista* (Editora CRV 2022).

Oliveira VE and Fernandez M, 'Política de Saúde no Governo Bolsonaro: desmonte e negacionismo' in Avritzer L, Kerche F and Marona M (eds), *Governo Bolsonaro: retrocesso democrático e degradação política* (Autêntica 2021).

Oliveira VE and Madeira LM, 'Judicialização da política no enfrentamento à COVID-19: um novo padrão decisório do STF?' (2021) 13 (35) Revista Brasileira de Ciência Política 1 <https://www.scielo.br/j/rbcpol/a/zVR7JRsKnppq8TBw9VLMPXx/?format=pdf> accessed 16 May 2023.

Oliveira VE and Rodrigues GMA, 'Federal Responses to Corona Pandemic: Brazil' (2021) 22 Jahrbuch des Föderalismus 161.

Ostrom E, *Understanding institutional diversity* (Princeton University Press 2005).

Ostrom E, 'A Long Polycentric Journey' (2010) 13 Annual Review of Political Science 1.

Pierre J and Peters BG, *Governance, Politics and the State* (2nd edn, Red Globe Press 2020).

Poirier J and Michelin J, 'Facing the coronavirus pandemic in the Canadian federation: Reinforced dualism and muted cooperation?' in Steytler N (ed), *Comparative federalism and COVID-19 Combating the Pandemic* (Routledge 2021).

Rhodes RAW, 'Understanding Governance: Ten Years On' (2007) 28 Organization Studies 1243.

Rodrigues GMA, 'Concurrent Power and Local Interest in Brazil's Federalism' in Steytler N (ed), *Concurrent Powers in Federal Systems: Meaning, Making, Managing* (Brill/Nijhoff 2017).

Rodrigues GMA, 'Les villes sont-elles des unités constituantes dans le fédéralisme brésilien?' in Mathieu F, Guénette D and Gagnon AG (eds), *Cinquante Déclinaisons de Féderalisme Théorie, Enjeux et Études de Cas* (Presses de l'Université du Québec 2020).

Rodrigues GMA, *Paradiplomacia: cidades e estados na cena global* (Desatino 2021).

Rodrigues GMA and others, 'Brazil and the fight against COVID-19: Strenghtening State and Municipal Powers' in Steytler N (ed), *Comparative Federalism and COVID-19: Combating the Pandemic* (Routledge 2021).

Souza C, 'Federal Republic of Brazil' in Kincaid J and Tarr GA (eds), *Constitutional Origins, Structure, and Change in Federal Countries* (McGill-Queen's University Press 2005).

Souza C, 'Regiões metropolitanas: reforma do regime político e vazio de governança' in Diniz E (ed), *Globalização, Estado e Desenvolvimento: dilemas do Brasil no novo milênio* (FGV 2007).

Souza C, 'Coordenação, uniformidade e autonomia na formulação de políticas públicas: experiências federativas no cenário internacional e nacional' (2019) 35 (suppl 2) Cadernos de Saúde Pública 1 <https://www.scielo.br/j/csp/a/45DWPg6xBf99zWHR57q4hcK/?lang=pt> accessed 16 May 2023.

Souza C and Fontanelli F, 'Antídotos institucionais do federalismo brasileiro: a COVID-19 mudou a dinâmica federativa?' in Avritzer L, Kerche F and Marona M (eds), *Governo Bolsonaro: retrocesso democrático e degradação política* (Autêntica Editora 2021).

Stoker G, 'Urban political science and the challenge of urban governance' in Pierre J (ed), *Debating governance: Authority, Steering, and Democracy* (Oxford University Press 2000).

Thuranira B and Frey K, 'Planning and Governance for Resilient Metropolises in Brazil and Germany – Arrangements for Institutional Collective Action' (2023) 15 urbe. Revista Brasileira de Gestão Urbana <https://www.scielo.br/j/urbe/a/kDFwVPf83MxKSTkxCy94YZc/?format=pdf&lang=en> accessed 16 May 2023.

Watts RL, 'Origins of Cooperative and Competitive Federalism' in Greer SL (ed), *Territory, Democracy and Justice: Regionalism and Federalism in Western Democracies* (Palgrave Macmillan 2006).

Whately M and Neves EMSC, *O município e a governança da água. Subsídios para a agenda municipal de cuidado com a água* (2017) <https://sinapse.gife.org.br/download/o-municipio-e-a-governanca-da-agua-subsidios-para-a-agenda-municipal-de-cuidado-com-a-agua> accessed 22 April 2024.

# PART 4

## *Country Reports*

CHAPTER 8

# The Weight of History

## *The Preservation of a Centralised Judiciary in the Spanish Decentralised State (and its Consequences)*

*Jordi Jaria-Manzano*

## 1 Introduction

The political transition which led Spain from an authoritarian political regime to a liberal democracy in 1978 was based on the assumption that the constitution-making power was vested in the Spanish nation as a historical subject, recognizing some kind of plurality leading to decentralisation through the procedures established in the Constitution (CE).[1] This vision led to a particular system of decentralisation, which is not based on a federal arrangement, but on a fundamental political decision adopted by the Spanish people as only constitution-making actor.[2] After the adoption of the Constitution, the possibilities in terms of political decentralisation enabled by the text were fulfilled in a few years, giving birth to 17 autonomous communities, with (theoretically) wide powers and some asymmetries. Nevertheless, this process of

1 Art 1.2 of the Spanish Constitution attributes 'national sovereignty' to the Spanish people, while defining a single political subject at the base of the system that is the Spanish nation. It expresses itself through the Spanish people, which would act as a representative body of the Spanish nation, which was already the constitutional substrate of the previous regime and is presented as the ultimate foundation of the current constitutional system. Consequently, the Spanish nation is the true sovereign power, the will on which the Constitution is based, as the preamble makes clear. With this background, Art 2 proclaims the 'indissoluble unity of the Spanish Nation' and then consecrates the right to self-government of 'nationalities and regions'.

2 The fact that the Spanish Constitution is based on an act of a single sovereignty and the derived character of the self-government of 'nationalities and regions' make clear that Spain is not a federal state and even cannot be one, unless a constitutional rupture takes place. See Miguel Herrero de Miñón, 'La posible diversidad de los modelos autonómicos en la Transición, en la Constitución española de 1978 y en los Estatutos de Autonomía' in Institut d'Estudis Autonòmics (ed), *Uniformidad o diversidad de las comunidades autónomas* (Viena Serveis Editorials 1995) 17.

© JORDI JARIA-MANZANO, 2024 | DOI:10.1163/9789004528581_010

decentralisation was dependent on historical assumptions vested in the identification of the subject of sovereignty in the Constitution.[3]

For this reason, decentralisation in Spain should not be understood as the result of a more or less sophisticated technical solution embedded in the Constitution of 1978, but the result of complex historical circumstances and processes of *longue durée*, which define the solution adopted, with its potentialities, its achievements, but also its challenges and shortcomings.[4] According to its historical background, the Spanish model of decentralisation shows a tension between the centripetal dynamics linked to the construction of the modern state and the centrifugal forces associated with identities formed through centuries, strongly reinforced with the particular evolution of the economic modernisation of Spain since the beginning of the 19th century.

One of the most notable characteristics of the centripetal dynamics of the Spanish constitutional history is the design of a national body of judges, associated with rationality, equality and proficiency. Such Judiciary was mostly left untouched with the Constitution of 1978. As Rosado Iglesias points out, the Judiciary follows a different path from the decentralisation operated in the legislative and executive branches, as far as the judicial function is attributed exclusively to '*jueces y magistrados, integrantes de ese Poder Judicial, independientes, inamovibles, responsables y sometidos únicamente al imperio de la ley* [judges and magistrates, integrating this Judicial Branch, independent, irremovable, responsible and submitted only to the rule of law]' and is operated according to the principle of unity of jurisdiction (*principio de unidad jurisdiccional*).[5] Judiciary remains a stronghold of the unitary state according to the tradition of Spanish state-building during the previous centuries.[6]

3 See Jordi Jaria-Manzano, 'La independència com a procés constituent. Consideracions constitucionals sobre la creació d'un estat català' (2015) 22 Revista d'Estudis Autonòmics i Federals 184, 185ff.

4 Besides the reference to the Spanish nation as the ultimate foundation of the Constitution, there are several examples of historicism in it, notably, the reference to the historical rights in the first additional provision of the Constitution, which is the constitutional basis for the particular regime of self-government of the Basque territories as well as the second transitory provision of the Constitution, which is linked with the restoration of the Catalan government in the exile as legitimate government through the Royal Decree Law 41/1977. The complexity of historical ties in the fabric of the Spanish Constitution results in tensions which are the subject of this paper.

5 See Gema Rosado Iglesias, '¿Es posible arbitrar fórmulas que acerquen el Poder Judicial a la realidad autonómica?' (2022) 35 Revista d'Estudis Autonòmics i Federals 53, 56.

6 According to Joan-Josep Vallbé, 'Descentralización judicial regional. Una exploración empírica del poder judicial regional en Europa occidental' (2022) 35 Revista d'Estudis Autonòmics i Federals 195, 220, most regions in Spain have a comparative high level of judicial self-government in the European context (a coefficient of 0,337). They are certainly far away

Nevertheless, the process of decentralisation produced different legal subsystems with a complex of principles and rules to be applied by the courts. Despite this, the Judiciary remained a single centralized power with little sensibility to the consequences of political decentralisation and particularly its legal implications, ie specific regional law. In my view, this is one of the most salient examples of the tension between the historical narratives lodged in the constitution: the centripetal dynamics of Spanish political modernization according with the French model and the centrifugal forces related to economic modernization in the periphery, particularly in Catalonia and the Basque Country. This is why I will focus on Spanish Judiciary in relation to the Autonomous Communities to show how history shapes constitutional arrangements regarding territorial distribution of power, making them path dependent and idiosyncratic.

A couple of decades ago, the question of adapting Judiciary, without changing its constitutional (centralized) nature, to the reality of decentralisation was debated politically and academically. To some extent, the decision of the Constitutional Court on the Catalan Statute of Autonomy in 2010 closed the debate, leaving things unchanged. Today the mismatch between a significantly decentralised system, even if it is under a strong centralizing pressure since the crisis of 2008, and the centralized Judiciary is still a problem, which shows the burden of the historical matrix of Spanish regionalism and its shortcomings, strongly underlined during the Catalan crisis of the last decade, when notorious tensions between different assumptions about constitutional identity, self-government and democracy were at display.[7] The known narratives on the construction of the Spanish liberal state as homogeneous nation of citizens and on the intrinsic diversity driving to a need of decentralisation are still feeding an unresolved tension providing a permanent source of political unrest.

of the federal units in Switzerland (cantons), with 1, and Germany (*Länder*), with 0,867, but above the results of Austria (0) and Belgium (0,067), both federal states. The level of shared judicial government between the central state and the subcentral unities is relatively low (0,333 for the Basque Country, Navarre, Ceuta and Melilla; and 0,167 for the rest), compared with the other federal states in Europe: Switzerland (1), Germany (1), Belgium (0,722), and Austria (0,500), according to Vallbé, ibid 226. Overall, it seems that empirically the Spanish Judiciary has a lower level of decentralisation than other decentralised states in Europe, with exception of Italy which renders 0 in the first coefficient and 0,167 in the second one.

7 The recentralization in the Spanish constitutional system has been hastened since the global financial crisis of 2008, linked to a wide range of measures of economic stimulus (and doubtful environmental sensitiveness) promoted by the Spanish central government. See on this, Jordi Jaria-Manzano, 'Constitución, desarrollo y medio ambiente en un contexto de crisis' [2017] Revista Catalana de Dret Ambiental 23ff <https://revistes.urv.cat/index.php/rcda/article/view/1810> accessed 19 January 2023.

Provided that in the constitutional process Judiciary has not undergone major change from the institutional point of view, the question arises whether it is actually suitable to adapt to deep transformations in the distribution of political power and, particularly, to the existence of a plurality of regulations provided by the autonomous communities. Thus, governing the Judiciary in a sensitive way according to territorial diversity is still a problematic aspect of the Spanish constitutional regime, which seems to have failed in adapting the jurisdiction to the cultural and legal plurality of the system. In fact, it seems that Judiciary has preserved to some extent the traditional centripetal dynamics of the previous Spanish constitutional regimes. This reveals how even a new constitutional framework seems to experience some path dependency and this seems to stress the importance of local context and background in the design and performance of each decentralised state.

To some extent, the intrinsic tension between the decentralisation process and the existence of a unitary Judiciary shows the ultimate contradiction between the historical project of the state-building in Spain as a process of modernisation and the existence of centrifugal dynamics that this project never achieved to eliminate, but that rather were encapsulated in the current Constitution to some extent. I will try to show this considering the pathway of the Judiciary in the Spanish constitutional history and its influence in the design provided by the Constitution of 1978, underlining its remarkable unsuitability to adapt to the pluralism created by the process of decentralisation, to show how historical dynamics affect the development of any system of territorial distribution of power and how path dependence can impede a long-term constitutional agreement to deal with diversity.

## 2 The Building Process of the Spanish Liberal State and the Design of the Judiciary

The reputation of Spanish judges during the *ancient régime* was not particularly good. An example for this is given by a French public servant during the Napoleonic occupation. The count Pelets de la Lozère, state councillor in charge of the 2nd *arrondissement* of the General Police of the Empire states the following in his *Rapport général sur la situation du Département des Bouches de l'Ebre*:

> Parmi les causes qui ont précipité le Royaume d'Espagne vers sa chute, on doit compter la corruption de l'ordre Judiciaire. La vénalité des charges avait amené la vénalité des Juges. Dans les dernières années du Régné de

Charles IV et à l'époque de la faveur du Prince de la Paix, la Justice s'achetait dans presque tous les Tribunaux supérieurs. (...) Là des Juges corrompus, sous le prétexte de défendre l'innocence opprimée, renvoyaient les coupables absolus, et avilissaient ainsi l'autorité et le caractère des Juges particuliers. On cite un grand nombre de jugements rendus par Royales Audiences de l'Espagne et de la Catalogne qui tous portent l'empreinte de la corruption des Juges.

[Among the causes which precipitated the Kingdom of Spain towards its fall, we must count the corruption of the Judiciary. The venality of the offices had brought the venality of the Judges. In the last years of the Reign of Charles IV and at the period of the favour of the Prince of the Peace, Justice was bought in almost all the Superior Courts. (...) During this time, corrupt Judges, under the pretence of defending oppressed innocence, dismissed the absolute culprits, and thus degraded the authority and character of the particular Judges. A large number of judgments rendered by Royal Audiences of Spain and Catalonia are cited, all of which bear the imprint of the corruption of the Judges.][8]

Given the situation of venality and corruption of Judiciary in modern Spain, the selection of judges was a controversial issue during the first decades of Spanish constitutionalism. Accordingly, the first Spanish Constitution (1812) confronted this situation with certain provisions. In Art 251 it foresaw that in order to be appointed as judge, applicants needed to have the Spanish citizenship and be at least 25 years old, but deferred any supplementary condition to the laws. In any case, it was clear that the Constitution envisaged a unified Judiciary, according to mechanical rationalism and the idea of a single legal order that inspired its drafters.[9]

However, the regulation of the selection of the members of Judiciary did not improve in the following decades, amid a messy constitutional situation with ordinary political violence, particularly during the decade of the thirties, with the first Carlist War.[10] In this context, there was a strong dependence of

---

8 Reproduced by Lluís M. de Puig i Oliver, *La identitat catalana en temps de Napoleó (1808–1814)* (Generalitat de Catalunya 2015) 322.

9 See Miguel Ángel García Herrera, 'Constitución de Cádiz y forma de Estado' in Juan Mª. Terradillos Basoco (ed), *La Constitución de 1812: Reflexiones jurídicas en la víspera del Bicentenario* (Diputación de Cádiz 2006) 32.

10 The Constitution of 1812 was in force until the return of King Ferdinand VII in 1814. It was restored in 1820 to be again abrogated in 1823. In 1834 the Royal Statute was passed

the appointed judges to the Executive branch, raising new doubts about the integrity and the impartiality of judges. Consequently, the ideal of a unified single professional body of judges gained approval in Spanish political scene as far as it was associated to the consolidation of a modern liberal state as a collective goal. For this reason, the solution of the judicial question became strongly linked to the construction of a unitary nation-state and, consequently, appeared in an inherent tension regarding the existing cultural and political diversity, particularly in some territories as the Basque Country and Catalonia.

Since the Constitution of 1812, the dominant goal in the development of Spanish constitutionalism is '*eliminar la tan temida y denostada pluralidad de fueros y sus perniciosos efectos en los tribunales* [to eliminate the much feared and reviled plurality of laws and its pernicious effects in the courts]', with the final aim of providing legal certainty and thus helping in the development of a modern capitalist economy.[11] Therefore, unity is linked to security and modernization. Thus, the Judiciary acquires a leading role in this process and, for this reason, its configuration becomes a sensitive issue in the 19th century Spain.

The selection of judges remained a problem until the Constitution of 1869, which bolstered a decisive change in the process of the selection of judges, with the introduction of a public examination process required for becoming a judge (with some exceptions that have existed in various forms until today, in any case remaining more or less residual).[12] This system of access had a

---

as a new Constitution, when in 1837 the Constitution of 1812 was put into force again to be substituted by a new Constitution in the same year, which was a full-fledged amendment of the one of 1812. In 1845, the Constitution of 1837 was substituted by a far more conservative Constitution in accordance with the hegemonic political forces of the time. This Constitution lasted until 1868, but was on the verge to be repealed by a new, more liberal Constitution in 1856, which although being completely drafted and conveniently approved, failed to enter into force.

11 See Clara Álvarez Alonso, 'Un rey, una ley, una religión (goticismo y constitución histórica en el debate constitucional gaditano)' [2000] Historia Constitucional 1, 18 <https://www.historiaconstitucional.com/index.php/historiaconstitucional/article/view/106/90> accessed 26 July 2023.

12 Art 94 of the 1869 Constitution provided the following: '*El Rey nombra los Magistrados y Jueces a propuesta del Consejo de Estado y con arreglo a la ley orgánica de Tribunales. El ingreso en la carrera judicial será por oposición. Sin embargo, el Rey podrá nombrar hasta la cuarta parte de Magistrados de las Audiencias y del Tribunal Supremo sin sujeción a lo dispuesto en el párrafo anterior, ni a las reglas generales de la ley orgánica de Tribunales pero siempre con audiencia del Consejo de Estado y dentro de las categorías que para estos casos establezca la referida ley.* [The King appoints the Magistrates and Judges at the proposal of the Council of State and in accordance with the Organic Act of Courts. Public examination will be the way of access to a judicial career. However, the King may appoint up to a quarter of the Magistrates of the Provincial Courts and the Supreme Court without being subject to the provisions of the preceding paragraph, nor to the general rules of the

powerful appeal, given the situation of political interference and corruption of the Judiciary at that moment, as far as it seemed to guarantee a certain objectivity in the selection and a particular proficiency regarding the selected ones. With this, a '*modelo burocrático de juez* [bureaucratic model of judge]'[13] was implemented. Accordingly, each judge is part of a public professional body that is accessed through a competitive public tender, where the legal knowledge of the candidate is assessed (or intended to be assessed).

The framework provided by the Constitution of 1869 was concretised in the provisional Act for the Organisation of the Judicial Branch the following year. Despite its 'provisional' status, this act was in force for more than a century, in different regimes as the Bourbon Restoration, the Second Republic and the Francoism. It was finally derogated in 1985. During this long period of time, the 1870 Act shaped the Spanish Judiciary and, particularly, contributed to the consolidation of a nationwide professional body of judges associated with political modernization and legal rationalisation. The Constitution of 1978, currently in force, did not implement any substantial modification regarding this historical configuration of the Judiciary, besides the obvious impact of the substantial changes in law derived from the transition from an authoritarian regime to a liberal democracy.

The 1870 Act had shaped the Spanish Judiciary in its main features, unaltered with the end of the Franco's dictatorship and the political transition that led to the current Constitution. Its main goal was to overcome the politicization and the interference of the Executive in the selection of judges, as far as this damaged their independence and prolonged the reviled state of corruption of the Judiciary already mentioned. One of the main measures to achieve a profound reformation was the implementation of a competitive access procedure, where the merit and ability of applicants should be examined, as pointed out above.

Public examination was strengthened as the predominant, almost exclusive, way of access to the judicial career during the last third of the 19th century and the first decade of the 20th century. Once effectively implemented, this system of selection allowed to consolidate a professional body of judges, despite the constitutional instability, creating a corporatist culture, based in the inner conviction that the selection process guaranteed the independence and skills of

---

Organic Act of Courts, but always with a hearing of the Council of State and within the categories that the aforementioned act establishes for these cases.]'.

13 See Rafael Jiménez Asensio, 'El acceso a la judicatura en España: evolución histórica, situación actual y propuestas de cambio' in Consejo General del Poder Judicial (ed), *El acceso a la función judicial: estudio comparado* (Consejo General del Poder Judicial 2001) 150.

the members of the Judiciary.[14] The prestige of the system of selection and the resulting body of professional judges increased over time, granting judges an image of professionalism and independence, which enabled them to become guarantors of the rule of law, even during Franco's dictatorship.

The existence of a single national body of professional judges, selected through a process which had gained a significant social approval, was perceived as a guarantee of professional proficiency and reliability and, consequently, of the equality of all citizens before the law. The exceptions of the public examination system required for the access to a judicial career were few and little significant, as the so-called *cuarto turno*, introduced during the Restoration, by the Act of 14 October 1882, allowing legal professionals with a consolidated career to be appointed as judges by the Executive.[15] Nevertheless, even the judges selected outside the public examination process were immovable and could get promoted according to criteria of seniority. Nevertheless, the Executive retained control regarding the appointment of Supreme Court judges.[16] Thus, the alternatives to the public examination did not modify the unity of the Judiciary.

In reality, the *cuarto turno* during the Bourbon Restoration showed a notorious politicization compared to the public examination, therefore justifying criticism. This gave way to a wide prevention regarding the alternatives to the public examination, consolidated through the years to result into significant reticence to any attempt in modifying the essential features of the design of the Judiciary as a single professional body and providing other ways of becoming a judge, particularly to legal professionals. Career judges are extremely reluctant to any reform affecting their configuration as a single national body as well as the system of selection that they had to pass. As far as public examination is perceived by them as a guarantee of their independence and proficiency, any attempt to reform is met with suspicion, if not rejection, by most of them and their professional associations.[17]

In any case, the unfortunate practice of the Restoration almost decisively eroded the possibilities of establishing ways of access different to public

14 See Jordi Jaria-Manzano, 'Selección, perfil profesional y formación inicial de los jueces en España' [2011] Revista De Educación Y Derecho <https://revistes.ub.edu/index.php/RED/article/view/1780> accessed 26 July 2023.

15 See Íñigo Cavero Lataillade, 'Artículo 122. La estructura organizativa del Poder Judicial' in Óscar Alzaga Villaamil (ed), *Comentarios a la Constitución española de 1978*, vol IX (Edersa 1998) 447.

16 See Jiménez Asensio (n 13) 150f.

17 See Jaria-Manzano (n 14) 4.

examination, a circumstance that influences the discussion about the design of the Judiciary even today, without much reason, since, obviously, politicization is not inherent to design alternative ways of access to the Judiciary, particularly regarding accredited legal professionals, who can contribute to open a mostly self-referential judicial profession. Indeed, public examination is invested with a nearly initiatory character that allows entry into an almost priestly body. The candidate, who passes the test, is considered invested with a sufficient professional training, which legitimizes her before society, and all-encompassing legal knowledge, which enables her to exercise jurisdiction in any imaginable field.[18]

Regarding the aim of this paper, it is important to keep the link between public examination, professional proficiency, rule of law and unity in mind, because this relation is crucial in the reception of the historical design of the Judiciary in the current Constitution and in the tensions that this creates regarding political decentralisation and cultural and legal pluralism. Consequently, reluctance regarding any attempt of reforming the Judiciary to adapt it to the necessities of decentralisation is strongly based in the dominant professional culture and the commonly shared beliefs about the adequacy of the historical design of the Judiciary as the ultimate guarantee of the rule of law.

To close this section, it should be remembered, that the two experiences of decentralisation in the Spanish contemporary history, during the First (1873–1874) and the Second Republic (1931–1939), have left little impression in the design of the Judiciary. The First Republic lasted too short and was too close to the Act of 1870 to leave any significant footprint. During the Second Republic, a Catalan Supreme Court (*Tribunal de cassació*) existed between 1934 and 1939, formed with judges selected among senior legal professionals without judicial background, as barristers or academics, but this experience was also forgotten when it came to decide on the design of the Judiciary in the Constitution of 1978, as we will see in the next section.

## 3 Judicial Unity and Political Decentralisation: A Permanent Challenge for the Constitutional System

As seen in the previous section, the existence of this single body of judges, fully consolidated over time and justified by the need to escape old malpractices,

18 See Alejandro Saiz Arnaiz, *La reforma del acceso a la carrera judicial en España: algunas propuestas* (Fundación Alternativas 2007) 16.

has been strengthened and did not experience any particular affectation with the entry into force of the Constitution of 1978, despite the fact that the new political regime opened the door to a significant process of political decentralisation. Art 122.1 of the Constitution creates, or rather accepts, a single body of professional judges, as it already existed. In fact, according to the constitutional principle of jurisdictional unity, no real decentralisation is possible regarding the Judiciary, which is configured as a single national body of career judges, as it has been usual since 1869.[19] In any case, the Constitution forbids a Judiciary of the Autonomous Communities, so that there is a single unitary Judiciary with full jurisdiction.[20]

Although a link between the national body of professional judges and the system of access was firmly established through public examination, the Constitution does not include any reference to the latter.[21] So, in principle, given the uniqueness of the Judiciary, there is no particular regulation in the Constitution preventing the adaption of the selection and training of judges to the pluralism created by the process of decentralisation. Even if the public examination system is not constitutionalized, the pre-existent judicial professional culture and organization is preserved to a great extent.[22] As a result, the new constitutional regime receives, justifies and consolidates the existing structure, including the design of the access and the career, which remains untouched.

The preservation of the main historical features of the Judiciary in the Constitution of 1978 is due to the relevance of the judicial unity in order to guarantee the rule of law, as it has been traditional since the 19th century, showing a surreptitious mistrust regarding decentralisation and heralding the intrinsic tension between centripetal and centrifugal dynamics in the system. From the organisational point of view, the most significant innovation of the Constitution of 1978 is the creation of a specific institution governing the Judiciary, the *Consejo General del Poder Judicial* (General Council of the

---

19 See Rosado Iglesias (n 5) 55.

20 See José-Pascual Ortells Ramos, 'La distribución territorial del poder del Estado como presupuesto constitucional de la reforma del Poder judicial' (1989) 2 Revista del Centro de Estudios Políticos y Constitucionales 265, 267.

21 See Jiménez Asensio (n 13) 162; Saiz Arnaiz (n 18) 7.

22 The fascination exerted by the public examination, both for the judges themselves and for many others, has led some authors to consider that it is constitutionalized, despite the fact that the Constitution obviously does not refer to it, nor to any another selection system for the Judiciary. See, for example, Jorge de Esteban, 'El Poder Judicial. Comentario introductorio al Título VI' in Óscar Alzaga Villaamil (ed), *Comentarios a la Constitución española de 1978*, vol IX (Edersa 1998) 272.

Judiciary), which has certain competences regarding the selection of judges (Art 122.2 CE).

In fact, a key element of the consensus for providing a seamless and pacific transition from Franco's dictatorship to a liberal democracy was to leave the existent public service structure untouched.[23] In case of the Judiciary this implied the conservation of the national body of judges, including the judges appointed during the dictatorship remaining in office. Accordingly, while some public servants working for the national Government were transferred to the newly created Autonomous Communities, which was the first step in the creation of the public service in each of them, judges remained a closed unified body with a high self-esteem derived from the prestige of the system of access to the career and rather refractory to the decentralisation process developed during the political transition and boosted by the Constitution of 1978. There is a Superior Court in each Autonomous Community since 1989, but it is part of the national Judiciary and its members are selected among judges, with an exception I will mention below.

It can hardly be surprising that, despite no particular constitutional provision referring to it, the traditional system of access by public examination remained untouched in the new regime. When the longstanding Act of 1870 was substituted by the new Organic Act of the Judiciary of 1985 (LOPJ), the traditional system of selection and promotion of judges was maintained, without taking into account the deep changes implied by the Constitution of 1978, particularly regarding the process of political decentralisation. Art 301.3 LOPJ establishes that '[*e*]*l ingreso en la Carrera Judicial por la categoría de juez se producirá mediante la superación de oposición libre y de un curso teórico y práctico de selección realizado en la Escuela Judicial* [the admission to the Judicial Career for the category of judge depends on passing a public examination process and then a theoretical and practical selection course held at the Judicial School]'.

This is important, because, even if the Constitution consecrates the unity of the Judiciary, contrasting with the decentralisation of the other two branches of government, there is no constitutional obligation of maintaining its specific historical features, particularly the system of selection. Its preservation secures that any significant consequence of decentralisation is expected to have an impact on Judiciary. We will see how the inertia of the tradition prevents

23 The 1977 Amnesty Act did not only extinguish the criminal responsibilities of those who had opposed the regime, but also of those corresponding to those who had committed crimes as public officials during the dictatorship, showing how little public administration was affected within the transition process to the current political regime.

judicial adaptation to the new territorial organisation and becomes one of the most salient elements of the tension between centripetal dynamics of Spanish constitutional history and the centrifugal tendencies encapsulated in the recognition of the right to self-government of 'nationalities and regions', according to Art 2 of the Constitution.

Art 301.7 LOPJ provides that '[*e*]*l Ministerio de Justicia, en colaboración, en su caso, con las comunidades autónomas competentes, podrá instar del Consejo General del Poder Judicial la convocatoria de las oposiciones, concursos y pruebas selectivas de promoción y de especialización necesarios para la cobertura de las vacantes existentes en la plantilla de la Carrera Judicial* [the Ministry of Justice, in collaboration, where appropriate, with the Autonomous Communities with corresponding powers, may urge the General Council of the Judiciary to call public examinations, competitions and selective tests for promotion and specialization necessary to cover existing vacancies in the staff of the Judicial Career]'. However, this provision has had little effect. The selection of judges is centralized and the system of public examination is still the main way of access. As far as this system is crucial in providing the professional culture and the legal knowledge to judges, it is worth to see how it works currently.

The last call for participation in the public examination process (Resolution of the Selection Committee of 28 October 2021) included 328 topics in different legal fields as constitutional law, private law, criminal law, etc. Items related to decentralisation were only mentioned in four of them.[24] In fact, the structure and subjects of the examination have been pretty much the same for years and the relevance of the law of the Autonomous Communities is not considered as relevant knowledge for future judges, giving a clear proof of the imperviousness of the selection process to the political decentralisation. As Fernández de Frutos has pointed out, '*cabe dudar de que en solo cuatro temas se pueda condensar la complejidad del Estado autonómico, y que la referencia a los derechos propios de las CC. AA. como un subapartado de un tema permita tener una visión real de la diversidad y amplitud de la regulación del derecho propio por las diferentes CC. AA.* [it is doubtful that the complexity of the decentralised State can be condensed in only four topics, and that the reference to the law of the different Autonomous Communities as a subsection of a particular lesson allows to have a real vision of the diversity and breadth of these different laws]'.[25]

24 See Marta Elena Fernández de Frutos, 'La incidencia del Estado autonómico en la selección y formación de jueces y magistrados' (2022) 35 Revista d'Estudis Autonòmics i Federals 239, 247.

25 ibid 247f.

The evolution of the selection process since 1985 clearly shows that the idea of a single national body of judges with little sensitiveness to pluralism and diversity has been reinforced while the decentralisation process advanced and consolidated. Since 1985, there has been no significant process in the design of a system for admission to the Judiciary; the system rather seems to be drawn into the past. The White Paper on Justice, approved by the plenary session of the General Council of the Judiciary on 8 September 1997, did not discuss the public examination as entrance to the judicial career, although it suggested the advisability of completing mere knowledge with other aspects, such as argumentation skills or legal culture. However, the system of access is not questioned profoundly.[26]

Once the candidate has passed the public examination, she has to follow the courses at Judicial School, where training is uniform with no particular attention to the place where the new judge should serve and where probably not only some legal specificities but full-fledged bodies of law in many areas and also an official language different from Spanish-Castilian exist.[27] With this background, the new judge is assigned to a concrete position in a courthouse, with an understandable lack of knowledge of the particular law and language (if there is one different from Spanish-Castilian) of the Autonomous Community where the courthouse is located, as there is no specific preparation for it.[28] Even more, when a judge takes her position in a particular Autonomous Community, there is no particular training regarding regional law.[29] The only impact of the legal (and cultural) diversity of the state in the assignation of the first position of the new judge is that those who have a proven knowledge of the law or the language of a particular Autonomous Community have preference to obtain a position there.[30]

This is a problem in some Autonomous Communities and, particularly in Catalonia, because there are only few local lawyers who decide to take the public examination to enter a judicial career. For this reason, most judges

26 See Consejo General del Poder Judicial, *Libro Blanco de la Justicia* (Consejo General del Poder Judicial 1997) 18ff.

27 See Fernández de Frutos (n 24) 260.

28 The previous knowledge about the law of a particular Autonomous Community, obtained for example by getting a law degree from a University located there, is only considered a qualification for obtaining a position in a courtroom as far as it is limited to private law, which only exists in few Autonomous Communities, while in the majority of them the private law in force is the Spanish Civil Code. Public law of the Autonomous Communities is simply ignored.

29 See Fernández de Frutos (n 24) 265.

30 ibid 250.

in Catalonia come from other Autonomous Communities and opt to leave Catalonia to their own region as soon as possible. Therefore, not only few judges are familiar with local law and language, but there is also a persistent lack of judges to the extent that Marta Elena Fernández de Frutos has spoken of judicial desertification in Catalonia.[31]

The problems caused by this general structure of selection and training are not solved with a certain process of access where local professionals have the possibility of acceding to the Judiciary. Actually, a particular way of access for local professionals to the civil and criminal division of the Superior Court in each Autonomous Community has been implemented through Art 330.4 LOPJ, according to which one out of three positions should be attributed to a renowned lawyer with more than ten years of professional practice in the Autonomous Community, selected by the General Council of the Judiciary from a list of three people proposed by the Parliament of the concerned Autonomous Community. This clearly seems not enough to secure an adequate knowledge of the law of the Autonomous Communities by the judges.

Consequently, although the power has been decentralised and the Autonomous Communities have generated their own legal systems with significant regulations in different areas of social life, the Judiciary has not only remained a unitary organisation, but has preserved a system of selection and training of its members which contributes very little in guaranteeing the knowledge of the law of the Autonomous Communities as well as the language in some of them, where Spanish (Castilian) is the official language along with the local language (Catalan, Basque or Galician), despite some concrete measures with little impact.[32]

As a consequence – provided that the judges gained the needed legal knowledge and professional culture during the process of selection and training – the bench is mostly unreceptive, even if the law of the Autonomous Communities is broadly applied by the territorial governments. Moreover, citizens in Autonomous Communities with an official language different from Spanish-Castilian can hardly take actions before courts in their own language, because there is no obligation for the judges to know any other language than

31 ibid 257f.

32 Regarding this, the Committee of Ministers of the Council of Europe has issued a number of recommendations since 2005 (the last of them in 2019), warning the Kingdom of Spain about its lack of compliance of the European Charter for Regional or Minority Languages in the field of justice. See Íñigo Urrutia Libarona, 'Administración de Justicia, doble oficialidad lingüística y derecho fundamental a la tutela judicial efectiva' (2022) 35 Revista d'Estudis Autonòmics i Federals 283, 309ff.

Spanish-Castilian and many of them are incapable of writing a judgment in an official language different from Spanish-Castilian.[33] As a result, the intrinsic tension between a unitary Judiciary and a decentralised legislation as consecrated in the Constitution has been sharpened over the years.

To add complexity to the situation, a strongly centralized professional body of judges meets a highly decentralised administrative support for the Judiciary. The judicial office, ie the administrative structure and the material support of each court, depends of the Autonomous Communities, with the exception of the Supreme Court and the *Audiencia Nacional*, a singular court with competence within the whole Spanish territory which is a residue of the judicial organisation of the dictatorship that is preserved although contested by many. Despite the Constitution assigning the administration of justice to the central institutions of the State, the Constitutional Court has accepted the competence of the Autonomous Communities regarding the administrative support to the Judiciary (introduced by the first Statutes of Autonomy, ie the Basque and the Catalan ones in 1979).[34]

## 4 The Shadow of History on a Doomed Reform

As explained in the previous section, it seems clear that there is a gap between the decentralised structure of the government and the imperviousness of the Judiciary regarding legal and cultural diversity, particularly regarding official languages different from Spanish-Castilian. Even if this gap is to some extent structural to the constitutional framework, achieving some kind of adaptation of the Judiciary to the reality of decentralisation has been discussed over the years. As the amendment of the Spanish Constitution is certainly very difficult,[35] the most realistic way to solve the problem would be legal reforms to improve the sensibility of the Judiciary to diversity, allowing a wider knowledge and application of the law of the Autonomous Communities and the use of the official languages different from Spanish-Castilian in the courts.

---

33 If we take, eg, Catalan language in Catalonia, statistical data shows that there were 14.455 judgments in Catalan (7.44 % of the total) in 2020, with a clear downward trend since 2004, when the maximum percentage of 20.63 % was reached. See Fernández de Frutos (n 24) 275.

34 ibid 242.

35 See Jordi Jaria-Manzano, 'La defensa de la Constitució com a relat i la crisi constitucional catalana' (2020) 31 Revista d'Estudis Autonòmics i Federals 65, 74ff.

In the first decade of this century, there was a serious attempt to improve the adaptation of the Judiciary to the decentralised structure of the government without touching the Constitution. This attempt was made through the reform of some statutes of autonomy, particularly the Catalan one, passed in 2006. The new Catalan Statute provided a detailed regulation of a singular institution, the *Consell de Justícia de Catalunya* (Council of Justice of Catalonia), conceived as an arm of the CGPJ, to which the Constitution attributes the government of the Judiciary, and some other provisions trying to improve the sensitiveness of the judges in Catalonia to local law and language. Before the new Catalan Statute, some authors had defended the idea of such a council as a possible way to promote the decentralisation process started with the Constitution of 1978 and the traditional unity of the Judiciary.[36]

Moreover, as underlined by the lawyers representing the Catalan Parliament before the Constitutional Court, the Council of Justice was not only conceived as an arm of the CGPJ, but also vested with merely consultive attributions carefully designed in accordance with the final decision power of the CGPJ and partly deferred to a further regulation in the LOPJ.[37] In this vein, the Catalan Council was not conceived as a Catalan institution, but as a body integrated in the CGPJ, similar to the so-called peripheral administration of the central government, which is located in a particular demarcation, as, for example, in an Autonomous Community, but integrated into the structure of the government.[38]

However, the Catalan Statute was challenged before the Constitutional Court, among others, by the MPs of the *Partido Popular*, a conservative and nationalist party, in the opposition at that time. The regulation on justice was one of the controversial issues addressed in the claim lodged by the conservative MPs.[39] Among many other things, the decision of the Constitutional

36 See Juan Antonio Xiol Ríos, 'Evaluación de los aspectos relacionados con la Administración de justicia en una futura reforma del Estatuto de Autonomía de Catalunya' in Institut d'Estudis Autonòmics (ed), *Estudios sobre la reforma del Estatuto* (Institut d'Estudis Autonòmics 2004) 269ff.

37 See Allegations of the Lawyers of the Parliament of Catalonia in the procedure of unconstitutionality on the Statute of Autonomy of Catalonia, delivered to the Constitutional Court on 30 July 2007 (2007) 215 <https://www.parlament.cat/document/actualitat/150159.pdf> accessed 26 July 2023.

38 See Mariano Baena de Alcázar, 'Artículo 103.1 y 2. Los principios reguladores y la estructura de la Administración' in Óscar Alzaga Villaamil (ed), *Comentarios a la Constitución española de 1978*, vol VIII (Edersa 1998) 407.

39 The Statute of Autonomy of Andalusia of 2007 included similar provisions on justice, also establishing a Council of Justice, but was never contested for this reason. In fact, it was passed by the *Cortes Generales*, the Spanish Parliament, with the support of the same MPs who challenged the Statute of Autonomy of Catalonia.

Court on the Catalan Statute defined a series of limits regarding the possibility of adapting the Judiciary to the decentralised structure derived from the Constitution, leaving most of the challenged provisions without effect, as far as they contradicted the Constitution.[40]

As a starting point of its judgment, the Constitutional Court endorsed a particular interpretation of the principle of jurisdictional unity, connecting this principle with the unity of sovereignty which is the basis of the Spanish Constitution.[41] From this, the Constitutional Court considers that there is no room for a Catalan Council of Justice, even if it was an arm of the CGPJ, as foreseen in the Statute. However, the Constitutional Court did not eliminate the Council but arguably change its competences.[42] The Court especially considered that the Catalan Council shall not have the power to: i) take part in the appointment of the chair of different courts; ii) appoint and dismiss temporary judges; iii) hold disciplinary competences regarding judges; iv) oversee the courts; and v) inform about appeals concerning administrative decisions of judges and courts in Catalonia.[43]

In any case, the attempt to combine the unity of the Judiciary with the diversity of laws and languages by taking them into account through a body depending on the CGPJ but based in Catalonia was fully disabled with the decision of the Constitutional Court. Nevertheless, the judgment of the Constitutional Court opened the door to the possibility of creating decentralised arms of the

40 See STC 31/2010.

41 ibid para 42. Art 1.2 of the Constitution attributes the sovereignty to the Spanish people. Accordingly, the self-rule of the Autonomous Communities is not original, as of the American states or the Swiss cantons, but derived from the Constitution, particularly from Art 2. As a consequence, the statutes of autonomy require the consent of the Spanish *Cortes* to enter into force, which differs from to the constitutions of the members of a federal state.

42 In his dissenting opinion to the judgment of the Constitutional Court (ibid para 11), Judge Javier Delgado Barrio pointed out the following: '*La Sentencia declara, y estoy de acuerdo, que es inconstitucional el Consejo de Justicia en cuanto órgano de gobierno del Poder Judicial y en cuanto órgano desconcentrado del Consejo General del Poder Judicial, que es lo único que el Consejo de Justicia es según el Estatuto, pero la Sentencia inventa un órgano nuevo, un Consejo de Justicia que es otra cosa, – un órgano de la Generalitat – para ejercer algunas de las funciones del Consejo de Justicia que creaba el Estatuto.* [The Judgment declares, and I do agree, that the Council of Justice as a governing body of the Judiciary and as a decentralised body of the General Council of the Judiciary, which is the only thing that the Council of Justice is according to the Statute, is unconstitutional, but the Judgment invents a new body, a Council of Justice that is something else – an organ of the Catalan Government – to exercise some of the functions of the Council of Justice that the Statute created.]'.

43 ibid para 48.

CGPJ in the different Autonomous Communities by amending the LOPJ, as far as it concluded that this decision cannot be made in the statutes of autonomy, but it is not constitutionally forbidden if the correct legal source is used.

In conclusion, the judgment of the Constitutional Court on the Catalan Statute almost eliminated all the innovations regarding the Judiciary, leaving the things mostly the same as they were before. During the long processing of the appeal, the reluctance of a significant part of the judges to any intervention of the Autonomous Communities in the Judiciary was also very transparent. The burden of the tradition and a strongly proud characterised professional culture have contributed to prevent any attempt to introduce provisions more friendly to decentralisation in the Judiciary until today. Currently, no constitutional amendment to transform the Judicial Branch is on the agenda and the debate about less ambitious reforms is extremely weak.

Until today, this possibility has not even been explored and the centripetal dynamics of the Judiciary have been maintained, if not even grown. The importance traditionally given to the unity of the Judiciary as a guarantee of the rule of law and the existence of a professional body of judges selected through a competitive procedure at national level have been decisive in the interpretation of the Constitution by the Constitutional Court, which has opted for sustaining the dynamics of tension in the system rather than soften them.

## 5 Final Remarks

Beyond the messy question of definition, two fundamental approaches can be delineated regarding federalism (or decentralisation). It can be seen as a technique or as a result. Federalism (or decentralisation) as a technique is related with the idea of manipulating the reality to achieve some goal. This approach starts from the assumption that there is a more or less open set of organisational tools to be applied to any reality in order to provide a sort of equilibrium between centripetal and centrifugal tendencies. This approach justifies the transplant of institutions, processes and rules, as far as they are supposed to offer a desired outcome in any given case.

Contrarily, federalism (or decentralisation) can be interpreted as a result. It is then attached to the idea that each system of decentralisation is the consequence of a complex set of factors that give a path-dependent solution, subjected to further tensions depending on how successful the difficult balance of these factors is. In this second view, each system is unique to some extent, with intrinsic genuine solutions. Accordingly, even accepting that some inspiration can be found in other models of decentralisation, this perspective stresses the necessity to understand the historical conditions of a given system in order to design solutions to achieve a particular outcome.

Spain has failed to undergo a real and robust decentralisation, asymmetric and evolutionary, in order to respond to the challenges posed both by the need of improving institutional performance in a world in crisis, and by particular demands of singular solutions, as existing in Catalonia and in the Basque Country.[44] There is an intrinsic and non-resolved tension between the unitary principle central to the process of political modernisation in Spain and the decentralisation process initiated with the Constitution of 1978. The most conspicuous feature of the well established link between unification and modernisation (ie, rationalisation) is the construction and consolidation of a unified body of judges.

According with the fundamental hallmarks characterizing the Judiciary in Spain, it has been mostly reluctant to integrate the consequences of the decentralisation process, even within the limits of the Constitution. The question remains unresolved and the strongly centralized configuration of the Judiciary prompts to significant shortcomings in the integration of (cultural and legal) diversity in the constitutional system. The tension between decentralised governments and unitary Judiciary in Spain shows the importance of political history in the construction, success and eventual failure of federal or quasi-federal covenants, and marks the fundamental area of tension in the Spanish regional state, which undergoes a profound crisis since a couple of decades.

## Bibliography

Allegations of the Lawyers of the Parliament of Catalonia in the procedure of unconstitutionality on the Statute of Autonomy of Catalonia, delivered to the Constitutional Court on 30 July 2007 (2007) <https://www.parlament.cat/document/actualitat/150159.pdf> accessed 26 July 2023.

Álvarez Alonso C, 'Un rey, una ley, una religión (goticismo y constitución histórica en el debate constitucional gaditano)' [2000] Historia Constitucional 1 <https://www.historiaconstitucional.com/index.php/historiaconstitucional/article/view/106/90> accessed 26 July 2023.

44 Spanish decentralisation certainly responded to different goals, and different actors imagined it in very different ways. See Pablo Lucas Verdú and Pablo Lucas Murillo de la Cueva, 'De la organización territorial del Estado. Comentario introductorio al Título VIII' in Óscar Alzaga Villaamil (ed), *Comentarios a la Constitución española de 1978*, vol X (Edersa 1998) 374.

Baena de Alcázar M, 'Artículo 103.1 y 2. Los principios reguladores y la estructura de la Administración' in Alzaga Villaamil Ó (ed), *Comentarios a la Constitución española de 1978*, vol VIII (Edersa 1998).

Cavero Lataillade Í, 'Artículo 122. La estructura organizativa del Poder Judicial' in Alzaga Villaamil Ó (ed), *Comentarios a la Constitución española de 1978*, vol IX (Edersa 1998).

Consejo General del Poder Judicial, *Libro Blanco de la Justicia* (Consejo General del Poder Judicial 1997).

De Esteban J, 'El Poder Judicial. Comentario introductorio al Título VI' in Alzaga Villaamil Ó (ed), *Comentarios a la Constitución española de 1978*, vol IX (Edersa 1998).

De Puig i Oliver LM, *La identitat catalana en temps de Napoleó (1808–1814)* (Generalitat de Catalunya 2015).

Fernández de Frutos ME, 'La incidencia del Estado autonómico en la selección y formación de jueces y magistrados' (2022) 35 Revista d'Estudis Autonòmics i Federals 239.

García Herrera MÁ, 'Constitución de Cádiz y forma de Estado' in Terradillos Basoco JM (ed), *La Constitución de 1812: Reflexiones jurídicas en la víspera del Bicentenario* (Diputación de Cádiz 2006).

Herrero de Miñón M, 'La posible diversidad de los modelos autonómicos en la Transición, en la Constitución española de 1978 y en los Estatutos de Autonomía' in Institut d'Estudis Autonòmics (ed), *Uniformidad o diversidad de las comunidades autónomas* (Viena Serveis Editorials 1995).

Jaria-Manzano J, 'Selección, perfil profesional y formación inicial de los jueces en España' [2011] Revista De Educación Y Derecho <https://revistes.ub.edu/index.php/RED/article/view/1780> accessed 26 July 2023.

Jaria-Manzano J, 'La independència com a procés constituent. Consideracions constitucionals sobre la creació d'un estat català' (2015) 22 Revista d'Estudis Autonòmics i Federals 184.

Jaria-Manzano J, 'Constitución, desarrollo y medio ambiente en un contexto de crisis' [2017] Revista Catalana de Dret Ambiental <https://revistes.urv.cat/index.php/rcda/article/view/1810> accessed 19 January 2023.

Jaria-Manzano J, 'La defensa de la Constitució com a relat i la crisi constitucional catalana' (2020) 31 Revista d'Estudis Autonòmics i Federals 65.

Jiménez Asensio R, 'El acceso a la judicatura en España: evolución histórica, situación actual y propuestas de cambio' in Consejo General del Poder Judicial (ed), *El acceso a la función judicial: estudio comparado* (Consejo General del Poder Judicial 2001).

Lucas Verdú P and Lucas Murillo de la Cueva P, 'De la organización territorial del Estado. Comentario introductorio al Título VIII' in Alzaga Villaamil Ó (ed), *Comentarios a la Constitución española de 1978*, vol X (Edersa 1998).

Ortells Ramos JP, 'La distribución territorial del poder del Estado como presupuesto constitucional de la reforma del Poder judicial' (1989) 2 Revista del Centro de Estudios Políticos y Constitucionales 265.

Rosado Iglesias G, '¿Es posible arbitrar fórmulas que acerquen el Poder Judicial a la realidad autonómica?' (2022) 35 Revista d'Estudis Autonòmics i Federals 53.

Saiz Arnaiz A, *La reforma del acceso a la carrera judicial en España: algunas propuestas* (Fundación Alternativas 2007).

Urrutia Libarona Í, 'Administración de Justicia, doble oficialidad lingüística y derecho fundamental a la tutela judicial efectiva' (2022) 35 Revista d'Estudis Autonòmics i Federals 283.

Vallbé JJ, 'Descentralización judicial regional. Una exploración empírica del poder judicial regional en Europa occidental' (2022) 35 Revista d'Estudis Autonòmics i Federals 195.

Xiol Ríos JA, 'Evaluación de los aspectos relacionados con la Administración de justicia en una futura reforma del Estatuto de Autonomía de Catalunya' in Institut d'Estudis Autonòmics (ed), *Estudios sobre la reforma del Estatuto* (Institut d'Estudis Autonòmics 2004).

CHAPTER 9

# The Making of Italian Regionalism

## *Foundation, Evolution and Perspective through a Compact among the Constituent Units*

*Paolo Colasante*

## 1 Premise: Where Do the Borders of the Italian Regions Come From?*

The decision to adopt a regional form of State is relatively recent in the Italian experience, as it dates back to the moment (1946–1947) when the Constituent Assembly was drafting the text of the Constitution which would constitute the fundamental Charter of the current Republic.

The reasons for this choice were various and, in summary, they can be traced back [1] to contingent political reasons to respond to autonomic tensions especially in some territories (Sicily, Sardinia and Valle d'Aosta), to prevent them from taking the form of secessionist requests; [2] to the heterogeneity of the country from both a geographical and socio-economic point of view; [3] to the desire to consolidate the regained democracy, as regionalism would have increased the participation of the populations concerned in political decisions, as well as facilitated a future reform of the central State.[1]

In outlining the borders of the Italian Regions, the Constituent Assembly did not adopt a historical-identity criterion, but relied on the territorial division

* Para 5 was added to the original version of the paper to tell about the recent developments concerning the implementation process of differentiated regionalism (Art 116 para 3 Italian Constitution).

1 See Antonio D'Atena, *Diritto regionale* (Giappichelli 2022) 10ff, as well as Sergio Bartole, 'Art. 116' in Giuseppe Branca (ed), *Commentario della Costituzione* (Zanichelli-Foro italiano 1985) 55ff and Paolo Giangaspero, 'La nascita delle Regioni speciali' in Stelio Mangiameli (ed), *Il regionalismo italiano dall'Unità alla Costituzione e alla sua riforma*, vol I (Giuffré 2012) 121ff. It is also useful to mention the following paper, which traces the 'seasons' of Italian special regionalism: Antonio D'Atena, 'Passato, presente … E futuro delle autonomie regionali speciali' [2014] Rivista AIC <https://www.rivistaaic.it/images/rivista/pdf/4_2014_D'Atena.pdf> accessed 26 July 2023; as well as Paolo Colasante, 'Unità e diversità nel (parziale) regionalismo asimmetrico italiano, alla luce della riforma costituzionale in itinere' [2015] Italian Papers on Federalism <https://www.ipof.it/wp-content/uploads/2021/06/Colasante-2015.pdf> accessed 25 July 2023.

© PAOLO COLASANTE, 2024 | DOI:10.1163/9789004528581_011

devised by Pietro Maestri in 1861 (subsequently revised in 1871[2]) used for statistical purposes only, as can be seen in the figure that follows.[3]

In fact, at the time of national unification, the project of subdividing the State into Regions was discarded and instead the Constituent Assembly opted for a unitary model inspired by the French one in which all powers belonged to the central government.

Nonetheless, a regional partition of the country was still necessary, albeit aimed at statistical purposes only and inspired by a principle of topographical cohesion, such as to make the compartments a mere grouping of provinces.[4]

The term Region (whose etymology dates back to the Latin verb 'regere' which means 'to govern') was then used for the first time in 1912 to rename the statistical compartments in the Italian Statistical Yearbook published in 1913. Since then, the Regions, even if not inserted in any way in the government structure of the State (neither to distribute the power of the central State over the territory, nor even as autonomous bodies), have officially become part of the Italian territorial division, albeit from a merely operational and statistical point of view.

2 See ISTAT, *Struttura e dinamica delle unità amministrative territoriali italiane – Dall'unificazione del Regno al 2017* (ISTAT 2018) *passim*. In fact, in the subdivision of 1861, the former Kingdom of the Two Sicilies included two statistical compartments: one coinciding with Sicily and the other coinciding with the entire continental part, therefore the South of Italy gave rise only to the statistical compartment of the 'Neapolitan Provinces', which roughly included the current Regions of Abruzzo, Molise, Campania, Puglia, Basilicata and Calabria. In 1871, this single compartment was then divided into the following: Abruzzi and Molise, Campania, Puglie, Basilicata and Calabria, all more or less coinciding with the current homonymous Regions, with the exception of the compartment of Abruzzi and Molise, which just at the beginning of the republican history coincided with the homonymous Region and was then split into the Abruzzi Region and the Molise Region with the constitutional law no 3 of 1963.

3 Taken from ibid 19.

4 ibid 52: 'This was the first statistical division of the Italian territory; the compartments thus defined were used for the official publications of the Central Statistical Office, a body directly subordinate to the State set up within the Ministry of Agriculture, Industry and Commerce. The statistical compartments were territorial subdivisions of a hierarchical level higher than the provinces, used for the first time for the dissemination of the data of 1861 census. They were born as a territorial structure designed exclusively for the publication of data, but they already appear as a disguised regional structure, being in any case made up of unions of provinces, grouped on the basis of territorial and socio-economic affinities. Therefore, it is immediately evident that statistical compartments and regions are different terms for identifying equivalent territorial aggregates. On the other hand, it can be stated that the regions, starting from 1861 and up to post-war period, were geographical entities considered exclusively as statistical units used for the dissemination of data'.

FIGURE 9.1 Territorial compartments of the Kingdom of Italy in 1871
SOURCE: ISTAT – ISTITUTO NAZIONALE DI STATISTICA (NATIONAL INSTITUTE OF STATISTICS).

Therefore, the Constituent Assembly, using the boundaries of the statistical compartments to delimit the territory of the new Regions of the Italian State as autonomous government entities, did not adopt an autonomous historical-identity criterion,[5] but relied on statistical principles (topographic, territorial,

5 Nonetheless, at least with reference to the special Regions, it is reasonable to think that a certain identity *idem sentire* existed since then due to their particular situation (island or border areas in which many communities were located), which, moreover, is the basis for the recognition of their different rate of autonomy.

socio-economic) which had guided a territorial division conducted for other purposes.

It has therefore been said[6] that in this case there is an *authoritative identification of the Regions* through an act of will of the constituent legislator and a consequent listing of the Regions, unlike, for example, the Spanish model, where the constitutional regulation provides for a bottom-up process of self-identification[7] of the *Comunidades Autònomas*.

Therefore, if one considers that the Italian State was founded in 1861 with a unitary approach and that, moreover, in 1946–1947 the foundation of the regional State took place 'from above', without valorizing any previous historical-identity division in any way, one easily reaches the conclusion that the Italian regional State neither was the result of a *Compact* (or *foedus*, if one prefers a Latin term) between Member States, as it cannot be traced back to the model of a federal State established through the aggregation of pre-existing States, nor of a – so to speak – anthropological-cultural *Compact*.

## 2 The Foundation of Federal States and Regional States and the Possible Declinations of the Compact among the Constituent Units

According to the classical theory, federal States are formed by aggregation, by virtue of an agreement – *Compact*,[8] according to the Anglo-Saxon expression, or *foedus* (pact), if one wishes to use the Latin lemma from which the modern word 'federation' derives – among pre-existing Member States[9] (*Constituent*

6 D'Atena 2022 (n 1) 32.

7 According to D'Atena 2022 (n 1) 32 that process 'avoids the greatest danger to which regionalization processes are exposed: the danger of the creation of artificial entities'. In relation to the issue of the Italian Regions as 'artificial' entities, see Carlo Desideri, *Regioni politiche e territori – Per una storia del regionalismo italiano* (Giuffré 2015) 101ff. On the Spanish regional self-identification process, see Omar Pallotta, 'Spagna' in Enzo Di Salvatore (ed), *Sistemi costituzionali europei* (Giuffré 2021) 388ff. This process is connected to the so-called *principio dispositivo*, on which see Enric Fossas Espadaler, *El principio dispositivo en el Estado autonòmico* (Marcial Pons Ediciones Jurídicas y Sociales 2007) *passim*.

8 In the recent literature on the concept of Compact for the creation of a federal State, it is worth mentioning the monographic work of David Benner, *Compact of the Republic – The League of States and The Constitution* (Life and Liberty Publishing Group 2015).

9 The issue has been investigated since the famous '*The Federalist Papers*', the 85 essays written between 1787 and 1788 by Alexander Hamilton, James Madison and John Jay using the pseudonym *Publius*. See for example no 39 (Madison): 'That it (the adoption of the Constitution) will be a federal and not a national act, as these terms are understood by the objectors, the act of the people as forming so many independent states, not as forming one aggregate nation is obvious from this single consideration, that it is to result neither from

*Units*), although there are federal experiences coming out from a historical itinerary exactly opposite to the traditional one and, therefore, they are the result not of a process of aggregation, but of decentralization of unitary States.[10]

Apart from the cases just mentioned, the American experience serves as a paradigm and historical precursor of all other federative processes that took place by aggregation.[11] Before the Federal Constitution of 1787, in fact thirteen sovereign entities (the former colonies) existed, which had proclaimed their independence in 1776 and, moreover, gave rise to an intermediate step, ie the Confederation (1777–1781), before uniting in the real federal State. The Confederation, as an association of States, still had to be placed in the context of international law (rather than constitutional law).

Neither was the historical path of Switzerland and Germany different from the American one, also with respect to the intermediate passage of the confederation,[12] nor was the Austrian one dissimilar, which developed after the defeat in the First World War and, in particular, in the transitional period 1918–2020, when the process of dissolution of the Austro-Hungarian Empire led the

---

the decision of a majority of the people of the union, nor from that of a majority of the states. It must result from the unanimous assent of the several states that are parties to it, differing no other wise from their ordinary assent than in its being expressed, not by the legislative authority, but by that of the people themselves'; and no 15 (Hamilton): 'There is nothing absurd or impracticable in the idea of a league or alliance between independent nations for certain defined purposes precisely stated in a treaty regulating all the details of time, place, circumstance, and quantity; leaving nothing to future discretion; and depending for its execution on the good faith of the parties. Compacts of this kind exist among all civilized nations, subject to the usual vicissitudes of peace and war, of observance and non-observance, as the interests or passions of the contracting powers dictate'.

10 For example, Belgium, regarding which – in the most recent Italian literature – we can refer to the contribution of Giacomo Delledonne, 'Belgio' in Enzo Di Salvatore (ed), *Sistemi costituzionali europei* (Giuffré 2021), which systematically and organically describes the functioning of the Belgian national order, including its federal structure.

11 Benner (n 8) 13 values the 'compact view of the Constitution' and dismisses the thesis according to which the United States were created by decision of one people. The thesis of the book according to the author (ibid 11) is that '[t]he central point presented in this book asserts that the creature – the United States Constitution, which established the federal government, cannot control the creator – the states that ratified it. The United States government was not created by 'one people', but instead by a conglomeration of several independent, sovereign states that delegated it certain limited powers, retaining all others'.

12 Respectively: the Confederation of Cantons of 1815 and the Swiss Federation of 1848; the German Confederation (*Deutscher Bund*) of 1815 (later dissolved in 1866) and the Federation of 1867–1871. On the historical-constitutional experience of Germany and on its federal structure, see the detailed analysis of Enzo Di Salvatore, 'Germania' in Enzo Di Salvatore (ed), *Sistemi costituzionali europei* (Giuffré 2021).

old German-speaking *Länder* of the Crown to assume a fundamental role in the formation of the new State, sanctioned with the 1920 Constitution.[13]

Apart from that, the formation of regional States, which historically is much more recent,[14] takes place in a different way: Normally, they are unitary States and become regional ones after a process of constitutional reform aimed at establishing some kind of decentralization.[15]

Exactly this has been the path of the Italian legal system, which has been a unitary State from the outset. After the liberal monarchic experience (1861–1922), Italy faced the twenty years of fascism (1922–1943), with a further centralization of the State. Finally, post-war the Constituent Assembly opted towards the regional model, which was then further consolidated as a result of the constitutional reforms of 1999–2001.

Other later examples of regional States are Spain with the 1978 Constitution; Portugal, whose 1976 Constitution established the autonomous Regions of the Azores and Madeira; Belgium, which has begun an evolution in this direction since the 1970s and now has indeed reached a special type of federal State. Finally, more recently, even the United Kingdom – starting with the referendums of 1997 – has embarked on a process of regionalization (devolution), which has led it to be now counted among the countries that have adopted a regional form of State.

In all these regional experiences, the *Constituent Units* of the States which have passed from a unitary to a decentralized form, are components of an originally unitary State to which some guarantees of autonomy have been conferred, but they did not possess the characteristic feature of statehood, which

---

13 On which see Paolo Colasante, 'Austria' in Enzo Di Salvatore (ed), *Sistemi costituzionali europei* (Giuffré 2021) in particular 487.

14 If we exclude the brief experience of the regional State introduced by the Constitution of the Spanish Republic of 1931, interrupted by the arrival of the regime led by Francisco Franco (1939), which restored the centralized unitary State, the Italian Republic of 1949 was the first State that assumed a regional structure.

15 For the sake of completeness, it should also be noted that, in addition to the different ways in which regional States and federal States arise, they have some differences that the literature has attempted to systematize, while emphasizing how characteristics of one type can recur in the other and vice versa. In this sense, see D'Atena 2022 (n 1) 14ff; Enzo Di Salvatore, 'Federalismo' in Stelio Mangiameli (ed), *Dizionario costituzionale – Dizionario sistematico* (Il Sole 24 Ore 2008) 20ff. More generally, with reference to the distinction between the federal State and the regional State, it is worth recalling both the dating back and some more recent literature, ie Gaspare Ambrosini, *Autonomia regionale e federalismo* (Edizioni italiane 1944); Mauro Volpi, 'Stato federale e Stato regionale: due modelli a confronto' (1995) 15 Quaderni Costituzionali 367; Giuseppe Di Genio, *Stato regionale versus Stato federale* (Giuffré 2005).

instead is normally present in the aggregation processes of the federal States. However, it should be noted that, with the exception of Italy, the regionalization of the mentioned States (Spain, Portugal, Belgium and the United Kingdom) took place 'from below', as this transformation was the answer to spontaneous independence movements of populations and territories and, therefore, has valued collective identities or pre-existing differentiated instances. In Italy, indeed, the literature has found a certain 'rate of artificiality' of ordinary autonomies, although it cannot be excluded that, to date, their concrete functioning has ended up acting as a 'constitutive factor of collective identities'.[16]

Therefore, some of these experiences (above all Belgium and the United Kingdom) are characterized by a common front of the Constituent Units aimed at requesting the satisfaction of independence movements corresponding to identity factors. In this sense – if it is true that the concept of federal Compact (ex ante) refers to the agreement among States with which a federation is established – the inverse process of the unitary State which transforms itself into a regional/federal State on the basis of independence movements widely present on the territory could be read as a (identity and not State) Compact matured ex post.

Despite their undeniable differences, it could be argued that the two kinds of Compact mirror each other: the ex ante one – which develops between pre-existing States – tends to create a central entity (the Federation) endowed with powers attributed to it by subtraction of those of the Constituent Units; the ex post one – which develops in the context of autonomous movements associated with the collective identity phenomena –, given the existence of the central entity (the unitary State), aims at downsizing the latter's role by adding competences to the Constituent Units (existing or yet to be established).

## 3 The 'Rate of Asymmetry' of Italian Regionalism. The Special Regions

The choice adopted by the Italian Constituent Assembly for a type of regional State converged in the formulation of art 5 of the Constitution,[17] which is

16 D'Atena 2014 (n 1) 6. According to the author, it is different to the case of the 'anthropological-cultural roots of Regions with special autonomy, which are based on solid collective identities, of which they constitute the institutional projection'.

17 On that provision see Carlo Esposito, 'Autonomie locali e decentramento amministrativo nell'art. 5 della Costituzione' in Carlo Esposito (ed), *La Costituzione italiana. Saggi* (Cedam 1954) 67ff; Giorgio Berti, 'Art. 5' in Giuseppe Branca (ed), *Commentario della Costituzione* (Zanichelli-Foro italiano 1985) 277ff.

undoubtedly the rejection of both the federal idea and the centralist idea. It founded a model of regionalism that is only partially asymmetrical, as 15 out of 20 Regions, which were actually established only in 1970, have an ordinary statute, therefore enjoying the legislative and administrative powers established by Title V of the Constitution in a homogeneous way, while the other 5 Regions with a special statute (in red in Figure 9.2) 'have special forms and conditions of autonomy pursuant to the special statutes adopted by constitutional law' (art 116 Italian Constitution).

Most of the Italian regions – where 85% of the Italian population resides – have homogeneous legislative and administrative powers directly provided for in art 117 and 118 of the Italian Constitution. The other (special) Regions (Valle d'Aosta, Trentino-Alto Adige, Friuli-Venezia Giulia, Sardinia and Sicily) have the powers provided for in their respective Statutes of autonomy, which are contained within constitutional laws of the national Parliament. Therefore, their revision is mainly left to a unilateral act of the central State and not to an authentically consensual method, so not even with respect to them one can speak of a method of 'aggregation' ascribable to the *foedus* or the *Compact* of the federations.

FIGURE 9.2 Italy – Regions with special autonomy. Percentage of population and GDP produced. The data relating to GDP cited in figures 9.2, 9.3 and 9.4 refer to 2019 and are extracted from the ISTAT institutional website <https://www.istat.it/it/> accessed 26 July 2023.

Despite the intention of strengthening Italian regionalism, the constitutional reform of 1999–2001 did not change this arrangement. In particular, the constitutional law no 3 of 2001 led to the overthrow of the principle of enumeration and the adoption of a division of powers pursuant to the federal tradition, but – unlike the federal Compact – not as a result of a unanimous decision of the Regions, but according to the ordinary procedure of constitutional revision, without any particular involvement of the entities that would have been the recipients of the new rules.

Indeed, the development of the regional model with the reforms of 1999–2001 (inspired by a federalist logic that was never fully implemented) proves once again that the fate of Italian regionalism is absolutely unrelated to a Compact among the Regions, depending instead on constitutional revision procedures almost entirely in the hands of the national legislator, also because there is no Chamber of Regions that deliberate them[18] and, in any case, the Regions are marginally and only possibly involved.[19]

Regarding the merits of the 2001 reform, it can be briefly noted that the original formulation of art 117 of the Constitution listed the regional competences, leaving the general legislative power to the State, while today the general competence belongs to the Regions (Art 117 para 4) and two enumerations contain the powers of the State: specifically, para 2 of Art 117 lists the 17 matters of exclusive State legislative competence and para 3 the 20 matters of concurrent competence between the State and the Regions, within which the legislation belongs to the Regions, while respecting the fundamental principles established by the national law.[20]

---

18 Unlike what happens in federal States, where there is a representative Chamber of the member States, which moreover participates in the process of revision of the constitution: D'Atena 2022 (n 1) 21.

19 In fact, pursuant to art 138 of the Constitution, at least five regional councils can request the holding of a confirmatory referendum on the constitutional revision bill already approved by the two Houses of Parliament. Nevertheless, where both Chambers approve the constitutional revision bill in second reading with a qualified majority of two thirds of their members, a referendum cannot be held and, therefore, the Regions cannot even exercise this (weak) power.

For the sake of completeness, it can also be remembered that, pursuant to art 121 of the Constitution, the regional councils are holders of the right of legislative initiative and, therefore, each council can formulate a bill – ordinary or constitutional – to the Parliament. However, this is an even weaker power, since, in the context of the legislative procedure, the right of initiative is not inserted in any of the moments in which a 'conditioning' of the national legislator can occur: neither in the deliberative phase, nor in the supplementary phase of the effectiveness.

20 The attribution of general or residual legislative power to the Regions was soon reduced in its potential scope due to its interpretation by the Constitutional Court. In this sense,

Even for the special Regions nothing changes, as they continue to see their autonomy regulated in their respective Statutes, while also enjoying the effects of the so-called more favorable clause[21] (art 10 of the constitutional law no 3 of 2001), according to which '(...) the provisions of the present constitutional law also apply to the Regions with special statute and to the autonomous provinces of Trento and of Bolzano [until the adaptation of the respective statutes] for the parts in which they provide for wider forms of autonomy than those already attributed'. In essence, the legal regime of the competences of the special Regions has remained unchanged, as it has always been left to the source of the Statute of autonomy (contained in a constitutional law) supplemented by the more favorable provisions contained in the new Title v. Moreover, according to the intentions of the legislator of 2001 this provision should have been temporary, but the lack of revision of the Statutes themselves has stabilized its effects, which have therefore become structural by now.

## 4 *It Follows.* The Asymmetry Clause of Art 116 Para 3 of the Italian Constitution: From Its Introduction to the End of the XVIII Legislature

The constitutional reform of 2001 introduced the seed of a division of powers into the constitutional text, potentially (albeit partially) determined by agreements between State and Region and, therefore, of a regional differentiation through the so-called asymmetry clause pursuant to Art 116 para 3 of the Constitution. It could be said that the activation of this clause – possible

---

it is useful to mention the following monographic works, which completely reconstruct what has been defined as the 'rewriting of Title V' of the Italian Constitution by constitutional case law: Filippo Benelli, *La "smaterializzazione" delle materie* (Giuffré 2006); Michele Belletti, *Percorsi di ricentralizzazione del regionalismo italiano nella giurisprudenza costituzionale – Tra tutela di valori fondamentali, esigenze strategiche e di coordinamento della finanza pubblica* (Aracne 2012); Simone Calzolaio, *Il cammino delle materie nello Stato regionale – La definizione delle competenze legislative nell'ordinamento costituzionale* (Giappichelli 2012); Gianluca Cosmelli, *Oltre i confini della "materia" – La potestà legislativa residuale delle regioni tra poteri impliciti e sussidiarietà* (Giuffré 2015).

21 On the interpretation of the most favorable clause and its developments in constitutional case law see D'Atena 2014 (n 1); Antonio Saitta, 'Gli Statuti delle Regioni speciali ieri, oggi e domani' in Editoriale Scientifica (ed), *Studi in onore di Franco Modugno*, vol IV (Editoriale Scientifica 2011); Eduardo Gianfrancesco, 'L'art. 10 della legge costituzionale n. 3 del 2001 ed i controlli nelle regioni ad autonomia speciale' (2002) 47 Giurisprudenza costituzionale 3312.

only for ordinary Regions[22] – would increase the rate of asymmetry of Italian regionalism, no longer limited exclusively to special autonomies, but extended to all Regions that wanted (and were able) to access this 'negotiation' form of downwards attraction of powers.

Specifically, Art 116 para 3 of the Constitution establishes that the ordinary Regions can be attributed 'additional special forms and conditions of autonomy' on the basis of a 'State Law, upon the initiative of the Region concerned, after consultation with the local authorities', which 'is approved by both Houses of Parliament with the absolute majority of their members, on the basis of an agreement between the State and the Region concerned'.[23]

This complex procedure, on which the Italian literature has widely debated since its introduction,[24] should therefore lead to a transfer of powers from the

---

22 This is the absolute majority and consolidated opinion. In the opposite direction Davide Galliani, 'All'interno del Titolo V: le "ulteriori forme e condizioni particolari di autonomia" di cui all'art. 116.3 Cost. riguardano anche le Regioni a Statuto speciale?' (2003) 31 Le Regioni 419.

23 For the sake of completeness, please note that the asymmetry clause also requires compliance with the principles set out in art 119 of the Constitution, which regulates regional financial autonomy.

24 In fact, although in the first decade following the Reform of Title V there were no concrete initiatives to implement the asymmetry clause, the literature has extensively dealt with the issue: Marcello Cecchetti, 'Attuazione della riforma costituzionale del Titolo V e differenziazione delle Regioni di diritto comune' [2002] Federalismi.it <https://www.federalismi.it/ApplOpenFilePDF.cfm?artid=813&dpath=document&dfile=ACFA98.pdf&content=Attuazione%2Bdella%2Briforma%2Bcostituzionale%2Bdel%2BTitolo%2BV%2Be%2Bdifferenziazione%2Bdelle%2BRegioni%2Bdi%2Bdiritto%2Bcomune%2B%2D%2Bstato%2B%2D%2Bdottrina%2B%2D%2B> accessed 26 July 2023; Francesco Palermo, 'Il regionalismo differenziato' in Tania Groppi and Marco Olivetti (eds), *La Repubblica delle autonomie* (Giappichelli 2003) 53ff; Andrea Morrone, 'Il regionalismo differenziato. Commento all'art. 116, comma 3, della Costituzione' (2007) 1 Federalismo fiscale 139; Marco Di Folco, 'Le differenziazioni ipotetiche: l'art. 116 della Costituzione' in Luciano Vandelli (ed), *Il governo delle regioni: sistemi politici, amministrazioni, autonomie speciali* (Il Mulino 2013) 419ff; Nicolò Zanon, 'Per un regionalismo differenziato: linee di sviluppo a Costituzione invariata e prospettive alla luce della revisione del Titolo V' in *Problemi del Federalismo* (Giuffré 2001). See also the monographic issue no 1 of the review Le istituzioni del federalismo (2008) 29, with the papers of: Roberto Bin, '"Regionalismo differenziato" e utilizzazione dell'art. 116, terzo comma, Cost. Alcune tesi per aprire il dibattito' 9; Antonio Ruggeri, 'La "specializzazione" dell'autonomia regionale: se, come e nei riguardi di chi farvi luogo' 21; Adele Anzon Demmig, 'Quale "regionalismo differenziato"?' 51; Giovanni Di Cosimo, 'Sui contenuti del regionalismo differenziato' 63; Pietro Ciarlo and Marco Betzu, 'Dal regionalismo differenziato al regionalismo pasticciato' 67; Enrico Carloni, 'Teoria e pratica della differenziazione: federalismo asimmetrico ed attuazione del Titolo V' 75; Lorenza Violini, 'Regionalismo differenziato e utilizzazione dell'art. 116, comma 3, Cost. (con particolare riguardo al regime dei diritti sociali)' 87; Girolamo Sciullo, 'Art. 116, comma 3, Cost. e beni culturali' 95; Ilenia Ruggiu, 'Il "ritorno" del principio di competenza?' 101.

State to the Region (or Regions) that has (or have) requested it. The material field susceptible of transfer is circumscribed by the same asymmetry clause, although its perimeter remains quite extensive, since, in addition to all the matters of concurrent competence between the State and the Regions,[25] powers in matters of justice (limited to the organizational requirements of the Justice of the Peace), education and protection of the environment, ecosystem and cultural heritage can be devolved.

The asymmetry clause has remained silent for a long time in the Italian legal system and, although it has not yet been implemented, there has been considerable attention in respect to its activation in the last years.

In particular, the recognition of forms of 'differentiated autonomy' pursuant to Art 116 para 3 of the Constitution has become the focus of the institutional debate on the relationship between the State and the Regions after the initiatives undertaken by the Lombardy, Veneto and Emilia-Romagna Regions in the final part of the XVII legislature (March 2013–March 2018). These initiatives merged into the signing of the so-called *pre-intese* (preliminary agreements).[26]

25 Art 117 para 3: 'Concurring legislation applies to the following subject matters: international and EU relations of the Regions; foreign trade; job protection and safety; education, subject to the autonomy of educational institutions and with the exception of vocational education and training; professions; scientific and technological research and innovation support for productive sectors; health protection; nutrition; sports; disaster relief; land-use planning; civil ports and airports; large transport and navigation networks; communications; national production, transport and distribution of energy; complementary and supplementary social security; harmonisation of public accounts and co-ordination of public finance and taxation system; enhancement of cultural and environmental properties, including the promotion and organisation of cultural activities; savings banks, rural banks, regional credit institutions; regional land and agricultural credit institutions. In the subject matters covered by concurring legislation legislative powers are vested in the Regions, except for the determination of the fundamental principles, which are laid down in State legislation'.

26 Reviving the debate in the literature (see n 24 for previous literature): Antonio D'Atena, 'L'art. 116, u.c., Cost. alla prova dell'applicazione. Profili procedimentali' (2018) 60 Rassegna parlamentare 185; Antonio D'Atena, 'Tra l'attuazione del regionalismo differenziato, la legge Delrio e le riforme da fare' (2019) 61 Rassegna parlamentare 639; Antonio D'Atena, 'A proposito della "clausola di asimmetria" (art. 116 u.c. Cost.)' [2020] Rivista AIC <https://www.rivistaaic.it/images/rivista/pdf/4_2020_14_D_Atena.pdf> accessed 26 July 2023; Lorenza Violini, 'I procedimenti per l'attuazione del regionalismo differenziato: luci e ombre dell'art. 116, comma 3, della Costituzione' [2019] Italian Papers on Federalism <https://www.ipof.it/wp-content/uploads/2021/04/Violini-Procedimenti-Regionalismo-differenziato.pdf> accessed 26 July 2023; Lorenza Violini, *Una forma di Stato a regionalismo differenziato? Percorsi e argomenti per l'attuazione dell'art. 116, III comma, Cost.* (Giappichelli 2021); Giovanni Tarli Barbieri, 'Verso un regionalismo differenziato o verso un regionalismo confuso? Appunti sulla (presunta) attuazione dell'art. 116, comma 3, Cost.' (2019) 12 Osservatorio sulle fonti 1; Giovanni Piccirilli, 'Gli "accordi preliminari" per la differenziazione regionale. Primi spunti sulla procedura da seguire per l'attuazione dell'art. 116, terzo comma, Cost.' [2018] Diritti regionali <https://www.dirittiregionali.it/wp-content/uploads/2018/04/documento-integrale-10.pdf> accessed 26 July 2023;

Eduardo Gianfrancesco, 'L'attuazione dell'art. 116, comma 3, Cost. Tra nodi problematici e prospettive evolutive del regionalismo italiano' [2020] Consulta online <https://giurcost.org/studi/gianfrancesco.pdf> accessed 26 July 2023; Stelio Mangiameli, 'Appunti a margine dell'art. 116, comma 3, della Costituzione' (2017) 49 Le Regioni 661; Vincenzo Baldini, 'Unità dello Stato e dinamiche delle autonomie territoriali' [2019] Federalismi.it <https://www.federalismi.it/ApplOpenFilePDF.cfm?artid=38884&dpath=document&dfile=29062019101047.pdf&content=Unit%C3%A0%2Bdello%2BStato%2Be%2Bdinamiche%2Bdelle%2Bautonomie%2Bterritoriali%2B%2D%2Bstato%2B%2D%2Bdottrina%2B%2D%2B> accessed 26 July 2023; Marco Olivetti, 'Il regionalismo differenziato alla prova dell'esame parlamentare' [2019] Federalismi.it <https://www.federalismi.it/ApplOpenFilePDF.cfm?artid=38243&dpath=document&dfile=19032019231006.pdf&content=Il%2Bregionalismo%2Bdifferenziato%2Balla%2Bprova%2Bdell%27esame%2Bparlamentare%2B%2D%2Bstato%2B%2D%2Bdottrina%2B%2D%2B> accessed 26 July 2023; Roberto Toniatti, 'L'autonomia regionale ponderata: aspettative ed incognite di un incremento delle asimmetrie quale possibile premessa per una nuova stagione costituzionale del regionalismo italiano' (2017) 49 Le Regioni 635; Daniele Coduti, 'Le fonti normative nella differenziazione regionale: una problematica ipotesi ricostruttiva' [2022] Federalismi.it <https://www.federalismi.it/ApplOpenFilePDF.cfm?artid=47134&dpath=document&dfile=04052022130312.pdf&content=Le%2Bfonti%2Bnormative%2Bnella-%2Bdifferenziazione%2Bregionale%3A%2Buna%2Bproblematica%2Bipotesi%2Bricostruttiva%2B%2D%2Bstato%2B%2D%2Bdottrina%2B%2D%2B> accessed 26 July 2023; Carlo Iannello, 'La piena sovranità del Parlamento nella determinazione dei contenuti e dei limiti dell'autonomia differenziata' [2019] Diritti regionali <https://www.dirittiregionali.it/wp-content/uploads/2019/09/documento-integrale-3.pdf> accessed 26 July 2023; Andrea Piraino, 'L'autonomia differenziata nella crisi del regionalismo italiano' in Adriana Apostoli, Mario Gorlani and Nadia Maccabiani (eds), *Quale rilancio per le autonomie territoriali* (Giuffré 2020); Raffaele Bifulco, 'I limiti del regionalismo differenziato' in Adriana Apostoli, Mario Gorlani and Nadia Maccabiani (eds), *Quale rilancio per le autonomie territoriali* (Giuffré 2020); Guido Rivosecchi, 'Il regionalismo differenziato nella Repubblica delle autonomie, con particolare riguardo ai profili procedurali' in Daniele Coduti (ed), *La differenziazione nella Repubblica delle autonomie* (Giappichelli 2022); Alessandro Morelli, 'L'incerta attuazione del regionalismo differenziato' in Daniele Coduti (ed), *La differenziazione nella Repubblica delle autonomie* (Giappichelli 2022) 101ff. See also issue no 3 of the Review Nuove autonomie (2020) 29, mainly dedicated to this topic with the papers of: Nicola Gullo, 'Notazioni sul regionalismo differenziato tra aspirazioni autonomistiche e solidarietà economico-sociale' 817; Valentina Prudente, 'L'utile attuazione dell'art. 116, co. 3, Cost. alla luce del principio di sussidiarietà' 837; Patrizia Accordino, 'Le "asimmetrie fiscali" tra Regioni italiane: stato dell'arte, criticità e prospettive' 853; Luca Dell'Atti, 'Effetti dell'autonomia differenziata sulla combinazione funzionale dei principi di sussidiarietà e leale collaborazione. Verso una riforma del regionalismo a Costituzione invariata' 867; Andrea Napolitano, 'Il ruolo (imprescindibile) delle camere per una corretta ed equa attuazione del regionalismo differenziato' 881; Claudia Bianca Ceffa, '"Non basta dire intesa". Ragionando sul principio di leale collaborazione fra Stato e Regioni nella prospettiva del regionalismo differenziato' 895; Giuseppe Carlo Ricciardi, 'Note sulla dimensione amministrativa del regionalismo differenziato' 907; Matteo Pressi, 'Autonomia regionale differenziata: un'occasione per ripensare l'area vasta' 919. With specific reference to the relationship between differentiated regionalism and special regionalism see Alessandro Morelli, 'Regionalismo differenziato e autonomia speciale: un quadro complesso' [2019]

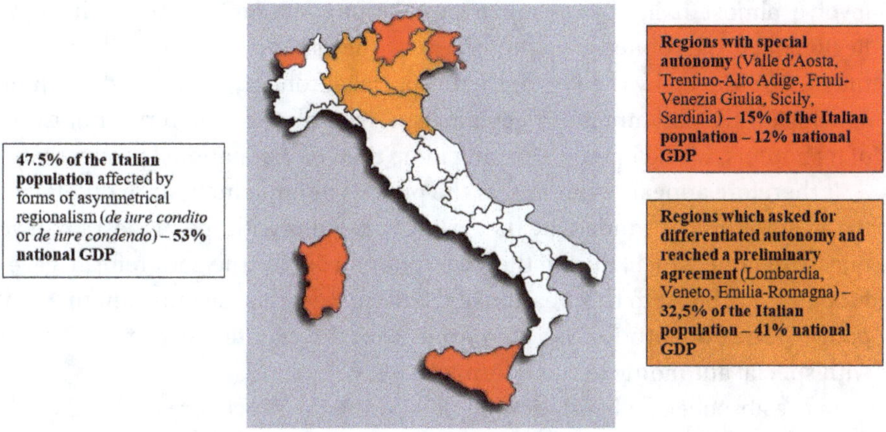


FIGURE 9.3 Italy – Regions with special autonomy and Regions that have reached preliminary agreements for the attribution of further forms of autonomy. Percentage of population and GDP produced.

Before illustrating the process followed to reach these preliminary agreements, which have not yet risen to the rank of agreements for the start of the parliamentary phase envisaged by Art 116 para 3 of the Constitution, Figure 9.3 shows the Regions with special autonomy and the ordinary Regions which at the time seemed to be closest to achieving differentiated autonomy pictured in different colors. Although these are different forms of autonomy, it is possible to note how the eventual achievement of differentiated autonomy by the Lombardy, Veneto and Emilia-Romagna Regions would lead to a considerable expansion of the rate of asymmetry of Italian regionalism from different points of view: geographical, as only 12 Regions out of 20 would remain subject to the general division of powers envisaged in the Constitution; demographical, since it would

Diritti regionali <https://www.dirittiregionali.it/wp-content/uploads/2019/11/documento-integrale-4.pdf> accessed 26 July 2023; Antonio Ruggeri, 'Attuazione dell'art. 116, III c., Cost. e prospettive della specialità regionale' [2020] Diritti regionali <https://www.dirittiregionali.it/wp-content/uploads/2020/01/documento-integrale-5.pdf> accessed 26 July 2023; Nicola Gullo, 'Le autonomie speciali nel prisma dell'attuazione dell'art. 116, co. 3, Cost.' [2022] Diritti regionali <https://www.dirittiregionali.it/wp-content/uploads/2022/04/documento-integrale-3.pdf> accessed 26 July 2023. With reference to the asymmetry clause within the so-called Renzi-Boschi constitutional bill, rejected by the electorate in December 2016, see Paolo Colasante, 'I meccanismi derogatori "di generale applicazione" del riparto delle competenze legislative fra Stato e Regioni nella riforma costituzionale in itinere: la clausola di asimmetria come limite all'esercizio della clausola di flessibilità/supremazia' [2015] Italian Papers on Federalism <https://www.ipof.it/wp-content/uploads/2021/06/Colasante-3_2015.pdf> accessed 26 July 2023.

involve almost half of the Italian population; economical, since the three Regions just mentioned constitute 41% of the national GDP and, if added to the GDP produced by the Regions with special autonomy, one would reach the conclusion that asymmetrical regionalism, regardless of the territorial extent of its borders, would end up affecting more than half of national productivity.

It therefore appears evident that the process of implementation of differentiated autonomy is 'guided' by the ordinary Regions with the highest tax revenues, the same which, during the preparatory work for the 2001 reform, gave a fundamental boost to the creation of the asymmetry clause pursuant to Art 116 para 3 of the Constitution as a compromise for the maintenance of the Regions with special autonomy in the reform of Title V.[27]

In the absence of a legislation implementing the procedure outlined by the Constitution,[28] the ways in which the three Regions activated the process pursuant to Art 116 para 3 were different.[29]

On 22 October 2017 – both in the Lombardy Region and in the Veneto Region – a referendum was held to ask citizens if they wanted that the respective Region started the process for the attribution of further forms and particular conditions of autonomy pursuant to the asymmetry clause[30] and in both

27 D'Atena 2020 (n 26) 313, who also says: 'The maintenance of these autonomies, and especially the preservation of the 'financial privilege' that accompanied them, was, however, in strong tension with the condition of the ordinary Regions with higher incomes, which, with the tax revenue produced in their territory, afford a well-being (measurable in terms of public expenditure per capita), from which their own citizens were (and are) excluded. This condition of unease manifested itself, in terms of paradigmatic evidence, in the Veneto Region, being an ordinary Region mainly bordering Regions with special autonomy'.

28 It seems useful to recall that at the time the only existing procedural rule was Art 1 para 571 of the budget law for 2014 (no 147 of 2013), pursuant to which: 'Also for the purposes of coordinating public finances, the Government takes action on the initiatives of the regions presented to the President of the Council of Ministers and to the Minister for Regional Affairs for the purposes of the agreement pursuant to article 116, third paragraph, of the Constitution within sixty days of receipt. The provision of the first sentence also applies to initiatives presented before the date of entry into force of this law in application of the principle of continuity of bodies and functions. In this case, the term referred to in the first sentence starts from the date of entry into force of this law'.

29 Regarding the process that is described hereafter see Camera dei deputati – Servizio Studi, *L'autonomia differenziata delle regioni a statuto ordinario* (28 September 2022) <https://www.camera.it/temiap/documentazione/temi/pdf/1104705.pdf?_1635237238195> accessed 26 July 2023.

30 On this topic see Lorenza Violini, 'L'autonomia delle Regioni italiane dopo i referendum e le richieste di maggiori poteri ex articolo 116, comma 3, Cost.' [2018] Rivista AIC <https://www.rivistaaic.it/images/rivista/pdf/Violini_4_2018.pdf> accessed 26 July 2023;

cases the answer was yes. The Emilia-Romagna Region instead took action following the initiative of the President of the Region, with the approval of the Regional Assembly, on 3 October 2017, with a resolution for the initiation of the procedure aimed at signing the agreement with the Government pursuant to Art 116 para 3 of the Constitution.

On 28 February 2018, the Government in charge at the time signed three separate preliminary agreements[31] (so-called *pre-intese*) with the Regions concerned, which identified the general principles, the methodology and a (first) list of matters in view of the definition of the final understanding.

Each preliminary agreement – if definitively approved – should be concluded for a period of ten years (art 2). The matters of priority regional interest to be negotiated were: protection of the environment and ecosystems; health protection; instruction; job protection; international relations and relations with the European Union. However, it was provided for that the negotiations could be extended to further matters of the subjects indicated and to other subjects (art 6).

At the beginning of the XVIII legislature (March 2018–October 2022) the three Regions that had signed the preliminary agreements expressed their willingness to expand the scope of the matters being transferred. In addition to that, other Regions officially expressed their intention to undertake the same path (Piedmont, Liguria, Tuscany, Umbria, Marche, Campania).[32]

Figure 9.4 shows how Italian asymmetrical (special and differentiated) regionalism would further expand, if these new requests were accepted: from a geographical point of view it would involve 14 Regions out of 20, which would correspond to 77% of the Italian population and 80% of the national GDP. However, it is interesting to see how the demands for autonomy aimed at the establishment of differentiated regionalism immediately expanded towards

---

Elisabetta Catelani, 'Nuove richieste di autonomia differenziata ex art. 116, comma 3, Cost.: profili procedimentali di dubbia legittimità e possibile violazione dei diritti' (2018) 11 Osservatorio sulle fonti 1. With regard to the initiative of the Veneto Region, it seems useful to recall the judgment of the Constitutional Court no 118 of 2015, which judged the constitutional legitimacy of the law regarding the introduction of a series of consultative referendums, including the one on the initiation of the procedure pursuant to Art 116 para 3 of the Constitution (the only one, indeed, that has not incurred in the declaration of constitutional illegitimacy).

31 Available on the website of the Regional Affairs Department of the Presidency of the Council of Ministers at the following link: <http://www.affariregionali.gov.it/comunicazione/notizie/2018/giugno/autonomia-differenziata-accordi-preliminari-con-le-regioni-emilia-romagna-lombardia-e-veneto/> accessed 26 July 2023.

32 The list of Regions that have made this request is taken from the aforementioned Chamber of Deputies file Camera dei deputati – Servizio Studi (n 29).

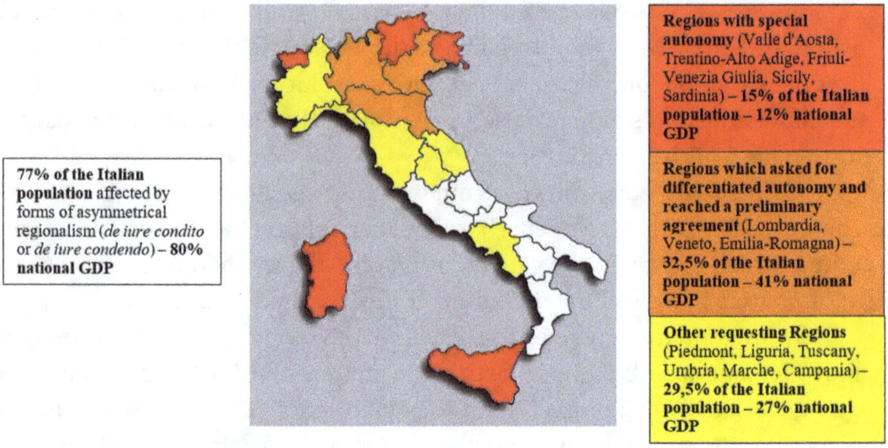


FIGURE 9.4 Italy – Regions with special autonomy, Regions that have reached preliminary agreements for the attribution of further forms of autonomy and Regions which asked for it. Percentage of population and GDP produced.

the other regions of Northern and Central-Northern Italy, going as far as to Campania, which is currently the only Southern Region to have formalized the request. This demonstrates once again how the acquisition of greater powers primarily interests the more developed areas of the country, even if it is probable that even the few remaining Regions will formulate their own requests, if the implementation process of differentiated regionalism – which has undergone an inevitable slowdown due to the pandemic and has been reactivated since the final part of the XVIII legislature[33] – should materialize.

## 5 *It Follows.* The Developments of Differentiated Regionalism in the XIX Legislature

With the start of the XIX legislature (October 2022) the process that should lead to the implementation of Art 116 para 3 of the Constitution has received new life, since the center-right government currently leading the country has placed it at the center of the political agenda.[34]

33 See once again Camera dei deputati – Servizio Studi (n 29).

34 This is a circumstance to which Italian public law literature has not remained indifferent. Specifically, in addition to the bibliography cited in the following footnotes, see Antonio D'Atena, 'Dove vanno le Regioni' [2022] Rivista AIC <https://www.rivistaaic.it/images/rivista/pdf/4_2022_09_D_Atena.pdf> accessed 26 July 2023; Silvio Gambino, 'Regionalismo

Nonetheless, it must be immediately observed that the debate is currently centered on – so to speak – the 'pre-conditions' for the implementation of differentiated regionalism, while from a concrete point of view the situation previously reached, where three Regions have signed preliminary agreements and other Regions have formally requested access to differentiated autonomy, remains unchanged.

The interest of the current parliamentary majority in the implementation process of the asymmetry clause has immediately been evident as it has dealt with it since the approval of the first budget law (Law No 197 of 2022), only two months within the beginning of the legislature. Specifically, it has been established that 'the attribution of further forms and particular conditions of autonomy referred to in article 116, third paragraph, of the Constitution, relating to subjects or areas of subjects referable (…) to civil and social rights which must be guaranteed throughout the national territory, is permitted only after the determination of the relative essential levels of services (LEP)' (Art 1 para 791 last sentence), also dictating a complex procedure for their determination (Art 1 para 792–801).[35]

---

'differenziato' e principi fondamentali della Carta' [2023] Diritti regionali <https://www.dirittiregionali.it/wp-content/uploads/2023/05/documento-integrale-4.pdf> accessed 26 July 2023; Luca Gori, 'L'autonomia regionale differenziata a partire dai lavori preparatori della riforma del Titolo V della Costituzione' (2023) 16 Osservatorio sulle fonti 59; Stelio Mangiameli, 'Errori e mancata attuazione costituzionale. A proposito di regionalismo e regionalismo differenziato' [2023] Diritti regionali <https://www.dirittiregionali.it/wp-content/uploads/2023/01/documento-integrale-4.pdf> accessed 26 July 2023. See also issue 1 of the review Italian Papers on Federalism (2023) <https://www.ipof.it/category/numero-1-2023/> accessed 26 July 2023, and issue 2 of the review Italian Papers on Federalism (2023) <https://www.ipof.it/category/numero-2-2023/> accessed 26 July 2023 among which the following papers should be highlighted: Roberto Di Maria, 'La procedura per la attuazione del c.d. "regionalismo differenziato": dalla marginalizzazione delle assemblee elettive e degli Enti locali, alla perplessa definizione dei l.e.p.' [2023] Italian Papers on Federalism <https://www.ipof.it/wp-content/uploads/2023/05/03_IPOF-1-23-Di-Maria.pdf> accessed 26 July 2023; Mario Gorlani, 'Regionalismo differenziato e materie oggetto di trasferimento: valutazioni politiche e criticità tecniche, organizzative e finanziarie' [2023] Italian Papers on Federalism <https://www.ipof.it/wp-content/uploads/2023/05/04_IPOF-1-23-Gorlani.pdf> accessed 26 July 2023; Antonino Iacoviello, 'Autonomia regionale e unità giuridica ed economica della Repubblica: i limiti costituzionali per l'attuazione dell'articolo 116, comma 3, della Costituzione' [2023] Italian Papers on Federalism <https://www.ipof.it/wp-content/uploads/2023/07/IPOF-2-23-Iacoviello.pdf> accessed 26 July 2023.

35 On that provision see Giulio Maria Salerno, 'Con il procedimento di determinazione dei LEP (e relativi costi e fabbisogni standard) la legge di bilancio

In fact, it is believed that the determination of the essential levels of services (LEP, *livelli essenziali delle prestazioni*) concerning civil and social rights could constitute a useful antidote to attenuate the criticisms of the detractors of the implementation process of differentiated regionalism, who leverage the risk of aggravation of the territorial gap existing in the country between the more developed Regions and those less strong from an economic-financial point of view, further weakening the latter. The establishment of the LEP would in fact act as a minimum and insurmountable threshold of the 'measure' of the civil and social rights guaranteed to all Italian citizens and, therefore, it would be guaranteed that no form of differentiation could affect its content.

The fact that the current Government has approved a bill containing 'Provisions for the implementation of the differentiated autonomy of Regions with ordinary statute pursuant to article 116, third paragraph, of the Constitution' (so-called *Calderoli* Bill) is equally relevant. The bill, which would regulate conditions and procedures for the implementation of differentiated regionalism, is currently discussed in the Senate of the Republic.[36]

Specifically, the bill, if approved, would regulate the procedure for approving the agreements between the State and the Region (art 2) and their duration

---

riapre il cantiere dell'autonomia differenziata' [2023] Federalismi.it <https://www.federalismi.it/ApplOpenFilePDF.cfm?eid=660&dpath=editoriale&dfile=EDITORIALE%5F10012023160745%2Epdf&content=Con%2Bil%2Bprocedimento%2Bdi%2Bdeterminazione%2Bdei%2BLEP%2B%28e%2Brelativi%2Bcosti%2Be%2Bfabbisogni%2Bstandard%29%2Bla%2Blegge%2Bdi%2Bbilancio%2Briapre%2Bil%2Bcantiere%2Bdell%E2%80%99autonomia%2Bdifferenziata&content_auth=%3Cb%3EGiulio%2BM%2E%2BSalerno%3C%2Fb%3E> accessed 26 July 2023; Enzo Balboni and Camilla Buzzacchi, 'Autonomia differenziata: più problemi che certezze' (2023) 16 Osservatorio sulle fonti 41; Marco Ladu and Lorenzo Spadacini, 'La nozione costituzionale di livello essenziale delle prestazioni tra potestà normativa e autonomia finanziaria delle Regioni' [2023] Italian Papers on Federalism <https://www.ipof.it/wp-content/uploads/2023/05/IPOF-2-23-Spadacini-Ladu.pdf> accessed 26 July 2023.

36 On which see Roberto Di Maria, 'Prime impressioni sulla bozza di disegno di legge per l'attuazione del c.d. "regionalismo differenziato" ex art. 116, co. 3, Cost.' [2023] Diritti regionali <https://www.dirittiregionali.it/wp-content/uploads/2023/03/documento-integrale-4.pdf> accessed 26 July 2023; Andrea Lollo, 'Prime note sul (nuovo) procedimento di attuazione del regionalismo differenziato' [2023] Diritti regionali <https://www.dirittiregionali.it/wp-content/uploads/2023/05/documento-integrale-20.pdf> accessed 26 July 2023; Marco Podetta, 'Il tentativo di attuazione dell'autonomia differenziata: dal disegno di legge Calderoli alla legge di bilancio per il 2023' [2023] Consulta online <https://giurcost.org/post/MARCO%20PODETTA/22634> accessed 26 July 2023; Vincente Pierluigi Grossi, 'L'evoluzione del ruolo della legge quadro nel sistema dell'art. 116, co. 3, Cost.: posizioni dottrinarie e funzione politica' [2023] Italian Papers on Federalism <https://www.ipof.it/wp-content/uploads/2023/05/IPOF-2-23-Grossi.pdf> accessed 26 July 2023.

(art 7), would contain further rules on the determination of LEP (art 3), would regulate the transfer of functions and the corresponding resources (art 4, 5, 6 and 8), as well as the equalization measures among different territories (art 9). The final provision of the bill (art 20) would be problematic, as in respect of special autonomies – excluded from the asymmetry clause according to the literal tenor of Art 116 of the Constitution – the so-called 'more favorable clause' could be applied pursuant to Art 10 of the Constitutional Law no 3 of 2001. Therefore, it would be necessary to extend the greater forms of autonomy thus attributed to the ordinary Regions also in their regard.[37]

## 6 Differentiated Regionalism as a Potential (Ex Post) Compact among Regions

More than one element leads us to believe that the implementation of differentiated regionalism will not be a process that concerns single (or few) Italian Regions. Similarly, to what happened in the Spanish case, in which there was a complete regionalization of the national territory, also in Italy a regional differentiation (overlapping ordinary regionalism) could end up to be tendentially inclusive of all regional realities.

Both what is happening in the current legislature and the previous events point in that direction. Starting from the latter, it should be noted that the preliminary agreements of February 2018 – stipulated with a very similar formulation – and the subsequent requests for access to differentiated autonomy by other Regions prove that from the regional side the process will probably take place not *uti singuli*, but *uti universi*. The Regions will not negotiate individually, representing their own specific peculiarities, but instead constitute a 'bloc' for autonomist demands, a – so to speak – new kind of Compact, of course ex post.[38]

Furthermore, the most recent developments corroborate this conclusion, in the sense that an attempt is being made to construct a 'horizontal' regulatory framework for an *undifferentiated* access to *differentiated* autonomy. Therefore, it is foreseeable that, when this framework is complete, the Regions will resume the movement previously interrupted and many of them

37 Indeed, there would also be many other remarks that should be made on these latest regulatory developments, but this is not the most appropriate forum, given that this paper has other purposes. Therefore, reference is made to the literature cited in the previous footnotes of this para (which was added later while updating the paper).

38 See above, para 2, especially the final part.

will simultaneously formulate a request for the attribution of further forms of autonomy, which will be followed by the simultaneity of the negotiations. This will induce the Government to treat the requesting Regions in a basically equal way. Therefore, the most probable outcome is that the contents of the agreements will be homogeneous and the eventual completion of the procedure envisaged by Art 116 para 3 of the Constitution will induce the remaining Regions to carry out the same path.

In essence, more than 70 years after the implementation of the constitutional provisions of the Regions in Italy (and more than 50 years after the concrete establishment of the ordinary ones), they could have the opportunity to be protagonists of a new evolution of Italian regionalism.

At the time of the foundation of Italian regionalism, the Constituent Assembly had the tradition of the pre-republican unitary State in mind, and therefore had to resort to an 'artificial' definition of the borders of the Regions, drawing on the pre-existing territorial subdivision for purely statistical purposes, and to a unilateral determination of the respective powers. Today those artificial entities are institutions that are embedded and well-known in our legal system and could therefore give rise to a regional 'bloc' that pushes towards the evolution of Italian regionalism thanks to the implementation of the asymmetry clause.

Unlike the founding Compact of the Federal State, this type of 'bloc' bearing autonomist demands would be an ex post Compact of partial 'revision' (since it is limited to a series of subjects) of the division of powers, through the use of a bargained source of law. Therefore, this process would be accompanied with an even higher involvement of the Regions than the one that would be achieved if the transfer of competences took place through the constitutional revision procedure, in which the regional position is almost irrelevant, given the absence of a Chamber of Regions. In any case, it would be qualitatively superior even if the latter existed, considering the bilateral nature of the law provided for in Art 116 para 3 of the Constitution.

In respect of the special Regions, a certain drag-and-drop effect has to be added, which, although lacking the possibility of activating the asymmetry clause, would certainly play an active part in equalizing their position with respect to the major forms of autonomy achieved in this way by the ordinary autonomy.

However, the next developments in the implementation process of differentiated regionalism have to be waited for to understand whether the asymmetry clause, created to enhance *uti singuli* autonomistic instances, can instead end up to be a source of general revision of Italian regionalism of a contractual nature through the activation of a unitary – *uti universi* – regional 'bloc' or – to use the typical federal language of American origin – a Compact between the Regions to modulate their autonomy ex post on the basis of an experience now dating back over time. This experience has therefore led each single Region to develop its own collective identity, regardless of the rate of artificiality that marked its formal establishment in 1948 (and the effective one in 1970). In fact, what we wanted to define here as an ex post Compact, although distinct from the Compact from which a federation originates and limited in the material field of application, shares the principle of self-determination which underlies it. In summary, a Compact not between pre-existing (sovereign) States, but between already existing (autonomous) constituent units. A Compact not for the exercise of a *constituent power*, but for the exercise of a *constituted power*.

## Bibliography


Accordino P, 'Le "asimmetrie fiscali" tra Regioni italiane: stato dell'arte, criticità e prospettive' (2020) 29 Nuove autonomie 853.

Ambrosini G, *Autonomia regionale e federalismo* (Edizioni italiane 1944).

Anzon Demmig A, 'Quale "regionalismo differenziato"?' (2008) 29 Le istituzioni del federalismo 51.

Balboni E and Buzzacchi C, 'Autonomia differenziata: più problemi che certezze' (2023) 16 Osservatorio sulle fonti 41.

Baldini V, 'Unità dello Stato e dinamiche delle autonomie territoriali' [2019] Federalismi.it <https://www.federalismi.it/ApplOpenFilePDF.cfm?artid=38884&dpath=document&dfile=29062019101047.pdf&content=Unit%C3%A0%2Bdello%2BStato%2Be%2Bdinamiche%2Bdelle%2Bautonomie%2Bterritoriali%2B%2D%2Bstato%2B%2D%2Bdottrina%2B%2D%2B> accessed 26 July 2023.

Bartole S, 'Art. 116' in Branca G (ed), *Commentario della Costituzione* (Zanichelli-Foro italiano 1985).

Belletti M, *Percorsi di ricentralizzazione del regionalismo italiano nella giurisprudenza costituzionale – Tra tutela di valori fondamentali, esigenze strategiche e di coordinamento della finanza pubblica* (Aracne 2012).

Benelli F, *La "smaterializzazione" delle materie* (Giuffré 2006).

Benner D, *Compact of the Republic – The League of States and The Constitution* (Life and Liberty Publishing Group 2015).

Berti G, 'Art. 5' in Branca G (ed), *Commentario della Costituzione* (Zanichelli-Foro italiano 1985).

Bifulco R, 'I limiti del regionalismo differenziato' in Apostoli A, Gorlani M and Maccabiani N (eds), *Quale rilancio per le autonomie territoriali* (Giuffré 2020).

Bin R, '"Regionalismo differenziato" e utilizzazione dell'art. 116, terzo comma, Cost. Alcune tesi per aprire il dibattito' (2008) 29 Le istituzioni del federalismo 9.

Calzolaio S, *Il cammino delle materie nello Stato regionale – La definizione delle competenze legislative nell'ordinamento costituzionale* (Giappichelli 2012).

Camera dei deputati – Servizio Studi, *L'autonomia differenziata delle regioni a statuto ordinario* (28 September 2022) <https://www.camera.it/temiap/documentazione/temi/pdf/1104705.pdf?_1635237238195> accessed 26 July 2023.

Carloni E, 'Teoria e pratica della differenziazione: federalismo asimmetrico ed attuazione del Titolo V' (2008) 29 Le istituzioni del federalismo 75.

Catelani E, 'Nuove richieste di autonomia differenziata ex art. 116, comma 3, Cost.: profili procedimentali di dubbia legittimità e possibile violazione dei diritti' (2018) 11 Osservatorio sulle fonti 1.

Cecchetti M, 'Attuazione della riforma costituzionale del Titolo V e differenziazione delle Regioni di diritto comune' [2002] Federalismi.it <https://www.federalismi.it/ApplOpenFilePDF.cfm?artid=813&dpath=document&dfile=ACFA98.pdf&content=Attuazione%2Bdella%2Briforma%2Bcostituzionale%2Bdel%2BTitolo%2BV%2Be%2Bdifferenziazione%2Bdelle%2BRegioni%2Bdi%2Bdiritto%2Bcomune%2B%2D%2Bstato%2B%2D%2Bdottrina%2B%2D%2B> accessed 26 July 2023.

Ceffa CB, '"Non basta dire intesa". Ragionando sul principio di leale collaborazione fra Stato e Regioni nella prospettiva del regionalismo differenziato' (2020) 29 Nuove autonomie 895.

Ciarlo P and Betzu M, 'Dal regionalismo differenziato al regionalismo pasticciato' (2008) 29 Le istituzioni del federalismo 67.

Coduti D, 'Le fonti normative nella differenziazione regionale: una problematica ipotesi ricostruttiva' [2022] Federalismi.it <https://www.federalismi.it/ApplOpenFilePDF.cfm?artid=47134&dpath=document&dfile=04052022130312.pdf&content=Le%2Bfonti%2Bnormative%2Bnella%2Bdifferenziazione%2Bregionale%3A%2Buna%2Bproblematica%2Bipotesi%2Bricostruttiva%2B%2D%2Bstato%2B%2D%2Bdottrina%2B%2D%2B> accessed 26 July 2023.

Colasante P, 'I meccanismi derogatori "di generale applicazione" del riparto delle competenze legislative fra Stato e Regioni nella riforma costituzionale in itinere: la clausola di asimmetria come limite all'esercizio della clausola di flessibilità/supremazia' [2015] Italian Papers on Federalism <https://www.ipof.it/wp-content/uploads/2021/06/Colasante-3_2015.pdf> accessed 26 July 2023.

Colasante P, 'Unità e diversità nel (parziale) regionalismo asimmetrico italiano, alla luce della riforma costituzionale in itinere' [2015] Italian Papers on Federalism <https://www.ipof.it/wp-content/uploads/2021/06/Colasante-2015.pdf> accessed 25 July 2023.

Colasante P, 'Austria' in Di Salvatore E (ed), *Sistemi costituzionali europei* (Giuffré 2021).

Cosmelli G, *Oltre i confini della "materia" – La potestà legislativa residuale delle regioni tra poteri impliciti e sussidiarietà* (Giuffré 2015).

D'Atena A, 'Passato, presente … E futuro delle autonomie regionali speciali' [2014] Rivista AIC <https://www.rivistaaic.it/images/rivista/pdf/4_2014_D'Atena.pdf> accessed 26 July 2023.

D'Atena A, 'L'art. 116, u.c., Cost. alla prova dell'applicazione. Profili procedimentali' (2018) 60 Rassegna parlamentare 185.

D'Atena A, 'Tra l'attuazione del regionalismo differenziato, la legge Delrio e le riforme da fare' (2019) 61 Rassegna parlamentare 639.

D'Atena A, 'A proposito della "clausola di asimmetria" (art. 116 u.c. Cost.)' [2020] Rivista AIC <https://www.rivistaaic.it/images/rivista/pdf/4_2020_14_D_Atena.pdf> accessed 26 July 2023.

D'Atena A, *Diritto regionale* (Giappichelli 2022).

D'Atena A, 'Dove vanno le Regioni' [2022] Rivista AIC <https://www.rivistaaic.it/images/rivista/pdf/4_2022_09_D_Atena.pdf> accessed 26 July 2023.

Dell'Atti L, 'Effetti dell'autonomia differenziata sulla combinazione funzionale dei principi di sussidiarietà e leale collaborazione. Verso una riforma del regionalismo a Costituzione invariata' (2020) 29 Nuove autonomie 867.

Delledonne G, 'Belgio' in Di Salvatore E (ed), *Sistemi costituzionali europei* (Giuffré 2021).

Desideri C, *Regioni politiche e territori – Per una storia del regionalismo italiano* (Giuffré 2015).

Di Cosimo G, 'Sui contenuti del regionalismo differenziato' (2008) 29 Le istituzioni del federalismo 63.

Di Folco M, 'Le differenziazioni ipotetiche: l'art. 116 della Costituzione' in Vandelli L (ed), *Il governo delle regioni: sistemi politici, amministrazioni, autonomie speciali* (Il Mulino 2013).

Di Genio G, *Stato regionale versus Stato federale* (Giuffré 2005).

Di Maria R, 'La procedura per la attuazione del c.d. "regionalismo differenziato": dalla marginalizzazione delle assemblee elettive e degli Enti locali, alla perplessa definizione dei l.e.p.' [2023] Italian Papers on Federalism <https://www.ipof.it/wp-content/uploads/2023/05/03_IPOF-1-23-Di-Maria.pdf> accessed 26 July 2023.

Di Maria R, 'Prime impressioni sulla bozza di disegno di legge per l'attuazione del c.d. "regionalismo differenziato" ex art. 116, co. 3, Cost.' [2023] Diritti regionali <https://www.dirittiregionali.it/wp-content/uploads/2023/03/documento-integrale-4.pdf> accessed 26 July 2023.

Di Salvatore E, 'Federalismo' in Mangiameli S (ed), *Dizionario costituzionale – Dizionario sistematico* (Il Sole 24 Ore 2008).

Di Salvatore E, 'Germania' in Di Salvatore E (ed), *Sistemi costituzionali europei* (Giuffré 2021).

Esposito C, 'Autonomie locali e decentramento amministrativo nell'art. 5 della Costituzione' in Esposito C (ed), *La Costituzione italiana. Saggi* (Cedam 1954).

Fossas Espadaler E, *El principio dispositivo en el Estado autonòmico* (Marcial Pons Ediciones Jurídicas y Sociales 2007).

Galliani D, 'All'interno del Titolo V: le "ulteriori forme e condizioni particolari di autonomia" di cui all'art. 116.3 Cost. riguardano anche le Regioni a Statuto speciale?' (2003) 31 Le Regioni 419.

Gambino S, 'Regionalismo 'differenziato' e principi fondamentali della Carta' [2023] Diritti regionali <https://www.dirittiregionali.it/wp-content/uploads/2023/05/documento-integrale-4.pdf> accessed 26 July 2023.

Gianfrancesco E, 'L'art. 10 della legge costituzionale n. 3 del 2001 ed i controlli nelle regioni ad autonomia speciale' (2002) 47 Giurisprudenza costituzionale 3312.

Gianfrancesco E, 'L'attuazione dell'art. 116, comma 3, Cost. Tra nodi problematici e prospettive evolutive del regionalismo italiano' [2020] Consulta online <https://giurcost.org/studi/gianfrancesco.pdf> accessed 26 July 2023.

Giangaspero P, 'La nascita delle Regioni speciali' in Mangiameli S (ed), *Il regionalismo italiano dall'Unità alla Costituzione e alla sua riforma*, vol I (Giuffré 2012).

Gori L, 'L'autonomia regionale differenziata a partire dai lavori preparatori della riforma del Titolo V della Costituzione' (2023) 16 Osservatorio sulle fonti 59.

Gorlani M, 'Regionalismo differenziato e materie oggetto di trasferimento: valutazioni politiche e criticità tecniche, organizzative e finanziarie' [2023] Italian Papers on Federalism <https://www.ipof.it/wp-content/uploads/2023/05/04_IPOF-1-23-Gorlani.pdf> accessed 26 July 2023.

Grossi VP, 'L'evoluzione del ruolo della legge quadro nel sistema dell'art. 116, co. 3, Cost.: posizioni dottrinarie e funzione politica' [2023] Italian Papers on Federalism <https://www.ipof.it/wp-content/uploads/2023/05/IPOF-2-23-Grossi.pdf> accessed 26 July 2023.

Gullo N, 'Notazioni sul regionalismo differenziato tra aspirazioni autonomistiche e solidarietà economico-sociale' (2020) 29 Nuove autonomie 817.

Gullo N, 'Le autonomie speciali nel prisma dell'attuazione dell'art. 116, co. 3, Cost.' [2022] Diritti regionali <https://www.dirittiregionali.it/wp-content/uploads/2022/04/documento-integrale-3.pdf> accessed 26 July 2023.

Iacoviello A, 'Autonomia regionale e unità giuridica ed economica della Repubblica: i limiti costituzionali per l'attuazione dell'articolo 116, comma 3, della Costituzione' [2023] Italian Papers on Federalism <https://www.ipof.it/wp-content/uploads/2023/07/IPOF-2-23-Iacoviello.pdf> accessed 26 July 2023.

Iannello C, 'La piena sovranità del Parlamento nella determinazione dei contenuti e dei limiti dell'autonomia differenziata' [2019] Diritti regionali <https://www.dirittiregionali.it/wp-content/uploads/2019/09/documento-integrale-3.pdf> accessed 26 July 2023.

ISTAT, *Struttura e dinamica delle unità amministrative territoriali italiane – Dall'unificazione del Regno al 2017* (ISTAT 2018).

Ladu M and Spadacini L, 'La nozione costituzionale di livello essenziale delle prestazioni tra potestà normativa e autonomia finanziaria delle Regioni' [2023] Italian Papers on Federalism <https://www.ipof.it/wp-content/uploads/2023/05/IPOF-2-23-Spadacini-Ladu.pdf> accessed 26 July 2023.

Lollo A, 'Prime note sul (nuovo) procedimento di attuazione del regionalismo differenziato' [2023] Diritti regionali <https://www.dirittiregionali.it/wp-content/uploads/2023/05/documento-integrale-20.pdf> accessed 26 July 2023.

Mangiameli S, 'Appunti a margine dell'art. 116, comma 3, della Costituzione' (2017) 49 Le Regioni 661.

Mangiameli S, 'Errori e mancata attuazione costituzionale. A proposito di regionalismo e regionalismo differenziato' [2023] Diritti regionali <https://www.dirittiregionali.it/wp-content/uploads/2023/01/documento-integrale-4.pdf> accessed 26 July 2023.

Morelli A, 'Regionalismo differenziato e autonomia speciale: un quadro complesso' [2019] Diritti regionali <https://www.dirittiregionali.it/wp-content/uploads/2019/11/documento-integrale-4.pdf> accessed 26 July 2023.

Morelli A, 'L'incerta attuazione del regionalismo differenziato' in Coduti D (ed), *La differenziazione nella Repubblica delle autonomie* (Giappichelli 2022).

Morrone A, 'Il regionalismo differenziato. Commento all'art. 116, comma 3, della Costituzione' (2007) 1 Federalismo fiscale 139.

Napolitano A, 'Il ruolo (imprescindibile) delle camere per una corretta ed equa attuazione del regionalismo differenziato' (2020) 29 Nuove autonomie 881.

Olivetti M, 'Il regionalismo differenziato alla prova dell'esame parlamentare' [2019] Federalismi.it <https://www.federalismi.it/ApplOpenFilePDF.cfm?artid=38243&dpath=document&dfile=19032019231006.pdf&content=Il%2Bregionalismo%2Bdifferenziato%2Balla%2Bprova%2Bdell%27esame%2Bparlamentare%2B%2D%2Bstato%2B%2D%2Bdottrina%2B%2D%2B> accessed 26 July 2023.

Palermo F, 'Il regionalismo differenziato' in Groppi T and Olivetti M (eds), *La Repubblica delle autonomie* (Giappichelli 2003).

Pallotta O, 'Spagna' in Di Salvatore E (ed), *Sistemi costituzionali europei* (Giuffré 2021).

Piccirilli G, 'Gli "accordi preliminari" per la differenziazione regionale. Primi spunti sulla procedura da seguire per l'attuazione dell'art. 116, terzo comma, Cost.' [2018] Diritti regionali <https://www.dirittiregionali.it/wp-content/uploads/2018/04/documento-integrale-10.pdf> acccessed 26 July 2023.

Piraino A, 'L'autonomia differenziata nella crisi del regionalismo italiano' in Apostoli A, Gorlani M and Maccabiani N (eds), *Quale rilancio per le autonomie territoriali* (Giuffré 2020).

Podetta M, 'Il tentativo di attuazione dell'autonomia differenziata: dal disegno di legge Calderoli alla legge di bilancio per il 2023' [2023] Consulta online <https://giurcost.org/post/MARCO%20PODETTA/22634> accessed 26 July 2023.

Pressi M, 'Autonomia regionale differenziata: un'occasione per ripensare l'area vasta' (2020) 29 Nuove autonomie 919.

Prudente V, 'L'utile attuazione dell'art. 116, co. 3, Cost. alla luce del principio di sussidiarietà' (2020) 29 Nuove autonomie 837.

Ricciardi GC, 'Note sulla dimensione amministrativa del regionalismo differenziato' (2020) 29 Nuove autonomie 907.

Rivosecchi G, 'Il regionalismo differenziato nella Repubblica delle autonomie, con particolare riguardo ai profili procedurali' in Coduti D (ed), *La differenziazione nella Repubblica delle autonomie* (Giappichelli 2022).

Ruggeri A, 'La "specializzazione" dell'autonomia regionale: se, come e nei riguardi di chi farvi luogo' (2008) 29 Le istituzioni del federalismo 21.

Ruggeri A, 'Attuazione dell'art. 116, III c., Cost. e prospettive della specialità regionale' [2020] Diritti regionali <https://www.dirittiregionali.it/wp-content/uploads/2020/01/documento-integrale-5.pdf> accessed 26 July 2023.

Ruggiu I, 'Il "ritorno" del principio di competenza?' (2008) 29 Le istituzioni del federalismo 101.

Saitta A, 'Gli Statuti delle Regioni speciali ieri, oggi e domani' in Editoriale Scientifica (ed), *Studi in onore di Franco Modugno*, vol IV (Editoriale Scientifica 2011).

Salerno GM, 'Con il procedimento di determinazione dei LEP (e relativi costi e fabbisogni standard) la legge di bilancio riapre il cantiere dell'autonomia differenziata' [2023] Federalismi.it <https://www.federalismi.it/ApplOpenFilePDF.cfm?eid=660&dpath=editoriale&dfile=EDITORIALE%5F10012023160745%2Epdf&content=Con%2Bil%2Bprocedimento%2Bdi%2Bdeterminazione%2Bdei%2BLEP%2B%28e%2Brelativi%2Bcosti%2Be%2Bfabbisogni%2Bstandard%29%2Bla%2Blegge%2Bdi%2Bbilancio%2Briapre%2Bil%2Bcantiere%2Bdell%E2%80%99autonomia%2Bdifferenziata&content_auth=%3Cb%3EGiulio%2BM%2E%2BSalerno%3C%2Fb%3E> accessed 26 July 2023.

Sciullo G, 'Art. 116, comma 3, Cost. e beni culturali' (2008) 29 Le istituzioni del federalismo 95.

Tarli Barbieri G, 'Verso un regionalismo differenziato o verso un regionalismo confuso? Appunti sulla (presunta) attuazione dell'art. 116, comma 3, Cost.' (2019) 12 Osservatorio sulle fonti 1.

Toniatti R, 'L'autonomia regionale ponderata: aspettative ed incognite di un incremento delle asimmetrie quale possibile premessa per una nuova stagione costituzionale del regionalismo italiano' (2017) 49 Le Regioni 635.

Violini L, 'Regionalismo differenziato e utilizzazione dell'art. 116, comma 3, Cost. (con particolare riguardo al regime dei diritti sociali)' (2008) 29 Le istituzioni del federalismo 87.

Violini L, 'L'autonomia delle Regioni italiane dopo i referendum e le richieste di maggiori poteri ex articolo 116, comma 3, Cost.' [2018] Rivista AIC <https://www.rivistaaic.it/images/rivista/pdf/Violini_4_2018.pdf> accessed 26 July 2023.

Violini L, 'I procedimenti per l'attuazione del regionalismo differenziato: luci e ombre dell'art. 116, comma 3, della Costituzione' [2019] Italian Papers on Federalism <https://www.ipof.it/wp-content/uploads/2021/04/Violini-Procedimenti-Regionalismo-differenziato.pdf> accessed 26 July 2023.

Violini L, *Una forma di Stato a regionalismo differenziato? Percorsi e argomenti per l'attuazione dell'art. 116, III comma, Cost.* (Giappichelli 2021).

Volpi M, 'Stato federale e Stato regionale: due modelli a confronto' (1995) 15 Quaderni Costituzionali 367.

Zanon N, 'Per un regionalismo differenziato: linee di sviluppo a Costituzione invariata e prospettive alla luce della revisione del Titolo V' in *Problemi del Federalismo* (Giuffré 2001).

# Index

www.ingramcontent.com/pod-product-compliance
Lightning Source LLC
LaVergne TN
LVHW010626300926
849162LV00001B/75
* 9 7 8 9 0 0 4 5 2 8 5 7 4 *